D1794773

NATURE WISDOM

NATURE WISDOM
MYSTICAL WRITERS OF THE BIG SUR-MONTEREY COAST

Richard Henry Dana
Robert Louis Stevenson
Gertrude Atherton
Jack London and 'The Bunch'
Robinson Jeffers
Jaime de Angulo
John Steinbeck
Eric Barker
Henry Miller

Plus a tribute to the 'blood conscious' pantheism of D. H. Lawrence and a
postscript on the 'organic psychology' of William James

ELAYNE WAREING FITZPATRICK

Xlibris Publishing
Indiana

Copyright © 2011 by Elayne Wareing Fitzpatrick. 91364-FITZ

ISBN: Softcover   978-1-4568-7287-8
       Hardcover   978-1-4568-7288-5

All rights reserved. No part of this book may be reproduced or transmitted in any form or by any means, electronic or mechanical, including photocopying, recording, or by any information storage and retrieval system, without permission in writing from the copyright owner.

Book Design: Carolyn Gambito

This book, a revised and expanded- in-color edition of a book originally titled *Shepherds of Pan on the Big Sur-Monterey Coast*, was printed in the United States of America.

To order copies of this book, contact:

Xlibris Corporation, 1-888-795-4274
www.Xlibris.com
Orders@Xlibris.com

Author's web site: www.capricornbrae.com

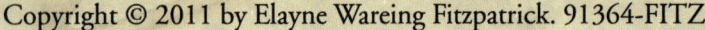

Nature Wisdom, The Cover, Elayne Wareing Fitzpatrick, and I.

The relationship began on Valentine's Day, 2011. We've been on a design roller coaster ever since. If you don't like roller coasters, compare our relationship with something mind-blowing in your own experience.

I liken design to a quote from Oliver Wendell Holmes. The quote came to me suddenly, just as I began typing this note: MAN'S MIND, ONCE STRETCHED BY A NEW IDEA, NEVER REGAINS ITS ORIGINAL DIMENSIONS. How does this apply to this book? Just bear with me.

The possibilities of design are endless. Since this *is* publishing, there is this need to succumb to popular preferences. Imagine months of deciding on the best fonts to be used, best point size, the best character and line spacing, the best font type to font type ratio, the best font type point size to font type point size ratio…the best

looking letter to be in drop cap on the lower third of the left or right page because a facing page spread *did* matter. The list goes on. Everything became a silent conversation between pages. Most days, we looked up to the cosmos for help. Still, we did need to get the book out!

So, after 238 days and then some, after finalizing and going through the entire internal layout, we reached the acme of design dilemma, the mother of all book design FAQs: *Is the cover perfect?* If only I had a dollar for every time this came up!

Confronted with choosing between two cover designs we liked, we resorted to polls. After what seemed like weeks of collecting opinions from various groups of ethnicity, degrees of kinship, and of course, the familiar assemblage of critical peers, the verdict came in, and — *Tada!* We finally decided on the design on the front cover of this book. But for posterity's sake, we decided to include this tale about *the cover-that-could-have-been.* By no means was it *the* lesser one. We just had to choose which would be appreciated most by the larger group of readers. The chosen cover seemed to be the safest, while the one pictured here (above) was the one favored by a select few of exceptionally different people (just four actually), including ourselves.

So -- behold *Nature Wisdom* in all its glory! To the eternally *Sunny Cynic,* Elayne Wareing Fitzpatrick, I say it has been an honor and a pleasure to have worked with you. I look forward to the next book. To the readers, *enjoy!*

Carolyn Gambito, Xlibris Designer

BY THE SAME AUTHOR

Dedicated to the memory of
Dr. Sterling M. McMurrin

STERLING M. MCMURRIN *was a noble mentor and charismatic friend of the author. For her, as for many of his other graduate students, he inspired inquiry and opened closed doors. A specialist in philosophy, history of ideas, and comparative religions, he authored several books and served as Commissioner of Education under President John F. Kennedy until he concluded he could 'do more good' in a university classroom. He served as Dean of the Graduate School and Chairman of the Department of Philosophy at the University of Utah when he wasn't linking back to his roots in Nature on an unpretentious family ranch in southern Utah. He wrote:*

"IT IS VERY DIFFICULT FOR US WITH OUR CONDITIONING to enter into [a] fellow-feeling for the universe. The imaginative child perhaps still enjoys it. And it has been suggested that it was, and for that matter still is, the attitude of the Pueblo civilization of the American Southwest. The Native American ... like the Oriental and ... the early Greeks, viewed Nature as the great principle for ordering of his life and sought in its mysterious forces not something to be captured and made to serve him, but harmonies that he might share to the profound satisfaction of his soul." (A History of Philosophy)

"WHEN WE COME RIGHT DOWN TO IT and insist on being honest with ourselves, for those of us whose passion for reason and reliable knowledge has robbed us of our enchantments, it appears that about all that is left is some kind of reverent naturalism ... the type of naturalism that makes a place, and a large place, for mind and moral values and for spiritual aspiration and commitment and insists that these are as real a part of Nature as are matter and physical events. This Naturalism can generate an authentic piety and reverence for life. And it can enable an individual to invest life with purpose and meaning." (Evolution, Religion and Human Hope)

Sterling M. McMurrin
(1914-1996)

The most beautiful and profound emotion we can experience is the sensation of the mystical. He to whom this emotion is a stranger, who can no longer wonder and stand rapt in awe, is as good as dead. To know that what is impenetrable to us really exists, manifesting itself as the highest wisdom and the most radiant beauty, which our dull faculties can comprehend only in their primitive forms – this knowledge, this feeling, is at the center of true religion.

Albert Einstein
(1879-1955)

CONTENTS

———◆———

———◆———

'*On the Edge*', mystic view of the Big Sur coast by Scottish watercolorist, Helen Jerene.

ABOUT THE COVER ARTIST: HELEN JERENE

From her Partington Ridge home on property once occupied by Big Sur's pioneer artists, Harrydick and Lillian Bos Ross, Scottish-born intuitive -- and self-taught watercolorist -- Helen Jerene captured the transcendental drama of the Big Sur-Monterey coast in an elegant mystical painting.

She called it *'On the Edge.'*
When told how her self-described 'Vision Painting' connects with the mystical Nature wisdom of the writers gathered together in this book, Helen graciously and enthusiastically offered her painting for the cover.
"There are no accidents,' she smiled. *"Perhaps it was meant to be."*

HELEN WAS BORN IN WICK, CAITHNESS, SCOTLAND, but she was brought up in Toronto, Canada, where she discovered she had a special passion for mathematics, a subject that has lent itself to mystical speculation dating back to Pythagoras and Plato.

Her use of this gift was originally pragmatic: She accepted a job as mathematics consultant for the Toronto Board of Education when Canada went metric. But it wasn't long before she realized that although she was 'making a good living,' she wasn't living in a way that was 'spiritually fulfilling.'

So she retreated to a place she hoped might help her to re-create herself – to rise like the mythical phoenix to a new life: Esalen Institute in Big Sur. There, inspired by the transcending beauty of California's Central Coast, she not only discovered a gift for painting, she also met the man who was to become her husband, Bruce Malcolm.

They lived together on Partington Ridge where she became 'passionate about color' and began to paint in a style that amazed them both. If spirits of Harrydick Ross and Henry Miller still hover on Partington, it's fun to speculate that they had an 'encouraging hand' in her fervor. Years before, these artists (a sculptor and a writer-turned-painter) had been stricken in similar ways.

Miller's voice was joyous. *"Paint as you like and die happy!"* he shouted from his mountain top. *"To paint is to love again!"*

Unlike Miller's playful child-like watercolors, Helen's painting took a more esoteric turn. Transformation began, she said, when she felt 'led' to the study of color wave lengths and the electromagnetic field around the body. Consequently, she came to believe that each individual's aura is a map of his or her state of being – mentally, physically, and spiritually.

She began to refer to her work as 'vision painting' because it is about "how we create the lives we live and wish to live' and how 'we ourselves are color -- walking rainbows.' She even began what she calls 'silent painting meditations.' Soon people were coming from all over to attend her Big Sur workshops at Esalen Institute and at Post Ranch and Ventana inns.

Like Larry Darrell, protagonist in W. Somerset Maugham's novel The Razor's Edge, Helen, has 'come down from the mountain' where she had painted her peace to share her wisdom with kindred spirits.

Today, she and her husband are in the United Kingdom living near the Aura Soma Institute in Tetford, England, where they share that wisdom with kindred spirits. At last check, each seemed to be wearing the contented smile of a bodhisattva.

(Photograph of Carmel's Tor House poet, Robinson Jeffers, by Leigh Wiener, 1956)

The greatest beauty is organic wholeness, the wholeness of life and things, the divine beauty of the universe. Love that, not man apart from that …

… Robinson Jeffers

A WORD ABOUT THIS BOOK

By a pantheistic experience I mean the experience of identity in difference between God and the world or God and the soul … It would indeed be an odd thing to suppose that a man cannot feel the wonder and terror and sublimity of the universe and its Maker without admitting his allegiance to some particular kind of metaphysics or theological dogma.

W. T. Stace,
Mysticism and Philosophy

When the late quantum chemist and Nobel laureate, Dr. Linus Pauling, admitted on a TV talk show that he didn't believe in God, there were dark murmurs from the studio audience. This wasn't what they had hoped to hear from the venerable scientist.

He was nearing ninety, and his disclosure flew in the face of a popularly held notion that, as death stares us down, even life-long unbelievers – like soldiers in foxholes – are apt to turn to a caring, protective God. Not Pauling. His perception, like that of Albert Einstein before him, was that divinity is revealed in the lawful harmony of the universe.

For these scientists, God was not the traditional rewarding and punishing 'Man Upstairs' of popular religion who concerns himself with the fate and doings of human beings. Quite the contrary. They saw God as the mysterious vitality, the infinite wisdom immanent in all creation -- or, as one philosopher[1] put it, "a harmony among irrational impulses."

Such esoteric perceptions may be satisfying to philosophers and to poetic mystics in the world's great religions. But it can be unsettling for the ordinary weekend churchgoer to think of God as an infinite cause/effect process perpetually struggling to harmonize recalcitrant polarities at every level of being. This sort of deity is unavailable for ordinary religious purposes and largely indifferent to our narrow human hopes and aspirations.

The idea that the word 'God' is a metaphor symbolizing the ultimate transcending mystery of Nature's eternal synergy – an interactive subatomic dance of necessary opposites that some call Love – doesn't fit orthodox patterns of religious belief.

But for a man like Pauling such an insight was natural. He spent years on the wave-beaten headlands of central California that gave rise to America's first Nature-honoring Bohemia. Under the spell of this alternately soft and violent seacoast, he sensed the power of divinity in Nature, symbolized by the ancient Greeks as the double-dealing 'all' god Pan, part human, part animal -- a little like themselves.

The Greeks alternately adored Pan for his canny charm and feared him as a trickster. He was a wonder and a holy terror – a whirling, dancing god -- a potent, vexatious, playful, protective, horned, hoof-stomping, flute-playing multifaceted marvel.

Whether seen as a bright, capricious youth romping in the forest with nymphs and satyrs -- or as a frightful, bearded, horny old man luring wayfarers with the magic of his pipes -- Pan represents the uneasy covenant between our most primitive instincts (love and hostility) and our extraordinary human capacity to reason, imagine, create, and transform. His aspects form a whole in whose image we are.

I like to think of the writers brought together in this book as 'shepherds' of Pan because, in varying ways, they share the perennial philosophy called 'pantheism.' Not only did they honor the dual aspects of Pan's psyche in themselves, they staunchly defended his favored habitats: places of pastoral simplicity and untamed landscape capable of reconciling disaffected humans with the essential, and therefore sacred, cycles of Nature.

These spiritual reconnections usually occur unexpectedly, in moments of perfect solitude. We can be stirred by 'Pan power' while walking in the wilds, perching on a crag overlooking the sea, imbibing a desert sunset, or simply tracing the patterns of bugs in a secluded garden.

When we are touched, love happens. We feel a kinship with everything around us, sublimely 'at home' in our natural surroundings. We experience, if only briefly, a basic conjugal relationship we know we can trust, no matter what.

Fleeting as the sensation may be, it is passionately religious, satisfying, difficult to express in words. Mystical. Something deep inside us seems to merge with a pervasive Presence. And, from that moment on, we know, intuitively, that we will never feel lonely again.

I experienced this transformative sort of thing just once, on a tranquil day in Big Sur, when I was feeling as lonely as the proverbial motherless child. But the episode was so impressive that I've empathized with the mystical feelings of others ever since, especially with experiences of the writers gathered together in this book.

To me, these writers were fellow seekers who had also discovered God in the necessary, pragmatic wisdom of Nature. Some even seem to have made, in their writings if not in their personal lives, what Aldous Huxley described as the "one effectively redemptive sacrifice, the sacrifice of self-will to make room for the knowledge of God."

Like indigenous people before them, they seem to have been transformed spiritually and compelled, almost instinctively, to fall in love outward with what the coast's poet laureate, Robinson Jeffers, called 'the divine beauty of the universe' and the 'beautiful, intolerable God who tortures himself to discover himself.'

Exalted by a vision of recalcitrant wildness and boundless intelligence straining together to maintain dynamic balance, they experienced God as the eternal reality that not only energizes everything, but invites our cooperation. God, for them, was no longer a being but the ground of all being, the all-encompassing unity of opposites that suffers, as we do, to create.

These writers – from Stevenson, London, Atherton, Lawrence, Jeffers, and Steinbeck to De Angulo, Barker and Miller – seemed 'reborn.' But now, as Jeffers put it, they were born "of the rock and of the air, not of a woman."

Even the sophisticated Harvard intellectual, George Santayana, felt obliged to comment, after a sojourn on this coast:

"I am struck in California by the deep and almost religious affection which people have for its influences … It is their spontaneous substitute for articulate art and articulate religion."

Anglican orientalist Alan Watts avowed here:

"I can feel like a Christian only when I am indoors. As soon as I get into the open air, I feel entirely out of relation with everything that goes on in a church – including both the worship and the theology."

Muckraking journalist Lincoln Steffens referred to the Monterey Peninsula as

"a heaven on earth to which the wise succeeders in life, wise enough to die before their time, go and live on – happily ever after," adding, *"But the beautiful people of Carmel, the good people of Pacific Grove do not know their state of bliss. The dead don't know they are dead."*

And looking down from Partington Ridge in Big Sur, Henry Miller was moved to write:

"This is the face of the world as the Creator intended it to look. How wonderful is the earth and the creatures which inhabit it! This is Heaven enough. Why ask for more?"

It may have been no accident that the Central California missions -- harsh as some of the padres may have been toward coastal Indians -- were founded by spiritual descendants of a great Christian mystic, St. Francis of Assisi. He was a medieval flower child who saw all living things as expressions of deity praising God by being just what they naturally are, despite society's 'norms.'

Today, many sensitive explorers are still smitten by the elemental beauty they find on this coast, despite encroachments of some overly zealous developers and of what Robert Louis Stevenson abhorred as "the flaunting caravanserai" way back in 1879.

Whether self-appointed advocates or reluctant prophets, the writers herein seem to have been touched by a palpable energy -- wild, primal, impersonal, yet somehow benign and comforting. 'Pan' power.

They were pantheists, or nature mystics, who non-intellectually experienced what they interpreted as 'holy' – an experience that resulted, if only momentarily, in a kind of 'peace that passeth all understanding.'

In trying to 'eff' the ineffable through literature, they serve to remind us that, with all our technological inventiveness, we humans are inextricably entwined in the palpable garments of God -- consummate Nature.

They caution that survival of God's most noble, and most dangerous, experiment – ourselves – may ultimately depend on our behavior toward each other and on our capacity to outlast the consequences of our own uprooted, short-sighted cleverness abetted by hubris and greed.

Their wisdom suggests that the divinity inherent in Nature is neither to be feared nor mastered, but understood and respected as God struggles, with us, to ameliorate, even harmonize, essential extremes.

They remind us that the divine Word is no 'respecter of persons' and is never 'politically correct.' Natural Law demands honesty, inclusiveness, courage, mindfulness, and wise measure in everything -- especially in procreation -- lest there be catastrophic consequences.

I believe that some of these 'shepherds' of Pan can serve as models for each of us to walk joyfully in our own way with a will-to-good, re-attuning ourselves to the infinite reciprocity that governs our world, remembering, as Robert Louis Stevenson put it, that "we are all God's scholars till we die."

Above all, their wisdom implies a mystical consciousness, latent in all of us, that invites contentment – a kind of at-one-ment or 'fellow feeling for the universe.' It motivates goodness and can enable us to return in the end to what was in the beginning, without shame or remorse.

Elayne Wareing Fitzpatrick

CARMEL VALLEY, CALIFORNIA
SUMMER, 2011

17

GOATPAN

Pan, the imperfect, the Legendary Christ.
Worshipping, we long to find some name to cling to.
Any, no matter how odd.
Reverence is all, the All God knows.
We revive what we can …
You Pan! Shape-shifting Dog of the Great Goddess,
Dance Master, Canine Kosmokrator.
The One who some believed to be the Sun itself.
Seven reeds and seven planets,
Syrinx and Echo, Elios and Moon,
Eternal sound, eternal chord, eternal chorus,
First star of heaven, Sirius, astronomical fact,
Egyptian God before all others.
Pan, the All God, the Orphic Compromise,
What shall we do with your many names,
With all that you have become?
Pan, you raucous goat god!
How could you stand it?
So many centuries of – blagh!
So little joy, so little sun.
They must have nearly done you in.
And how they stole from you!
Friends! Poems first, of course, then music.
Apollo – prophecy.
Hermes – your flute.
You never got angry, no.
Well, with everyone else perhaps, seldom with them.
And you even had sense enough to die young once,
Squatting, life between your legs.
Thanes, across the sea, said,
'The Great God Pan is dead …' Never!
The world is dying of hubris, Pan.
The world is dying of itself.
A goat god squats -- that old perverse, habitual lord --
Planning a comeback, scratching his soul, as he should.

BILL MINOR
(PROFESSOR EMERITUS, MONTEREY PENINSULA COLLEGE)

RETURN TO BEGINNINGS

When the familiar but remote God of our youth,
God of our faith,
Crumbles and is no longer here and close at heart,
The headlong flight begins;
A flight for meaning and purpose,
A reason for all the effort and the folly,
All the writings stored against the time of crisis
That seem to have been inescapably programmed
To end in failure, disgrace and rejection.
When the patterns we have carefully traced out
For God to follow are ignored by God;
When any alley cat can stare at and evaluate
A king stripped of his royalty;
When storms and the gathering darknesses
Bewilder with their intensity and their might;
When the soul is confronted by knives and clubs
Wielded by power that cannot hear the victim's pleas,
The soul is alone at last.   The soul is finally a soul!
Often, in such terrible times, the God of faith,
The God of our youth, is gone without a trace,
And the God of Nature begins like a dripping promise
And hope rises like some great cosmic kite
To a height that commands all the soul's attention.
Then the soul cannot be without sensing
The stir of God in the mountains, clouds and seas,
In the long-there goodness of the ordinary,
Whether of birds or people or things.
God makes a last ditch stand
In the darkness the soul has created;
God ministers to the wounds the soul has inflicted on the soul.
The crimes we lay on God are the crumpled hopes
That have left us low and wet
And at the mercy of our enemies.
Bending and kneeling over the sorry condition of the soul,
Tenderness, Warmth, and Healing gaze down in love
And begin to refashion, to create new life from old ashes.
The stupefied soul feels a stirring no pulse ever knew,
A response of strength, of understanding
That gives no answers but swathes itself in the holiest wonder.

JOSEPH CLOONAN
(CATHOLIC PRIEST AND LATE POET LAUREATE OF CARMEL VALLEY)

CHAPTER I

BETWEEN DESERT AND SEA:
D. H. LAWRENCE AND PAN

My individualism is really an illusion. I am part of the great whole, and I can never escape. But I can deny my connections, break them, and become a fragment. Then I am wretched. What we want is to destroy our false, inorganic connections, especially those related to money, and re-establish the living organic connections with the cosmos, the sun and earth, with mankind and nation and family.

D. H. LAWRENCE 'PAN IN AMERICA'

I t may seem odd to begin this book with words of a British expatriate, D. H. Lawrence, who experienced the power of Pan in Taos, New Mexico, *not* on California's Big Sur-Monterey coast.

But there are important links between that desert country and this coast.

Each place attracts passionately creative individuals aspiring to live in closer harmony with nature like the American Indians before them.

Lawrence and his Taos patroness, Mabel Dodge -- married to a relatively sophisticated Pueblo Indian, Tony Luhan -- were the original catalysts for an ongoing exchange of aesthetes between the two places.

Among them were Carmel's Tor House poet, Robinson Jeffers; and Big Sur's fabled outlander, Jaime de Angulo, medical doctor, Jungian psychiatrist, and story-telling linguist-anthropologist.

Lawrence did visit California -- and rejected it -- complaining, *"There seemed a strange brutality in the spirit of the western coast and I felt: O, let me get away!"*

He moved on to New Mexico.

When de Angulo showed up in Taos, Lawrence was indignant. He rejected de Angulo as '*strange and brutal*' like California, despite the two men's common interest in Indians, nature, and writing.

Adobe home in Taos, New Mexico, where Mabel Dodge Luhan hosted visiting artists and writers.

Lawrence even became ill and left the room when the dashing de Angulo threw off his shirt and flexed his impressive back muscles in the presence of Lawrence's delighted wife, Frieda.

Later Lawrence whispered to Mabel, *"He's not quite all right. You must keep an eye on him. Next time he'll rip his trousers off, I wouldn't wonder!"*

De Angulo remained unruffled. He wrote

Author talking with Chief of Taos Pueblo during a gathering at the home of Southwest writer Frank Waters

to his wife: *"I like [Lawrence] very much, strange duck that he is [but] I would like to see more of Mr. Luhan, go walking with him, or sit in the sun with him … I find his face full of an illuminating beauty … There is something very strengthening and assuaging in his presence."*

Luhan returned the compliment. He even broke with native tradition and introduced de Angulo to some Pueblo secrets paving the way for a pregnant meeting of Swiss psychoanalyst Carl Jung with Pueblo tribal elders. But more of that anon.

As for Jeffers, he and Lawrence had philosophic links but never met. Lawrence died in Italy in 1930 while Mabel was in Carmel visiting Jeffers and his wife Una.

Mabel tried to persuade Jeffers to come to Taos to fill the void left by Lawrence's death. Jeffers obliged, mainly to please Una who liked Mabel and her Bohemian friends.

But Jeffers took to Taos about as much as Lawrence had taken to California. He complained of the heat, was annoyed by the tourists, and took no comfort in encounters with some uprooted Indians he referred to as "empties." He wrote:

"Certainly, there was never religion enough, nor beauty nor poetry here to fill Americans. Only the drum is confident, it thinks the world has not changed. Apparently only myself and the strong tribal drum and the rock head of Taos mountain, remember that civilization is a transient sickness."

Nevertheless, for Jeffers, as for de Angulo, there was one redeeming factor in Taos: feelings of kinship with Tony Luhan who honored their friendship by presenting the poet with a sacred eagle feather.

"From one chief to another chief," the Indian declared.

This kinship notwithstanding, both Jeffers and de Angulo preferred their California Indians to the Pueblos. De Angulo put it this way:

"These Indians are petrified in an attitude of submissive obedience to a labyrinth of secret rules and orders. They have no individualities at all, not a shred of initiative. The Navajos and Apaches preyed on them too long. Too long they have been penned in their pueblos like sheep in a pen, distilling the intricate pattern of religious symbolism.

"I long to breathe freely with my California Indians and their oneness with nature. They don't need so many ceremonies to understand the life of the world in the trees, in the rivers, in the rocks."

(Sketch courtesy of *The D. H. Lawrence Society of North America Newsletter*, Volume 39, Fall 2010.)

For both coastal homesteaders, Pan only piped in California. Not so with Lawrence. He discovered Pan in America's Southwest after years of tarrying in the earth's beautiful places, hungering for experience that would strike him as *religious* – for something *deep down in the senses, inexplicable and inscrutable."*

Seized, at last, by the archetypal Pan in Taos, he shared his pantheistic experience with the rest of us in 'Pan in America.'

The following is an abbreviated version of Lawrence's powerful essay which sets the stage for subsequent chapters in this book:

"AT THE BEGINNING OF THE CHRISTIAN ERA, *voices were heard off the coast of Greece, out to sea, on the Mediterranean, wailing: 'Pan is dead! Great Pan is dead!'*

"The father of fauns and nymphs, satyrs and dryads and naiads was dead, with only the voices in the air to lament him. Humanity hardly noticed ...

"Lurking among the leafy recesses, he was almost more demon than god. To be feared, not loved or approached ... you might dimly see him in the night, a dark body within the darkness.

"And then, it was a vision filling the limbs and the trunk of a man with power, as with new strong mounting sap. The Pan power! You went on your way in the darkness secretly and subtly elated with blind energy, and you could cast a spell, by your mere presence, on women and on men. But particularly on women.

"In the woods and the remote places ran the children of Pan, all the nymphs and fauns of the forest and the spring and the river and the rocks ... the nymphs, running among the trees and curling to sleep under the bushes, made the myrtles blossom more gaily, and the spring bubble up with greater urge, and the birds splash with a strength of life. And the lithe flanks of the faun gave life to the oak groves, the vast trees hummed with energy. And the wheat sprouted like green rain returning out of the ground, in the little fields, and the vine hung its black drops in abundance, urging a secret.

"GRADUALLY MEN MOVED INTO CITIES. And they loved the display of people better than the display of a tree. They liked the glory they got of overpowering one another in war ... and the vanity of ideas.

"So Pan became old and grey-bearded and goat-legged, and his passion was degraded with the lust of senility. His power to blast and to brighten dwindled ... Till at last the old Pan died, and was turned into the devil of the Christians ... It is a most strange ending for a god with such a name. Pan! All! That which is everything has goat's feet and a tail! With a black face! This is really curious.

"Yet this is all that remained of Pan, except that he acquired brimstone and hell-fire for many, many centuries. The nymphs turned into the nasty-smelling witches of a Walpurgis night, and the fauns that danced became sorcerers riding the air, or fairies no bigger than your thumb.

"But Pan keeps on being reborn, in all kinds of strange shapes. There he was, at the

Renaissance.[editor's note: Michelangelo's sculpture of 'Moses' with unmistakable horns that suggest the dual nature of man and deity as symbolized by Pan] And in the eighteenth century he had quite a vogue. He gave rise to an 'ism,' and there were many pantheists. Wordsworth one of the first. They worshipped Nature in her sweet-and-pure aspects …

"And then he crossed over to the young United States: I mean Pan did. Suddenly he gets a new name. He becomes the Oversoul, the Allness of everything … Here in America … old Pan is still alive.

"W"hen Pan was greatest, he was not even Pan. He was nameless and unconceived, mentally. Just as a small baby new from the womb may say Mama! Dada! Whereas in the womb it said nothing; so humanity, in the womb of Pan, said naught. But when humanity was born into a separate idea of itself, it said Pan.

"In the days before man got too much separated off from the universe, he was Pan, along with all the rest. As a tree still is. A strong-willed, powerful thing-in-itself, reaching up and reaching down.

"With a powerful will of its own it thrusts green hands and huge limbs at the light above, and sends huge legs and gripping toes down, down between the earth and rocks, to the earth's middle … the tree is asserting itself as much as I am.

"It gives out life, as I give out life. Our two lives meet and cross one another, unknowingly; the tree's life penetrates my life, and my life the tree's. We cannot live near one another, as we do, without affecting one another.

"The tree gathers up earth power from the dark bowels of the earth, and a roaming sky-glitter from above. And all unto itself, which is a tree, woody, enormous, slow but unyielding with life, bristling with acquisitive energy, obscurely radiating some of its great strength.

Michelangelo's horned 'Moses'

"It vibrates its presence into my soul, and I am with Pan … I have become conscious of the tree, and of its interpenetration into my life.

"Long ago, the Indians must have been even more acutely conscious of it, when they blazed it to leave their mark on it. I am conscious that it helps to change me, vitally …

"Of course, if I like to cut myself off, and say it is all bunk, a tree is merely so much lumber not yet sawn, then in a great measure I shall be cut off. So much depends on one's attitude.

"One can shut many, many doors of receptivity in oneself; or one can open man doors that are shut. [But] all that goes to the primitive savageness of a pine tree, goes also to the strength of man …

"What can a man do with his life but live it? And what does life consist in, save a vivid relatedness between the man and the living universe that surrounds him?

"Yet man insulates himself more and more into mechanism, and repudiates everything but the machine and the contrivance of which he himself is master, God in the machine.

"Morning comes, and white ash lies in the fire-hollow, and the old man looks at it broodingly.

'The fire is gone,' he says in the Pan silence that is so full of unutterable things.

"Look! There is no more tree. We drank his warmth, and he is gone. He is way, way off in the sky, his smoke is in the blueness, with the sweet smell of a pine wood fire, and his yellow flame is in the sun. It is morning, with the ashes of night. There is no more tree. Tree is gone.

"But perhaps there is fire among the ashes. I shall blow it, and it will be alive. There is always fire, between the tree that goes and the tree that stays. 'One day I shall go – '

"So they cook their meat, and rise, and go in silence. This is Pan, the Pan mystery, the Pan power.

"What can men who sit at home in their studies, and drink hot milk and have lamb's wool slippers on their feet, and write anthropology, what can they possibly know about men, the men of Pan?

"Among the creatures of Pan there is an eternal struggle for life, between lives. Man, defenseless, rapacious man, has needed the qualities of every living thing, at one time or other.

"The hard, silent abidingness of rock, the surging resistance of a tree, the still evasion of a puma, the dogged earth-knowledge of the bear, the light alertness of the deer, the sky-prowling vision of the eagle; turn by turn man has needed the power of every living thing.

"Tree, stone, or hill, river, or little stream, or waterfall, or salmon in the fall – man can be master and complete in himself, only by assuming the living powers of each of them, as the occasion requires.

"He used to make himself master by a great effort of will, and sensitive, intuitive cunning, and immense labor of body.

"Then he discovered the 'idea.' He found that all things were related by certain laws. The moment man learned to abstract, he began to make engines that would do the work of his body.

"So, instead of concentrating upon his quarry, or upon the living things which made his universe, he concentrated upon the engines or instruments which should intervene between him and the living universe, and give him mastery.

"This was the death of the great Pan. The idea and the engine came between man and all things, like a death. The old connection, the old Allness, was severed, and can never be ideally restored. Great Pan is dead.

"Yet what do we live for, except to live?

Man has lived to conquer the phenomenal universe. To a great extent he has succeeded. With all the mechanism of the human world, man is to a great extent master of all his life, and of most phenomena.

"And what then? Once you have conquered a thing, you have lost it. Its real relation to you collapses. A conquered world is no good to man. He sits stupefied with boredom upon his conquest.

"We need the universe to live again, so that we can live with it. A conquered universe, a dead Pan, leaves us nothing to live with.

"You have to abandon the conquest, before Pan will live again. You live to live, not to conquer. What's the good of conquering even the North Pole, if after the conquest you've nothing left but an inert fact?

"Better leave it a mystery.

"It was better to be a hunter in the woods of Pan, than it is to be a clerk in a city store ...

"[But] it is useless to glorify the savage. He will kill Pan with his own hands, for the sake of a motor-car. And a bored savage, for whom Pan is dead, is the stupefied image of all boredom. And we cannot return to the primitive life, to live in tepee and hunt with bows and arrows.

"Yet live we must. And once life has been conquered, it is pretty difficult to live. What are we going to do, with a conquered universe?

"The Pan relationship, which the world of man once had with all the world, was better than anything man has now. The savage today, if you give him the chance, will become more mechanical and unloving than any civilized man.

"But civilized man, having conquered the universe, may as well leave off bossing it. Because, when all is said and done, life itself consists in a live relatedness between man and his universe: sun, moon stars, earth, trees, flowers, birds, animals, men, everything – and not in a 'conquest' of anything by anything. Even the conquest of the air makes the world smaller, tighter, and more airless.

"And whether we are a store-clerk or a bus- conductor, we can still choose between the living universe of Pan, and the mechanical conquered universe of modern humanity.

"The machine" has no windows. But even the most mechanized human being has only got his windows nailed up, or bricked in."

D. H. LAWRENCE RANCH IN TAOS, HIS BURIAL PLACE, AND FAVORITE OLD PINE TREE

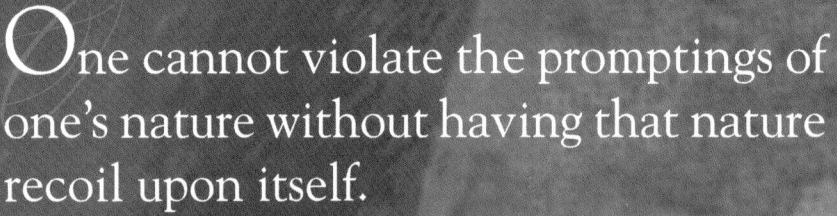

One cannot violate the promptings of one's nature without having that nature recoil upon itself.

… Jack London
(White Fang)

CHAPTER II

MONTEREY FROM THE SEA:
RICHARD HENRY DANA

RICHARD HENRY DANA, JR. was the first, since Sebastian Vizcaino's visit in 1602, to view the Big Sur-Monterey coast from the sea and write about it. He heard the mystical piping of Pan more than a century ago.

Richard Henry Dana (Photograph from Harvard Classics edition, *Two Years Before the Mast*)

Pan called him to adventure when he was very young, but he failed to incorporate the call into the remainder of his life -- and lived to regret it.

"We ought to have been travelers, had no profession and no home, and roamed over the world together, like two civilized and refined gypsies," he said to his wife near the end of his life.

His lament serves as a caution.

Dana was the son of a poet and essayist -- and grandson of the first American minister to Russia. He elected to become a common seaman for about as long as Henry David Thoreau spent in the woods – and for similar reasons.

Thoreau's deliberate sojourn resulted in Walden. Dana's was chronicled in *Two Years Before the Mast*.

When he finished the book in 1840, he had lauded Monterey as "decidedly the pleasantest and most civilized-looking place in California."

But then he traded what might have been a natural and adventurous career in journalism for a more 'respectable' job as a lawyer. The consequence of not following his natural, more spiritual 'gut inclination' was poor health, brought on by stresses of urban living.

Years later, hoping to be revitalized by fresh sea air, he embarked on another voyage, with an eye toward revisiting that 'pleasantest' little Spanish town.

It didn't happen.

When the ship's captain approached Monterey Bay, he only mentioned it to his passengers and sailed on north to San Francisco. It seems that Monterey wasn't important enough anymore to drop anchor there.

"No," Dana sighed in a postscript to a new edition of his book, "Monterey, the prettiest town on the coast, and its capital and seat of customs, had got no advantage from the great changes, and was out of the way of commerce and of the travel to the mines and great rivers, and was not worth stopping at."

The following are excerpts are a word picture from Dana's early nineteenth century observations of Monterey:

"The bay of Monterey is very wide at the entrance, being about twenty-four miles between the two points, Ano Nuevo at the north and Pinos at the south, but narrows gradually as you approach the town, which is situated in a bend, or large cove, at the southeastern extremity, and about eighteen miles from the points, which makes the whole depth of the bay.

"The shores are extremely well wooded, (the pine abounding upon them), and as it was now the rainy season, everything was as green as nature could make it, -- the grass, the leaves, and all; the birds were singing in the woods, and great numbers of wild-fowl were flying over our heads.

"Here we could lie safe from the southeasters. We came to anchor within two cable lengths of the shore, and the town lay directly before us, making a very pretty appearance; its houses being plastered, which give a much better effect than those of Santa Barbara, which are of a mud-color. The red tiles, too, on the roofs, contrasted well with the white plastered sides and with the extreme greenness of the lawn upon which the houses – about an hundred in number – were dotted about, here and there, irregularly.

"There are in this place, and in every other town which I saw in California, no streets, or fences, (except here and there a small patch was fenced in for a garden) so that the houses are placed at random upon the green, which, as they are of one story and of the cottage form, gives them a pretty effect when seen from a little distance.

"It was a fine Saturday afternoon when we came to anchor, the sun about an hour high, and everything looking pleasantly. The Mexican flag was flying from the little square Presidio, and the drums and trumpets of the soldiers, who were out on parade, sounded over the water, and gave great life to the scene.

"Everyone was delighted with the appearance of things. We felt as though we had got into a Christian (which in the sailor's vocabulary means 'civilized') country …

"We landed the agent and passengers, and found several persons waiting for them on the beach, among whom were some, who, though dressed in the costume of the country, spoke English; and who, we afterwards learned, were English and Americans who had married and settled in the country …

"The Californians are an idle, thriftless people, and can make nothing for themselves. The country abounds in grapes, yet they buy bad wines made in Boston and brought round by us, at an immense price, and retail it among themselves at a 'real' (12 l/2 cents) by the small wine glass.

"Their hides, too, which they value at two dollars in money, they give for something which costs seventy-five cents in Boston; and buy shoes (like as not, made of their own hides, and which have been carried twice around Cape Horn) at three or four dollars, and "chicken-skin" boots at fifteen dollars apiece. Things sell, on an average, at an advance of nearly three hundred per cent upon the Boston prices …

"Monterey, as far as my observation goes, is decidedly the pleasantest and most civilized-looking place in California. In the centre of it is an open square, surrounded by four lines of one-story plastered buildings, with half a dozen cannon in the centre; some mounted, and others not.

"This is the 'Presidio,' or fort. Every town has a presidio in its centre; or rather, every presidio has a town built around it; for the forts were first built by the Mexican government, and then the people built near them for protection.

"The presidio here was entirely open and unfortified. There were several officers with long titles, and about eighty soldiers, but they were poorly paid, fed, clothed, and disciplined.

"The governor-general, or, as he is commonly called, the 'general,' lives here; which makes it the seat of government …

"No Protestant has any civil rights, nor can he hold any property, or, indeed, remain more than a few weeks on shore, unless he belong to some vessel.

"Consequently, the Americans and English who intend to remain here become

Catholics, to a man; the current phrase among them being, --"A man must leave his conscience at Cape Horn."

"But to return to Monterey, the houses here, as everywhere else in California, are of one story, built of clay made into large bricks, about a foot and a half square and three or four inches thick, and hardened in the sun. These are cemented together by mortar of the same material, and the whole are of a common dirt-color. The floors are generally of earth, the windows grated and without glass; and the doors, which are seldom shut, open directly into the common room; thee being no entries.

"Some of the more wealthy inhabitants have glass to their windows and board floors; and in Monterey nearly all the houses are plastered on the outside.

"The better houses, too, have red tiles upon the roofs. The common ones have two or three rooms which open into each other, and are furnished with a bed or two, a few chairs and tables, a looking-glass, a crucifix of some material or other, and small daubs of paintings enclosed in glass, and representing some miracle or martyrdom.

"They have no chimneys or fire-places in the houses, the climate being such as to make a fire unnecessary; and all their cooking is done in a small cook-house, separated from the house.

"The Indians ... do all the hard work, two or three being attached to each house; and the poorest persons are able to keep one, at least, for they have only to feed them and give them a small piece of coarse cloth and a belt, for the males; and a course gown, without shoes or stockings, for the females ...

"The men in Monterey appeared to me to be always on horseback. Horses are as abundant here as dogs and chickens were in Juan Fernandez. There are no stables to keep them in, but they are allowed to run wild and graze wherever they please, being branded, and having long leather ropes called 'lassos,' attached to their necks and dragging along behind them, by which they can be easily taken ...'There are probably no better riders in the world ...

"They frequently give exhibitions of their horsemanship in races, bull-baitings, etc. ...

"Monterey is also a great place for cock-fighting, gambling of all sorts, fandangos, and every kind of amusement and knavery ...

Nothing but the character of the people prevents Monterey from becoming a great town.

"The soil is as rich as man could wish; climate as good as any in the world; water abundant, and situation extremely beautiful. The harbor, too, is a good one, being subject only to one bad wind, the north; and though the holding-ground is not the best, yet I heard of but one vessel's being driven ashore here ... Yet this was from the carelessness or ignorance of the captain, who paid out all his small cable before he let go his other anchor."

Dana's Monterey was ceded to the 'Gringos' in 1848 and was capital of California until 1854 when offices for the business of running the state were moved to Sacramento.

Consequently, the little town was fortunate enough to be by-passed by mainstream America's growing commercial interests. Residents still fight to keep it that way. That's why Pan continues to hang around.

Hidden in the body of Lawrence Clark Powell's California Classics – in an essay about another shepherd of Pan, Jack London -- are two tantalizing sentences:

"Among the London manuscripts in the Huntington Library is an unpublished introduction to 'Two Years Before the Mast.' It is one of the finest tributes ever written to the truth and the power of Dana's classic."

Apparently, London had mailed his critique too late for inclusion in the 1911 edition of the Dana classic.

The Huntington Library gave permission to copy the manuscript, and the Jack London Estate in Glen Ellen, California, allowed it to be printed here, for the first time, on the following page, just as London wrote it:

JACK LONDON
GLEN ELLEN,
SONOMA COUNTY,
CALIFORNIA, U.S.A.
1731 words

O nce in a hundred years is a book written that lives not alone for its own century but which becomes a document for the future centuries. Such a book is Dana's. When Marryat's and Cooper's sea novels are gone to dust, stimulating and joyful as they have been to generations of men, still will remain "Two Years Before the Mast."

Paradoxical as it may seem, Dana's book is the classic of the sea, not because there was anything extraordinary about Dana, but for the precise contrary reason that he was just an ordinary, normal man, clear-seeing, hard-headed, controlled, fitted with adequate education to go about the work. He brought a trained mind to put down with untroubled vision what he saw of a certain phase of work-a-day life. There was nothing brilliant nor fly-away about him. He was not a genius. His heart never rode his head. He was neither overlorded by sentiment nor hag-ridden by imagination. Otherwise he might have been guilty of the beautiful exaggerations in Melville's "Typee" or the imaginative orgies in the latter's "Moby Dick." It was Dana's cool poise that saved him from being spread-eagled and flogged when two of his mates were so treated; it was his lack of abandon that prevented him from taking up permanently with the sea that prevented him from seeing more than one poetical spot, and more than one romantic spot on all the coast of Old California. Yet those apparent defects were his strength. They enabled him magnificently to write, and for all time, the picture of the sea-life of his time.

Written close to the middle of the last century, such has been the revolution worked in man's method of trafficking with the sea that the life and conditions described in Dana's book have passed utterly away. Gone are the crack clippers, the driving captains, the hard-bitten but efficient foremast hands. Remain only crawling cargo tanks, dirty tramps, grey-hound liners, and a somber, sordid type of sailing ship. The only records broken today by sailing vessels are those for slowness. They are no longer built for speed, or are they manned before the mast by as sturdy a sailor stock, nor aft the mast are they officered by sail-carrying captains and driving mates.

Speed is left to the liners, who run the silk, and tea, and spices. Admiralty courts, boards of trade, and underwriters frown upon driving and sail-carrying. No more are the free-and-easy, dare-devil days, when fortunes were made in fast runs and lucky ventures, not alone for owners, but for captains as well. Nothing is ventured now. The risks of swift passages cannot be abided. Freights are calculated to the last least fraction of per cent. The captains do no speculating, no bargain-making for the owners. The latter attend to all this, and by wire and cable rake the ports of the seven seas in quest of cargoes, and through their gents make all business arrangements.

It has been learned that small crews only, and large carriers only, can return a decent interest on the investment. The inevitable corollary is that speed and spirit are at a discount. There is no discussion of the fact that in the sailing merchant marine the seamen, as a class, have sadly deteriorated. Men no longer sell farms to go to sea. But the time of which Dana writes was the heyday of fortune-making and adventure on the sea — with the full connotation of hardship and peril always attendant.

It was Dana's fortune, for the sake of the picture, that the 'Pilgrim' was an average ship, with an average crew and officers, and managed with average discipline. Even the hazing that took place after the California coast was reached, was of the average sort. The 'Pilgrim' savored not in any way of a hell-ship.

The captain, while not the sweetest-natured man in the world, was only an average down-east driver, neither brilliant nor slovenly in his seamanship, neither cruel nor sentimental in the treatment of his men. While, on the one hand, there were no extra liberty days, no delicacies added to the meager forecastle fare, nor grog or hot coffee on double watches, on the other hand the crew was not chronically crippled by the continual play of knuckle-dusters and belaying pins. Once, and once only, were men flogged or ironed – a very fair average for the year 1834, for at that time flogging on board merchant vessels was already well on the decline. The difference between the sea-life than and now can be no better epitomized than in Dana's description of the dress of the sailor of his day:

"The trousers right around the hips, and thence hanging long and loose around the feet, a superabundance of checked shirt, a low-crowned, well-varnished black hat, worn on the back of the head, with half a fathom of black ribbon hanging over the left eye, and a peculiar tie to the black silt neckerchief."

Though Dana sailed from Boston only three-quarters of a century ago, much that is at present obsolete was then in full sway. For instance, the old word 'larboard' was still in use. He was a member of the 'larboard' watch. The vessel was on the larboard tack. It was only the other day, because of its similarity in sound to 'starboard,' the 'larboard' was changed to port. Try to imagine "All larboard bowlines on deck!" being shouted down into the forecastle of a present day ship. Yet that was the call used on the 'Pilgrim 'to fetch Dana and the rest of his watch on deck.

The chronometer, which is merely the least imperfect time-piece man has devised, makes possible the surest and easiest method by far of ascertaining longitude. Yet the 'Pilgrim' sailed in a day when the chronometer was just coming into general use. So little was it depended upon that the Pilgrim carried only one, and that one, going wrong at the outset, was never used again. A navigator of the present would be aghast if asked to voyage for two years from Boston, around the Horn to California, and back again, without a chronometer. In those days such a proceeding was a matter of course, for those were the days when dead reckoning was indeed something to reckon on, when running down the latitude was a common way of finding a place, and when lunar observations were direly necessary. It may be fairly asserted that very few merchant officers of today ever make a lunar observation, and that a large percentage are unable to do it.

"Sept. 22nd, upon coming on deck at seven bells in the morning we found the other watch aloft throwing water upon the sails, and looking astern we saw a small, clipper-built brig with a black hull heading directly after us. We went to work immediately, and put all the canvas upon the brig which we could get upon her, rigging out oars for studding-sail yards; and continued setting down the sails by buckets of water shipped up to the mast head. She was armed, and full of men, and showed no colors."

The foregoing sounds like a paragraph from "Midshipman Easy" or the "Water Witch," rather than a paragraph from the soberest, faithfulest, and most literal chronicle of the sea ever written. And yet the chase by a pirate occurred, on board the brig 'Pilgrim', on September 22nd, 1834 – something like only two generations ago.

Dana was the thorough-going type of man, not overbalanced and erratic, without quirk or quibble of temperament. He was efficient, but not brilliant. His was a general all-around efficiency. He was efficient at the law; he was efficient at college; he was efficient as a sailor; he was efficient in the mater of pride, when that pride was no more than the pride of a forecastle hand, at twelve dollars a month, in his seaman's task well done, in the smart ailing of his captain, in the cleanness and trimness of his ship.

There is no sailor whose cockles of the heart will not warm to Dana's description of the first time he sent down a royal yard. Once or twice he had seen it done. He had got an old hand in the crow to coach him. And then, the first anchorage at Monterey, being pretty thick with the second mate, he got him to ask the mate to be sent up the first time the royal yards were struck. "Fortunately," as Dana describes it, "I got through without any word from the officer; and heard the 'well done' of the mate, when the yard reached the deck, with

31

as much satisfaction as I ever felt at Cambridge on seeing a 'bene'' at the foot of a Latin exercise.''

   This was the first time I had taken a weather ear-ring, and I felt not a little proud to sit astride of the weather yard-arm, past the ear-ring, and sing out 'Haul out to leeward!''' He had been over a year at sea before he essayed this able seaman's task, but he did it, and he did it with pride. And with pride, he went down a four-hundred foot cliff, on a pair of top-gallant studding-sail halyards bent together, to dislodge several dollars worth of stranded bullock hides, though all the acclaim he got from his mates was: "What a d-----d fool you were to risk your life for half a dozen hides!"

   In brief, it was just this efficiency in pride, as well as work, that enabled Dana to set down, not merely the photograph detail of life before the mast and hide-droghing on the coast of California, but of the unvarnished, simple psychology and ethics of the forecastle hands who droghed the hides, stood at the wheel, made and took in sail, tarred down the rigging, holystoned the decks, turned in all-standing, grumbled as they cut about the kid, criticized the seamanship of their officers, and estimated the duration of their exile from the cubic space of the hide-house.

Jack London
GLEN ELLEN, CALIFORNIA
AUGUST 13, 1911

Jack London and his 'mate woman' Charmian working on a manuscript

CHAPTER III

PRE-GRINGO CALIFORNIA:
GERTRUDE ATHERTON

GERTRUDE HORN ATHERTON was one of those rare humans destined to follow her own natural instincts, with or without society's approval. She was the quintessential Bohemian.

Atherton was born on San Francisco's Rincon Hill in 1857 to a mother she described as 'in hysterics' while pregnant and to a father who 'took to drink.'

The marriage lasted three years, during which time her father encouraged flamboyance by teaching little Gertrude to stand on the dinner table and kick plates into the laps of astounded guests.

"Undoubtedly," she quipped, "[these] abnormal conditions caused that dislocation of particles, or rotten spot in the brain, or whatever it may be that produces fiction."

That 'rotten spot' was offset under the relatively stable influence of a grandfather who provided her with books that catalyzed an aptitude for writing.

When she was nineteen, she married the wealthy George Atherton (they met when he came to court her mother) whom she later described as "one of the most important incidents of my school life" – a man who "talked a lot but never said anything."

Fortunately for both, perhaps, he died at sea, leaving her a rather merry widow who was already a published writer. (She had anonymously written her first scandalous novel, The Randolphs of Redwoods, to make money on her own because she considered her husband a tightwad.)

She was fond of repeating a questionable story. To wit: that she was made aware of her husband's demise only after his corpse had been left on her doorstep, pickled in a barrel of rum for preservation on its journey home.

Even by today's standards, Gertrude Atherton would be considered outrageous. But she was also intelligent, beautiful, original – as charming and impish as Pan.

She never married again. Why? "I invariably discovered," she wrote, "that an absorbing interest in a new man afforded a mental stimulation which inspired a book; and as soon as the book was ready to be born, the man ceased to interest me. Having served his purpose, he was tactfully or abruptly discarded. More enemies. It was Heine who said, 'A woman always writes with one eye on some man and the other eye on the paper'… but

Gertrude Atherton in 1916
(Bancroft Library archives)

I wrote better when I grew independent of this particular form of stimulation."

She fascinated, sometimes shocked, readers on both sides of the Atlantic.

In the early 1920's, for example, she wrote a novel called Black Oxen based on rejuvenation of her own love life by glandular therapy.

An incipient interest in pantheism was tapped when she and her husband left the San Francisco Bay area to settle in for a year at Rancho Milpitas, an Atherton family retreat. This was near the old San Antonio mission just east of Big Sur on what is now the Hunter Liggett Military Reservation.

Not only was she charmed by the natural beauty of the area, she also experienced her first view of poverty and the resentment it instills. This, during some trouble with Mexican squatters on the ranch.

A novel, Los Cerritos, was the result of her deepening insight. It was published in 1890 and anticipated John Steinbeck's 1933 novel To a God Unknown and Frank Norris' The Octopus.

While the heroine of Los Cerritos paid homage to the redwood, Steinbeck's hero honored the oak. Atherton's novel had a passionately happy ending; Steinbeck's conclusion was just as passionately tragic.

The Atherton lovers were able to harmonize with their environment and remain balanced; the Steinbeck protagonists got out of sync and met a tragic end.

Atherton expounded on her budding pantheism in Los Cerritos while living in a convent at Boulogne, France where she had retreated to regenerate after her husband's death.

Then, stimulated in the late 1880's by a paragraph in the literary column of a London newspaper questioning why California writers "neglect the old Spanish life of that state [which] is a mine of wealth waiting for some bright genius to pan out," she decided to become that genius.

She booked passage home immediately to begin researching the ways of early Californians before the Americans took over.

What she discovered was transformed into delightful, psychologically insightful romantic tales against a backdrop of moonlight meriendas, splendid balls, horse races, bear and bull fights, love and death.

Stories that had first appeared in British magazines were initially collected in a volume called Before the Gringo Came.

Later, the title was changed by American publishers to The Splendid Idle Forties.

In 1902, Atherton dedicated this book to fellow artists in the Bohemian Club of San Francisco

Lawrence Clark Powell wrote about her in California Classics:

"She was enchanted by the beauty of the Monterey-Carmel area, as Dana had been in the 1830's. [Robert Louis] Stevenson in the 1870's, and as Mary Austin, George Sterling, Robinson Jeffers, and John Steinbeck were yet to be."

Nor was she a stranger to Mabel Dodge Luhan's colony of artists at Taos. Mabel had even admitted in a letter that this energetic feminist was her heroine.

In a novel quite different from her treatment of Monterey before the Gringo arrived – Patience Sparhawk and Her Times – Atherton anticipated the violent action of the twisted characters in some of Robinson Jeffers' coastal narratives.

Patience was a lonesome Carmel Valley farm girl who lived near the mouth of the Carmel River with a drunken mother she had tried to throttle.

The young people of Monterey saw her as an outcast, so she spent much of her time as a solitary, walking on the Carmel beach, climbing rocks at Point Lobos and viewing the coast on moonlit nights from the tower of the old mission. Her best friend was an old gray owl she fed and named Solomon.

The novel is particularly interesting because, in it, Atherton described the countryside before Carmel became a retreat for writers and artists. She wrote:

"A great bleak mountain loomed on the other side of the valley. It was as steep as if the ocean had gnawed it flat, but only the peaceful valley lay under; out in the ocean it tapered to an immense irregular mass of rock over which the breakers leapt and fought. Carmel River sparkled peacefully beneath its moving willows. The blue bay murmured to the white sands with the peace of evening. Close to the little beach the old Mission hung its dilapidated head. Through its yawning crevices the rank grass grew. Only the tower still defied elements and vandals, although the wind whistled through its gaping windows and the silver bells were no more. The huts about the church had collapsed like old muscles, but in their ruin still whispered the story of the past."

Like Mary Austin, Atherton was able to see and write 'the other side of the story.'

That is, Atherton did for pastoral life among the Spanish-speaking people on this coast before the Yankees came what Austin did for the Indians before the Spaniards arrived.

In 'The Pearls of Loreto,' one of the tales in The Splendid Idle Forties (published with the subtitle 'Stories of Old California'), Atherton wrote:

"'[Life in Monterey] is the gayest, the happiest, the most careless life in the world,' thought Pio Pico, shutting his teeth, as he looked about him. 'But how long will it last? Curse the Americans! They are coming.'"

And in 'The Ears of Twenty Americans,' she put these damning words into the mouth of a Monterey woman:

"God of my soul! Do not speak of hope to me. Hope? For what are those three frigates, swarming with a horde of foreign bandits, creeping about our bay? For what have the persons of General Vallejo and Judge Leese been seized and imprisoned? Why does a strip of cotton, painted with a gaping bear, flaunt itself above Sonoma?

"Oh, abomination! Oh, execrable profanation! Mother of God, open thine ocean and suck them down! Smite them with pestilence if they put foot in our capital! Shrivel their fingers to the bone if they dethrone our Aztec Eagle and flourish their stars and stripes above our fort!

"O California! That thy sons and thy daughters should live to see thee plucked like a rose by the usurper!

"And why? Why? Not because these piratical Americans have the right to one league of our land; but because, Holy Evangelists! They want it!

"Our lands are rich, our harbours are fine, gold veins our valleys; therefore we must be plucked. The United States of America are mightier than Mexico, therefore they sweep down upon us with mouths wide open.

"Holy God! That I could choke but one with my own strong fingers … O that I were a man! That the women of California were men!"

Powell reports that it was Gertrude Atherton, not Irving Stone (to whom the credit has been given), who pioneered the historical biographical novel. She developed her own writing style, he said, through studying techniques of two other California-inspired writers, Stevenson and Dana.

But if you were to ask the writer herself about her mentors, she would probably have mentioned the Brontes as her idols. That's because she went to their home in Haworth, Yorkshire to live for awhile during the 1890's.

Yet there's little doubt that the charm of Stevenson and the historical presence of Dana, sparked her all-too-female curiosity and craving for adventure. Reading them, she saw a way to indulge her own lust for living and for swashbuckling romance – all under the guise of research.

One of Atherton's greatest gifts was her ability to get inside the troubled heads of some of the more sensitive Franciscan padres who ministered to Indians and Spaniards alike on the Central California coast.

She wondered why the padres would even contemplate a better life hereafter while living amidst such harmonious expressions of Pan right here and now!

They were, after all, followers of the greatest spiritual revolutionary in Western history, St. Francis of Assisi, who had tried very hard to substitute the idea of kinship of all life, including man, for the traditional Biblical notions of man's apartness from nature and of nature's subservience to man.

For example, one of Atherton's characters, young Padre Arroyo, 'loved his mission children, but he loved Nature more.'

Another, an old priest, tearfully admitted, after sixty years of repressing his natural instincts, 'Paulo! Paulo! ... would that I had been thou!' upon discovering that Father Paulo had succumbed to sexual lust for one of Pan's nymphs, in the shadow of the Santa Lucia redwoods.

In the final chapter of Los Cerritos, Atherton anthropomorphized the towering redwoods, embraced as friends by **her heroine, as 'gray and stern,'** setting 'their heads against the coming blasts' and bracing 'their rigid arms.'

She wrote, 'They might succumb to man and steel, but Nature had no enemy to pit against them.'

The rustic heroine's erstwhile lover, ultimately disenchanted by so-called civilization, seeks her out among her beloved redwoods, intent on abandoning urbane life to share her pastoral ways.

He proposes a relatively isolated mode of being together which (to the dismay, perhaps, of some humanists and feminists among us) she passionately accepts. He proposes:

"I have given it much thought in lonely nights since we parted; but I have lived widely, I have known the redwoods, and I think I am right. I want you to have no friend, or even an acquaintance, but myself ... We both have work to do ... you must have no one to depend upon for your pleasure, your diversion, your entertainment, or happiness, you must have no companion but myself. This is not jealousy, Carmelita, unless it be a jealous desire for your good.

"I have drunk of all the wines that flow from the fountain of life. There is nothing in society, nothing in friendship, nothing even in personal contact with great minds. Their written words are always the best part of them. Friends have other friends ... Society is a bubble to be pricked, not blown. So I have come to this conclusion: that the only chance of happiness lies in the isolated companionship of mated souls.

"Nor can I see anything selfish in such a life. I fail to remember ever having done any man good by listening to his tiresome opinions or to his string of woes that he had poured into a dozen ears before mine ... Does all this sound selfish to you, Carmelita? Aside from my own desires, I have planned for your good with all the sense and experience I possess. With people in general you have nothing in common, and in that minor world we call society you would be wretched and disgusted. You would not understand nor be understood.

"But 'life' in its free and educating sense you shall know and feel that no woman stands before you ... Shall we live in this forest until we have absorbed its mighty symbolism and the mystery of the redwoods? We shall know that primeval union ..."

It was the element of gratitude for Nature's splendor and for the possibilities of joyous fulfillment in a natural way of life that intrigued Gertrude Atherton, with all her contrary ways.

Pan allowed her more years than most to, at least, write out her instinctual longings..

When she died in San Francisco in 1948, she was 91 years old, member of the famed Bohemian Club, founder and president of the San Francisco branch of the American Poets, Playwrights, Editors, Essayists and Novelists (P.E.N.), and widely recognized as the grand dame of American literature.

Gertrude Atherton, far right, and a friend, tennis champion Helen Wills, left, at 1926 luncheon honoring Pueblo Native American chiefs at Montalvo, James Phelan's country estate in California's Santa Clara Valley, which served as a 'retreat' to satisfy Atherton's recurring 'escapist' yearnings. (Photo from Bancroft Library archives)

The true Bohemian, a creature lost to view under the imaginary Bohemians of literature ... lives wholly to himself, does what he wishes, and not what is thought proper, buys what he wants for himself, and not what is thought proper, works at what he believes he can do well and not what will bring him in money or favour. You may be the most respectable of men, and yet a true Bohemian. And the test is this: A Bohemian, for as poor as he may be, is always open-handed to his friend. He knows what he can do with money and how he can do without it ... I may starve my appetites and control my temper for the sake of those I love; but society shall take me as I choose to be, or go without me ...

... ROBERT LOUIS STEVENSON
(1850-1894)

CHAPTER IV

FROM EDINBURGH TO MONTEREY:
ROBERT LOUIS STEVENSON AND PAN

RLS and Fanny as they were when they met

California's central coast, for many, is a Neverland. It's a state of mind, a state of nature. It's a place where we can retreat, if only for a little while, when the rest of the world gets rough. Here, the child in us can play, and the adult can reflect in an atmosphere of natural acceptance.

Pan, that venerable old goat-god of things that grow, likes it here. And so does his counterpart, Peter Pan, Sir James M. Barrie's personification of the wild child in all of us who resists growing up.

When Robert Louis Stevenson crossed ocean and plains from Scotland to Monterey in 1879 to win back the woman he loved, he had the mind set of a young Peter Pan. When he left California, he was married to Fanny Matilda Osbourne and the wise old Pan became his guide.

Stevenson's incipient pantheism came to full flower during his encounter with this coast. It was an agonizing, ecstatic experience that won the lady but nearly cost him his life, as he put it, '*under the wide and starry sky*' of Carmel Valley.

He matured here. His writing became more muscular. Yet he was to retain a boyish charm in his work and in his personality that eventually prompted a watchful Barrie to characterize him as a man who wouldn't grow up. Accordingly, Barrie would use him as a model for Peter Pan in 1904, ten years after Stevenson's untimely death.

When the Stevensons dropped out of polite Victorian society in 1888 to live among natives of Western Samoa, RLS corresponded with Barrie, a persistent critic, who regarded Stevenson as '*still a boy wondering what he is going to be.*'

Barrie saw him as '*playing at pirates*' and summarized Stevenson's philosophy: "*We are but as the* light-hearted birds. This is our moment of being; let us play the intoxicating game of life beautifully, artistically, before we fall dead from the tree."

Yet he was taken, like everyone else, with Stevenson's "indescribable charm to which we give our hearts," unwittingly alluding to his yet-to-be-born Peter Pan.

Barrie wrote that RLS "wanders the by-ways of literature without any fixed address. Too much of a truant to be classified with the other boys, he is only a writer of fiction in the sense that he was once an Edinburgh University student because now and again he looked in at his classes when he happened to be that way."

It could hardly have escaped his attention that Stevenson had found his 'Wendy' in the adventurous-but-motherly Fanny, a budding artist and writer, who had been raised on the American frontier and was his senior by about a dozen years.

Stevenson met and fell in love with her in Barbizon, an idyllic art colony in the Fontainebleau forest south of Paris. But she left him in Paris and returned to San Francisco with her children hoping to rebuild a failing marriage.

The strain led to a nervous collapse in Monterey where she'd gone to think things over. Stevenson's heroism in coming there convinced her that she should leave her philandering husband and return to Europe with RLS.

Barrie didn't know, then, that Stevenson's British editors were censoring his post-California writings to keep his 'proper' image intact.

Essays -- more brawny ones influenced by his American experience (e.g. 'The Amateur Emigrant'; 'Across the Plains'; 'The Silverado Squatters') and his life in Samoa (e.g. 'The Beach of Falesa') -- attest to this.

The following word pictures from essays in 'The Old Pacific Capitol' illustrate his sensitivity to Nature and to the indigenous people on the Big Sur-Monterey coast:

"In front of the town, the long line of sea-beach trends north and northwest, and then westward to enclose the bay. The waves which lap so quietly about the jetties of Monterey grow louder and larger in the distance; you can see the breakers leaping high and white by day; at night, the outline of the shore is traced in transparent silver by the moonlight and the flying foam; and from all around, even in quiet weather, the low, distant, thrilling roar of the Pacific hangs over the coast and the adjacent country like smoke above a battle.

"These long beaches are enticing to the idle man. It would be hard to find a walk more solitary and at the same time more exciting to the mind.

"Crowds of ducks and sea-gulls hover over the sea. Sand-pipers trot in and out by troops after the retiring waves, trilling together in a chorus of infinitesimal song. Strange sea-tangles, new to the European eye, the bones of whales, or sometimes a while whale's carcass, white with carrion —gulls and poisoning the wind, lie scattered here and there along the sands.

"The waves come in slowly, vast and green, curve their translucent necks, and burst with a surprising uproar that runs, waxing and waning, up and down the long key-board of the beach. The foam of these great ruins mounts in an instant to the

Scenes today behind the inn at Grez Sur Loing, south of Paris, just as it was when RLS and Fanny romanced there

*Inn at Barbizon where RLS boarded as it
is today*

ridge of the sand glaciers, swiftly fleets back again,
and is met and buried by the next breaker.

"The interest is perpetually fresh. On
no other coast that I know shall you enjoy, in
calm, sunny weather, such a spectacle of Ocean's
greatness, such beauty of changing colour, or such
degrees of thunder in the sound. The very air is
more than usually salt by this Homeric deep.

"In shore, a tract of sand-hills borders on
the beach. Here and there a lagoon, more or less
brackish, attracts the birds and hunters. A rough,
spotty undergrowth partially conceals the sand.
The crouching, hardy, live oaks flourish singly or in
thickets – the kind of wood for murderers to crawl
among – and here and there the skirts of the forest
extend downward from the hills with a floor of turf
and long aisles of pine-trees hung with Spaniard's
Beard.

"Through this quaint desert the railway
cars drew near to Monterey from the junction at
Salinas City – though that and so many other things
are now forever altered – and it was from here that
you had the first view of the old township lying in
the sands, its white windmills bickering in the chill,
perpetual wind, and the first fogs of the evening
drawing drearily around it from the sea.

"The one common note of all this country
is the haunting presence of the ocean. A great faint
sound of breakers follow you high up into the inland
canons; the roar of water dwells in the clean, empty
rooms of Monterey as in a shell upon the chimney;
go where you will, you have but to pause and listen
to hear the voice of the Pacific.

"You pass out of the town to the southwest,
and mount the hill among pine woods. Glade,
thicket, and grove surround you. You follow
winding sandy tracks that lead nowhither. You see
a deer; a multitude of quail arises. But the sound
of the sea still follows you as you advance, like that
of wind among the trees, only harsher and stranger
to the ear; and when at length you gain the summit,
out breaks on every hand and with freshened vigour
that same unending, distant, whispering rumble of
the ocean; for now you are on the top of Monterey
peninsula, and the noise no longer only mounts to

43

you from behind along the beach towards Santa Cruz, but from your right also, round by Chinatown and Pinos lighthouse, and from down before you to the mouth of the Carmello river. The whole woodland is begirt with thundering surges.

"The silence that immediately surrounds you where you stand is not so much broken as it is haunted by this distant, circling rumour. It sets your sense upon edge; you strain your attention; you are clearly and unusually conscious of small sounds near at hand; you walk listening like an Indian hunter; and that voice of the Pacific is a sort of disquieting company to you in your walk …

"But it is the Pacific that exercises the most direct and obvious power upon the climate. At sunset, for months together, vast, wet, melancholy fogs arise and come shoreward from the ocean. From the hill-top above Monterey the scene is often noble, although it is always sad.

"The upper air is still bright with sunlight; a glow still rests upon the Gabelano Peak; but the fogs are in possession of the lower levels; they crawl in scarves among the sand hills; they float, a little higher, in clouds of a gigantic size and often of a wild configuration; to the south, where they have struck the seaward shoulder of the mountains of Santa Lucia, they double back and spire up skyward like smoke. There their shadow touches, colour dies out of the world. The air grows chill and deadly as they advance. The trade-wind freshens, the trees begin to sigh, and all the windmills in Monterey are whirling and creaking and filling their cisterns with the brackish water of the sands. It takes but a little while till the invasion is complete.

"The sea, in its lighter order, has submerged the earth. Monterey is curtained in the night in thick, wet, salt, and frigid colds, so to remain till day returns; and before the sun's rays they slowly disperse and retreat in broken squadrons to the bosom of the sea. And yet often when the fog is thickest and most chill a ,few steps out of the town and up the slope, the night will be dry and warm and full of inland perfume …

"In a comparison between what was and what is in California, the praisers of times past will fix upon the Indians of Carmel. The valley drained by the river so named is a true Californian valley, bare, dotted with chaparral, overlooked by quaint, unfinished hills. The Carmel runs by many pleasant farms, a clear and shallow river, loved by wading kine; and at last, as it is falling towards a quicksand and the great Pacific, passes a ruined mission on a hill.

"From the mission church the eye embraces a great field of ocean, and the ear is filled with a continuous sound of distant breakers on the shore.

"But the day of the Jesuit has gone by, the day of the Yankee has succeeded, and there is no one left to care for the converted savage. The church is roofless and ruinous, sea-breeze and sea-fogs, and the alternation of the rain and sunshine, daily widening the breaches and casting the crockets from the wall. As an antiquity in this new land, a quaint specimen of missionary architecture, and a memorial of good deeds, it had a triple claim to preservation from all thinking people; but neglect and abuse have been its portion. There is no sign of American interference, save where a head-board has been torn from a grave to be a mark for pistol-bullets.

"So it is with the Indians for whom it was erected. Their lands, I was told, are being yearly encroached upon by the neighbouring American proprietor, and with that exception no man troubles his head for the Indians of Carmel.

"Only one day in the year, the day before our Guy Fawkes, the padre drives over the hill from Monterey; the little sacristy, which is the only covered portion of the church, is filled with seats and decorated for the service; the Indians troop together, their bright dresses contrasting with their dark and melancholy faces; and there, among a crowd of unsympathetic holiday-makers, you may hear God served with perhaps more touching circumstances than in any other temple under heaven.

"An Indian, stone-blind and about eighty years of age, conducts the singing; other Indians compose the choir; yet they have the Gregorian music at their finger-ends, and pronounce the Latin so correctly that I could follow the meaning as they sang. The pronunciation was odd and nasal, the singing hurried and staccato. "In saecula saeculo-ho-horum," they went, with a vigorous aspirate to every additional syllable.

"I have never seen faces more vividly lit up with joy than the faces of these Indian singers. It was to them not only the worship of God, or an act by which they recalled and commemorated better days, but was besides an exercise of culture, where all they knew of art and letters was united and expressed.

"And it made a man's heart sorry for the good fathers of yore who had taught them to dig and to reap, to read and to sing, who had given them European mass-books which they still preserve and study in their cottages, and who had now passed away from all authority and influence in that land – to be succeeded by greedy land-thieves and sacrilegious pistol-shots. So ugly a thing may our Anglo-Saxon Protestantism appear beside the doings of the Society of Jesus.

"But revolution in this world succeeds to revolution. All that I say in this paper is in a paulo-past tense. The Monterey of last year exists no longer. A huge hotel has sprung up in the desert by the railway.

"Three sets of diners sit down successively to table. Invaluable toilettes figure along the beach and between the live oaks; and Monterey is advertised in the newspapers, and posted in the waiting-rooms at railway stations, as a resort for wealth and fashion.

"Alas for the little town! It is not strong enough to resist the influence of the flaunting caravanserai, and the poor, quaint, penniless native gentlemen of Monterey must perish, like a lower race, before the millionaire vulgarians of the Big Bonanza."

Prophet though he was -- and sad as it may be that today's traffic noises drown out surf sounds in Monterey – at least one positive change has occurred:

Stevenson's words shamed citizens into restoring the old Carmel mission. Now it serves spiritual needs of residents and tourists alike, not to mention a host of Bach Festival-goers from around the world.

But for our purposes here, it seems important to note that Stevenson's soul had been 'properly prepared' for his experience with Nature in this part of America by the shaggy east coast Transcendentalist poet, Walt Whitman.

Whitman had cast a spell on RLS from afar, just as Stevenson's adventurous nature-loving spirit would touch Jack London, Gertrude Atherton, and John Steinbeck in years to come.

RLS praised Whitman in essays that revealed his own pantheistic leanings as much as his mentor's. He explained:

"[Whitman] is not against religion; not, indeed, against any religion. He wishes to drag with a larger net, to make a more comprehensive synthesis, than any or than all of them put together. In feeling after the central type of man, he must embrace all eccentricities; his cosmology must subsume all cosmologies, and the feelings that gave birth to them; his statement of facts must include all religion and all irreligion, Christ and Buddha, God and the devil … the whole world as it is, physical, and spiritual, and historical, with its good and bad, with manifold inconsistencies, is what he wishes to set forth, in strong picturesque, and popular lineaments, for the understanding of the average man."

For Whitman, he went on, "Each person is, for himself, the keystone to his own character without apology; he sees 'that the elementary laws never apologize.'"

Both concluded that everything in life is naturally inclined to follow the bent of its own being as Nature struggles to maintain dynamic balance through rearrangement and renewal of an infinite variety of beings. Both recognized the mutuality of each independent life.

When Stevenson wrote that Whitman's ideal man "must not only be strong, free, and self-reliant … but his freedom must be bounded and his strength perfected by the most intimate, eager, and long-suffering love for others," he was also alluding to his own ideal.

And when Whitman urged, "Re-examine all you have been told at school or church, or in any book, and dismiss whatever insults your own soul," Stevenson did just that.

He had discovered, even as a child, that

Carmel's Mission to the Indians as it looked in 1909 after Stevenson's words initiated its renovation

the traditional theistic concept of God as an all-knowing and caring -- albeit rewarding and punishing, even vengeful father figure 'up there' -- didn't satisfy his precocious intellect.

"Who made God?" he would ask his Calvinist indoctrinators.

As if to thank the poet who opened his mind, RLS penned one of the most beautiful tributes ever paid the double-aspected all-god of Nature, long before D. H. Lawrence had discovered this trickster in Taos. The following are excerpts from Stevenson's 'Pan's Pipes':

"THERE IS AN UNCOUTH, OUTLANDISH STRAIN throughout the web of the world, as from a vexatious planet in the house of life. Things are not congruous and wear strange disguises: the consummate flower is fostered out of dung, and after nourishing itself awhile with heaven's delicate distillations, decays again into indistinguishable soil; and with Caesar's ashes, Hamlet tells us, the urchins make dirt pies and filthily besmear their countenance ...

"The Greeks figured Pan, the god of Nature, now terribly stamping his foot, so that armies were dispersed; now by the woodside on a summer noon trolling on his pipe until he charmed the hearts of upland ploughmen. And the Greeks, in so figuring, uttered the last word of human experience.

"To certain smoke-dried spirits, matter and motion and elastic aethers and the hypothesis of this or that other spectacled professor, tell a speaking story; but for youth and all ductile and congenial minds, Pan is not dead, but of all the classic hierarchy alone survives in triumph; goat-footed, with a gleeful and an angry look, the type of the shaggy world; and in every wood, if you go with a spirit properly prepared, you shall hear the note of his

Carmel-by-the-Sea today, a charming tourist haven, just as RLS predicted

pipe. For it is a shaggy world, and yet studded with gardens ... fruitful and austere; a rustic world; sunshiny, lewd, and cruel.

"Earth wages open war against her children, and under her softest touch hides treacherous claws. The cool waters invite us in to drown; the domestic hearth burns up in the hour of sleep, and makes an end of all. Everything is good or bad, helpful or deadly, not in itself, but by its circumstances. For a few bright days in England the hurricane must break forth and the North Sea pay a toll of populous ships.

"And when the universal music has led lovers into the paths of dalliance, confident of Nature's sympathy, suddenly the air shifts into a minor, and death makes a clutch from his ambuscade below the bed of marriage. For death is given in a kiss; the dearest kindnesses are fatal; and into this life, where one thing preys upon another, the child too often makes its entrance from the mother's corpse.

"It is no wonder, with so traitorous a scheme of things, if the wise people who created for us the idea of Pan thought that of all fears the fear of him was the most terrible, since it embraces all.

"And still we preserve the phrase: a panic terror.

"To reckon dangers too curiously, to hearken too intently for the threat that runs through all the winning music of the world, to hold back the hand from the rose because of the thorn, and from life because of death; this it is to be afraid of Pan.

"Highly respectable citizens who flee life's pleasures and responsibilities and keep, with upright hat, upon the midway of custom, avoiding the right hand and the left, the ecstasies and the agonies, how surprised they would be if they could hear their attitude mythologically expressed, and knew themselves as tooth-chattering ones, who flee from Nature because they fear the hand of Nature's God!

"Shrilly sound Pan's pipes; and behold the banker instantly concealed in the bank parlour! For to distrust one's impulses is to be recreant to Pan.

"There are moments when the mind refuses to be satisfied with evolution, and demands a ruddier presentation of the sum of man's experience. Sometimes the mood is brought about by laughter at the humorous side of life, as when, abstracting ourselves from earth, we imagine people plodding on foot, or seated in ships and speedy trains, with the planet all the while whirling in the opposite direction, so that, for all their hurry, they travel back-foremost through the universe of space.

"Sometimes it comes by the spirit of delight, and sometimes by the spirit of terror. At least, there will always be hours when we refuse to be put off by the feint of explanation, nicknamed science; and demand instead some palpitating image of our estate, that shall represent the troubled and uncertain element in which we dwell, and satisfy reason by the means of art.

"Science writes of the world as if with the cold finger of a starfish; if is all true; but what is it when compared to the reality of which it discourses? Where hearts beat high in April, and death strikes, and hills totter in the earthquake, and there is a glamour over all the objects of sight, and a thrill in all noises for the ear, and Romance herself has made her dwelling among men?

"So we come back to the old myth, and hear the goat-footed piper making the music which is itself the charm and terror of things; and when a glen invites our visiting footsteps, fancy that Pan leads us thither with a gracious tremolo; or when our hearts quail at the thunder of the cataract, tell ourselves that he has stamped his hoof in the nigh thicket."

Even before Stevenson wrote this tribute, his growing affinity with the ambiguous god of Nature was evident.

As early as 1872 -- when his health, as usual, was not good -- he wrote the following, all aglow after taking a three mile walk in the Dunblane countryside:

"[Thank God] *for making me and the birds and everything just as they are and not otherwise."*

Then he celebrated "*the grass, and the fir trees, and the crows, and the sheep, and the sunshine, and the shadows of the fir trees.'*

A friend, Will Low, had likened RLS to Pan early on, observing that he wasn't handsome until he spoke, but then came "*the appeal of the vivacious eyes, the humour or pathos of the mobile mouth, with its lurking suggestion of the great god Pan."*

When Rosaline Masson wrote *The Life of Robert Louis Stevenson* (1923), she described his writing style as being like "*the reed music of Pan, thin and fine and emotional, piping through the*

Western Samoa today, largely unchanged since the Stevensons built their own 'Neverland' there.

Stevenson's swimming grotto near Vailima where RLS played on his beloved flute, in tune with Pan

shining trees and awakening, with a sudden intensity, the soul of the hearer."

Fortunately, Fanny Stevenson shared her husband's love for Nature. Not only had she sought solace early on in the Fontainebleau forest -- and later by the sea in Monterey -- she was blissful working in the garden of their Vailima plantation in Western Samoa. She admitted in a secret journal:

"Louis says that I have the soul of a peasant, not so much that I love working in the earth and with the earth, but because I like to know that it is my own earth that I am delving in. Had I the soul of an artist, the stupidity of possessions would have no power over me. He may be right. I would as soon think of renting a child to love as a piece of land. When I plant a seed or a root, I plant a bit of my heart with it and do not feel that I have finished when I have had

48

my exercise and amusement.

"But I do feel not so far removed from God when the tender leaves put forth and I know that in a manner I am a creator. My heart melts over a bed of young peas, and a blossom on my rose tree is like a poem written by my son.

"After I had made a perfect garden and it had been sold and bought several times, I beheld it ploughed up, the vines torn down, my trees cut for firewood, the flowers uprooted – planted in potatoes. I could not have felt worse had I seen my favorite riding horse, hock-kneed and ruined, dragging the plough.

"After all, I believe we present in our home the best of it. We possess something deep and strong and never the evanescent sports of the artist.

"I love the earth not only when she is beautiful but when she is called ugly. I cannot play with her and love her. My things, my house have favored me, and I cannot loosen the strings that bind us without something breaking."

One can imagine Louis impishly piping, Pan like, on his beloved flageolet as Fanny cultivated her garden.

There was, of course, much more to Stevenson's philosophy than his Pan-loving aspects. He could not only relate to the Pan-child in all of us, he could peer into the darkest corners of our psyches and help us to see what is really there.

His greatest gift, as one friend, Sidney Colvin, put it, was the ability to be "child, boy, young man and old man at all times." Colvin observed that RLS "never seemed to be cramped like the rest of us at any given time of life, within the limits of his proper age."

Fact is that RLS believed it is our duty to acknowledge all facets of ourselves, to be free, to pay our way, to be good -- and to do what gives us joy -- because there is so little time allotted us on this earth.

But he was no Pollyanna. His characteristic other-side-of-the-coin perception was:

"In his own life … a man is not to expect happiness, only to profit by it gladly when it shall arise … Life is not designed to minister to a man's vanity … Friendships fall through, health fails, weariness assails him; year after year, he must thumb the hardly varying record of his own weakness and folly. It is a friendly process of detachment. When the time comes that he should go, there need by few illusions left about himself. 'Here lies one who meant well, tried a little, failed much.' Surely that may be his epitaph, of which he need not be ashamed."

Ultimately, he attained the challenge of his own philosophy. He wanted death to find him 'flushed with hope and planning vast foundations.'

Death complied. Stevenson died swiftly of a stroke, a relatively satisfied man deeply involved in his summum bonum and doing something he'd never been known to do before – mixing mayonnaise for a salad!

Fanny mourned his death for awhile. She feared that without Louis she was nothing.

But it wasn't long before she was applying his philosophy to herself, declaring, "I would rather go the wheel and be broken than be preserved on a dusty shelf!" (Later, Jack London, a devotee of the Stevensons, would similarly aver, "I'd rather be ashes than dust.")

Suffice it to say that, wherever RLS and Fanny happened to be, they lived with derring-do. Despite chronic illness, RLS was able to create an enchanted atmosphere, drawing on his own internal poetry – the language of his fertile emotions.

What's more, he managed to muster enough swashbuckling courage to nobly practice what he preached.

The man didn't spend his life trying to change the world. He changed worlds. He and his mate sailed away on the *Casco* -- posh forerunner of Captain Hook's *Jolly Roger* -- to find their own *Treasure Island* in a South Pacific paradise where they could put foundations under their dreams.

But for those who protest, "I can't change worlds and I'm getting disillusioned – if not downright depressed – by the confounding stuff of life," Stevenson suggests another way out.

We can embrace what he called our 'Brownies,' those primal promptings and conflicting emotions that, true as they may be, trouble the great heart of man.

Then, with the help of our imaginative faculty, we, too, might discover a kind of perverse-but-frisky joy in the struggle to manage and transform the worst of them.

This, *'humbly hopeful,'* as Stevenson put it, *'that we may prove heroes.'*

He summed it all up in 'The Lantern-Bearers,' an essay praised for its charm, as well as for its insight, by none other than William James, father of American psychology. [There is a 'Postscript' on the relevance of James at the end of this book.]

In this essay, Stevenson describes a childhood pastime *'in a certain easterly fish-village'* where he spent holidays with his family.

At night, he would sally forth with village boys – each equipped with a tin bull's eye lantern hidden under his buttoned topcoat – to *'some hollow of the links where the wind might whistle overhead'* or into *'the belly of a ten-man lugger.'*

There, they would crouch together and *'delight themselves with inappropriate talk.'*

But the real essence of this bliss, he suggested, was *'to walk by yourself in the black night … and all the while, deep down in the privacy of your fool's heart, to know you had a bull's-eye at your belt, and to exult and sing over the knowledge.'*

Stevenson believed that this *'bull's-eye'* – the imaginative, creative spark ignited by the tussles of multifarious *'Brownies'* in all of us – is the spice of life to its possessor. And even though a person's life, to an outsider, may seem prosaic, or no more than *"a rude round of mud,"* he reminds us, *"there will be some golden chamber at the heart of it, in which he dwells delighted … He will have some kind of a bull's-eye at his belt."*

This arch-Bohemian concludes: **"A man's true life, for which he consents to live, lies altogether in the field of fancy. "The clergyman, in his spare hours, may be winning battles; the farmer sailing ships; the banker reaping triumph in the arts – all leading another life, plying another trade from that they chose."**

Therefore, he shouts: **"Find out where joy resides and give it a voice far beyond singing! For to miss the joy is to miss all."**

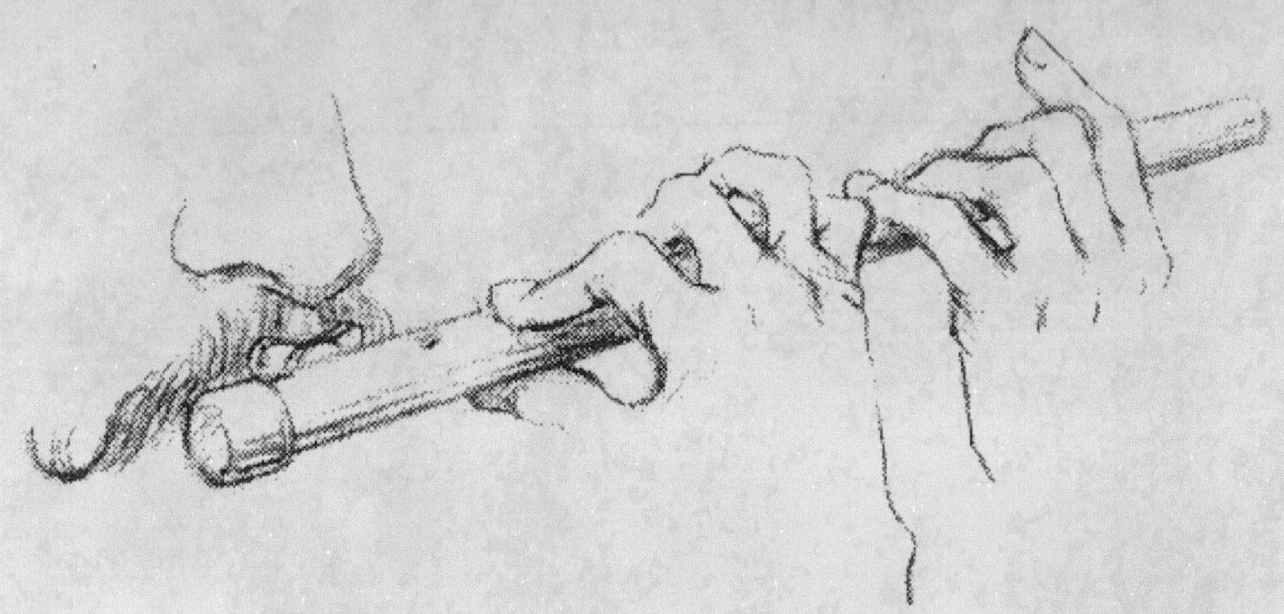

Sketch by Shell Fisher

VAILIMA CLAN (TOP); VAILIMA AS IT LOOKED WHEN RLS AND FANNY BUILT IT

RLS Centenary at Mt. Vaiea grave, 1994

STEVENSON'S VAILIMA RESTORED, 1994

Centenary images, from Aggie Grey's to Vailima, Christmastide

RLS in his study at Vailima, 1891

Samoan images while 'traveling backward'

PHOTOS FROM THE AUTHOR'S VISIT TO WESTERN SAMOA.
THE ISLAND IS INDEPENDENT, AND, UNLIKE MONTEREY,
RELATIVELY UNCHANGED SINCE THE TIME OF RLS

CHAPTER V

CARMEL'S NATURE BOHEMIANS:
JACK LONDON AND 'THE BUNCH'

The original poet laureate of San Francisco, George Sterling, is usually credited with the founding of America's first community of Nature Bohemians, Carmel-by-the-Sea.

But novelist Mary Austin and photographer Arnold Genthe, who joined Sterling in Carmel, insisted that storyteller Jack London actually motivated the movement.

After all, they argued, it was London -- home from adventures in the Klondike and basking in world praise of his epic novel, *Call of the Wild* -- who had influenced Sterling.

This, because London had preached so passionately about the virtues of a pastoral life away from urban ant heaps.

Sterling took his buddy's bait and became the first significant writer to buy land in Carmel (1905), attracting other aesthetes to what would eventually become known as California's '*seacoast of Bohemia.*'

As for Monterey, it was still a picturesque village at the time, but, since Robert Louis Stevenson's stopover, it had been more of a home to painters than to writers. That was because painters could make a good living doing seascapes to sell to those '*millionaire vulgarians of the Big Bonanza,*' as RLS had characterized guests-to-be at the posh Del Monte Hotel.

Sterling -- raised in the charming little port town called Sag Harbor, on New York's

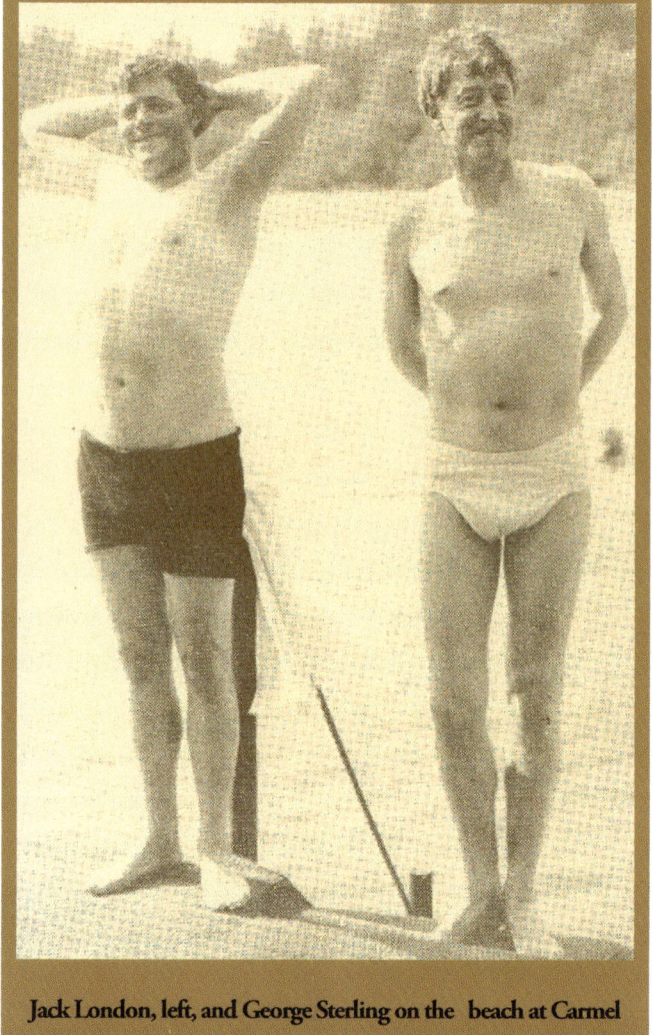

Jack London, left, and George Sterling on the beach at Carmel

Long Island that was to shelter John Steinbeck in his old age -- sought a middle ground somewhere between the hassles of city life and the dangers of wilderness after several years in the San Francisco Bay area. Carmel proved to be that golden mean.

He built a house on an acre here and described it this way:

"It's about a thousand feet from the old Carmel Mission, and a half a mile from the bay ... My 'living room' is 30 by 18 ft., finished' in oiled redwood, and with a huge fireplace and chimney, the chalk-rock for which I obtained by making several trips to a ranch a few miles up the Carmel Valley.

"The house is on a knoll at the edge of a large pine forest, half a mile from the town of Carmel. It affords a really magnificent view of the Carmel Valley and River, and of the wild and desolate mountains beyond them. I'm half a mile from the ocean (Carmel Bay), which is blue as a sapphire, and has usually a great surf; and I'm four miles from Monterey.

"Here a soft wind is always in the pines. It sounds like a distant surf, just as the surf sounds like a wind in pine trees. In Carmel, too, the air is always mild ... There are many beautiful things to see here, mostly appertaining to the reefs, cliffs, and ocean."

In putting this foundation under his dream, he became a virtual pied piper for an exodus of creatives who fled San Francisco after the earthquake and fire of 1906. Most of them were city bred writers and artists who hoped, like Sterling, to live a deeper life surrounded by the relatively unspoiled beauty of the Big Sur-Monterey coast.

Here was a landscape so perfectly balanced between extremes that there would be no need to spend time or money on improving it. Nor would they have to go far from their houses to heed the call of the wild -- hunting, swimming, fishing, walking, climbing – returning to the joys of their youth.

They considered themselves 'Bohemians,' but not the romantic 'starving-artist- in-a-garret' type.

With their interest in living close to nature as independent entities, ready to socialize and help each other when needed, they fit Robert Louis Stevenson's definition in 'Lay Morals' of a 'true' Bohemian. Stevenson wrote:

"The true Bohemian, a creature lost to view under the imaginary Bohemians of literature ... lives wholly to himself, does what he wishes, and not what is thought proper, buys what he wants for himself, and not what is thought proper, works at what he believes he can do well and not what will bring him in money of favour. You may be the most respectable of men, and yet a true Bohemian. And the test is this: a Bohemian, for as poor as he may be, is always open-handed to his friend; he knows what he can do with money and how he can do without it."

Apropos of this, Sterling and London had been early members of San Francisco's Bohemian Club. It was formed in 1872 by newspaper reporters and other men who had a passion for the arts and literature, including a handful of avant-garde businessmen.

Club headquarters was in the city, but members liked to get together in the woods for midsummer "jinks" (a Scottish drinking game). Ultimately, they purchased acreage in a redwood grove bordering the Russian River for camping and high-spirited 'self-entertainment.'

They declared themselves carefree and *blissfully indifferent to the value of money'* during Pan-worshipping romps among the redwoods.

But they soon discovered they couldn't continue to function without recruiting some wealthy members.

Attracting them was easy. The well-to-do, including a number of military top brass, were all too eager to join a private club where they could occasionally get away from restrictive lives to cut loose with some 'respectable' free spirits.

But, after the turn of the century, there was an ironic twist. Club members gradually excluded rank and file reporters for 'privacy' reasons. After that, the Club was well on its way toward becoming the playground for rich and powerful capitalists that we know today.

But today's Club is a far cry from the original community of creative socialists envisioned by London and his friends, where there were to be *'neither arrogant rich nor desperate poor,'* and where Apollonian intellectuals could freely express their Dionysian emotions with the help of Pan and a little red wine.

The 1906 quake destroyed the Bohemian

clubhouse. It took four years to rebuild. By then, however, London and Sterling had settled down in their own personal 'sacred grove' retreats in Carmel.

Here, these 'shepherds of Pan' hoped to become full-time 'pagans' --- refugees from what Sterling described as 'the cruel atmosphere of cities' where men were 'beat upon and semi-submerged by temptations to folly and luxury.'

In Carmel, on the other hand, they could hear the surf sounds and wind whistling through pines, instead of traffic noise.

London was always part of the Carmel 'bunch,' but he didn't root with them. He wanted more territory.

When he found his own 'mate-woman' -- a plucky journalist named Charmian Kittredge – he married her, and began construction of his own idea of paradise on acreage near Glen Ellen, north of San Francisco.

He explained why he didn't stay on the Big Sur-Monterey coast through a character, Mark Hall, in a semi-autobiographical novel called *The Valley of the Moon*:

"It's beautiful down beyond the Sur. I've been all over those redwood canyons, and the place is alive with game. The government land is there, too. But you'd be foolish to settle. It's too remote. And it isn't good farming land, except in patches in the canyons."

London's dream was a lot more ambitious than Sterling's. He wanted his homestead to be closer to 'working folks' so he could catalyze the building of what he hoped would become a self-sufficient socialist community.

His goal was noble, but the people who worked the ranch with him were never quite as capable as he needed them to be. And he had one big problem: he 'wanted it all right now.'

An insightful British biographer, Andrew Sinclair, speculated about London's intensity in his biography, *Jack* (1977). He quoted London as saying:

"The ultimate word is 'I like.' It is 'I like' that makes the drunkard drink and the martyr wear a hair shirt; that makes one man a reveler and another man an anchorite; that makes one man pursue fame, another gold,

another love, and another God. Philosophy is very often a man's way of explaining his own 'I like.'"

But Sinclair saw 'I like' a little differently: *"What of a man who wanted drink and revolution, revelry and intense study, fame, gold, love, and faith in mankind all at once, as Jack did? He could only try to do everything simultaneously, at the waste of his energy, at the eventual cost of his life. 'I like' is the cry of the child, not the voice of the grown man, which is 'I accept.'"*

That may well be, but near-manic intensity is often a characteristic of genius. Be that as it may, Sinclair was correct on at least one count: There was a lot of 'Peter Pan' in Jack London. There's little doubt that he was, indeed, a locked-out child ever searching for immediate gratification while trying to look out for everybody else. Like many ambitious Americans, London was impatient, more interested in short term benefits than in long term consequences.

When his ill-fated voyage into the South Seas on the *Snark* (in the wake of his mentor Robert Louis Stevenson) ended -- and he discovered he couldn't keep on 'doing it all at once' – when his body began to give the lie to his delusion that he could put anything into it and get away with it -- there was yet another blow.

The night before he and his 'mate-woman' were to move into their big, comfortable stone and redwood dream house (dubbed 'Wolf House' by George Sterling) the house burned, leaving only the stone walls and pillars standing.

Not long after this, a self-administered overdose of pain killer during an agonizing illness took him out of the game.

It seems that, sooner or later, Nature corrects the notion that if a little is good, a lot is better. London had been committing symbolic suicide for years by over-working, over-adventuring, over-eating, over-drinking, over-smoking, over-spending, over-writing, over-controlling, and finally over-medicating.

Like Melville's Captain Ahab, he was 'a wonder, a grandeur, and a woe.' His hubris brought him down as surely as any hero in ancient Greek tragedy.

But what a man he was! What a boy, too. He was an admitted alcoholic, too early for the camaraderie of Alcoholics Anonymous. He was probably manic-depressive, too early for lithium.

He was also a consummate socio-biologist – long before 'plain biology of Homo Sapiens' and the natural laws governing instinctive human behavior had became a major science.

Criticized for projecting human feelings onto animals, he replied:

"Let us be very humble. We who are so very human are very animal ... You must not deny your relatives, the other animals. Their history is your history, and if you kick them to the bottom of the abyss, to the bottom of the abyss you go yourself."

What's more, he was a budding Jungian, just beginning to understand himself and his work in light of the nature writings and psychoanalytic concepts of Dr. Carl Jung, when his physical pain became unbearable.

There was so much for him to live for, but even his 'mate woman' couldn't slow him down. There is an especially heart-rending passage in Charmian's *Book of Jack London*:

"'But you don't have to do it, mate,' I said, trying to stir his spirit. 'Always remember that you make all this work and overwork for yourself, and it must be because you choose to do rest. My ancient argument, you know!'

"There followed a colloquy upon relative values, and then he stood up abruptly, came around the small table, and flung himself on the couch into my arms.

"'Mate Woman, Mate Woman, you're all I've got, the last straw for me to cling to, my last bribe for living ... you must understand. If you don't understand, I'm lost. You're all I've got.'

"'I do understand,' I cried. 'I understand that there's too much for you to do, and that you're straining too hard to get it done ... You are going too fast. You are too aware. And you are ill. Something will snap if you don't pull up ... We can't go on this way!'"

Unfortunately, London was unable to reconcile his own disharmonies.

Made as we are in the image of Pan, self balance is essential. But to achieve it – well, Walt Whitman, who was at the height of his poetic fame when both London and Sterling were born, set an example: *"I loaf and invite my soul."* But London didn't pay attention.

One day Henry Miller left his perch in Big Sur to visit the London ranch at Glen Ellen. He exclaimed: *"Here is the nearest thing to Paradise I've ever seen in America."*

When his guide at the ranch told him London had been too busy to live there very much, Miller shook his head: *"He made a Paradise for himself and then locked himself out."* Miller didn't know then that he would do the same thing to himself in leaving Big Sur.

If the very ones who inspire us to make our own Paradise here on this earth have no taste for it when they find it themselves -- if the enlightenment we search for is a disappointment when we find it – we'd better have enjoyed the search. Jack London did. And, as we shall see, so did Henry Miller.

As for the less ambitious Sterling, he just wanted to live '*naturally and quietly*' in Carmel, inviting friends to visit '*only as I want them* [and] *find out for myself whether or not one can exist on little money and less society.*'

He had thrived on being to London what the quiet, pen-pushing Nikos was to the lusty Zorba the Greek. But their nicknames for each other belie this fact.

Jack dubbed George 'Greek' because Sterling was a solemn poet with an aquiline nose, steeped in the classics -- more like a Nikos. And George called Jack 'Wolf' because of ebullient, earthy qualities associated these days with Zorba types.

If the poet had been a woman, there's little doubt that the author of *Call of the Wild* would have declared him his 'other half' and married him.

But he wasn't female. And George's jealousy of his buddy's new-found 'mate-woman,' may have been another factor in the founding of Carmel's seacoast of Bohemia.

At least biographer Sinclair thought so. **He suggested that an act involving what Sterling appears to have interpreted as rejection by London** led directly to the move and eventuated in Sterling's becoming unchallenged leader of the Bay Area 'Crowd', or 'Bunch', which followed him to Carmel. Sinclair wrote:

"Now, in the summer of 1905, Wolf rejected his worshipping Greek and the Crowd for Charmian and Glen Ellen and the hills of Sonoma. The Greek felt betrayed and complained bitterly that his dream of living beside his Wolf had been destroyed.

"'No, I am afraid that the dream was too bright to last,' Jack wrote back to him. 'Our being near each other. If you don't understand now, some day sooner or later you may come to understand. It's not through any fault of yours, nor through any fault of mine. The world and people just happen to be so made.'"

Deeply wounded, if not angry, the 36-year-old Sterling -- a renegade Catholic seminarian-turned-realtor in the Bay area -- asserted his independence from London by assuming the role of alpha male to other members of 'The Bunch.'

Sterling had not only become bored with the world of business, he was determined to tame a growing appetite for wine, women and adventure he had acquired while carousing with London.

Besides, he'd been hailed by his mentor, Ambrose Bierce, then literary arbiter of the west coast, as poet laureate of San Francisco and needed time and space to write.

Jack London (far right), his wife Charmian Kittredge (left center), and 'The Bunch' in San Francisco about to set sail for the South Seas on '*The Snark*' following the route taken by Robert Louis Stevenson and Fanny on their own vessel, '*The Casco.*'

At least that's the way he explained his 'drop out' behavior to the skeptical Bierce, protesting, "Well, you see [now] why I must raise vegetables, Belgian hares, hens and the fruit of their wombs, squabs and gold fish, 'keep a bee,' raid mussel-reefs, and cultivate a taste for rice – not to mention cold water and 'just one girl.'"

That girl was his wife, Carrie, who had been jealous of London, accusing him of teaching her husband to run after other women and of urging him to leave his secure real estate job in the employment of a rich uncle.

But their new habitat failed to curb Sterling's drinking and lusting. He missed his 'Wolf' who had followed the example of RLS and sailed away into the South Pacific with his own 'mate-woman.'

What's more, Ambrose Bierce wrote a harsh, critical letter to Sterling, then went to Mexico in 1913 and disappeared forever.

As if that weren't enough, Sterling's frustrated wife left him, returning to Carmel for just one more try that didn't work. Unable to live with or without the man she adored, she divorced him in 1915, the year before an ailing London died from that self-administered overdose of morphine.

When Carrie committed suicide in 1918, Sterling was completely devastated. He traveled to New York, drank a lot, returned to the west coast, and wrote more poems, sheltered by his peers at the Bohemian Club.

A bright spot was development in the early 1920s of a friendship with poet Robinson Jeffers.

In writing a critique – 'Robinson Jeffers: The Man and the Artist' – Sterling launched Jeffers' career as a popular poet and inadvertently passed on his own position as California's leading poet to the younger man.

Sterling ended his life in 1926. Ill, and extremely depressed, he retreated to his quarters at the Bohemian Club and swallowed a vial of cyanide.

Club members, who had been attending a dinner in honor of critic H. L. Mencken (another protégé of Bierce) discovered charred remnants of a poem near his body: 'Deeper into the darkness can I peer than most, yet find the darkness still beyond.'

When Robinson and Una Jeffers arrived in Carmel in 1914, they happened upon what Jeffers described as "a group of trees, circular about a stone fireplace that looked like an altar, and each of the tall trunks hung with a skull, a cow's or a horse's, high up under the gloom of the boughs. It looked to us like the last of the sacred groves, deserted at last."

They had come across the grove in the Epicurean garden Sterling had abandoned after Carrie's death.

But the two poets didn't meet for several years. When they did, they took to each other immediately. Sterling became a frequent visitor at Jeffers' own retreat -- Tor House and Hawk Tower. He even planted one of the cypress trees in Jeffers' private grove on Carmel Point.

When Jeffers heard of his friend's suicide, he shook his head: "God carries the load for a Stoic, the impersonal power of nature must carry it for another, but the Epicurean must carry it for himself."

The current poet laureate of San Francisco, Lawrence Ferlinghetti, once described Sterling as "a kind of leashed Swinburne."

1925 snapshot of Robinson Jeffers and George Sterling, taken by Una Jeffers

Sterling did share the pantheism of Swinburne, but, as with Swinburne, Sterling's writing style is not popular today. Too much flowery sentiment, perhaps, not to mention a lot of ye's and thou's. The following poems by Sterling serve to illustrate:

Beneath the Redwoods

O Trees! So vast, so calm!
Softly ye lay
On heart and mind today
The unpurchaseable balm.
Ere yet the wind can cease,
Your mighty sigh
Is spirit of the sky –
Half sorrow and half peace.
Mourn ye your brothers slain,
That now afar
From hush and dews and star
Man barters for his gain?
Mourn them with all your boughs,
For I must mourn,
In seasons yet unborn,
The cares that they will house.

Spring In Carmel (Excerpts)

O'er Carmel fields in the springtime the sea-
gulls follow the plow.
White, white wings on the blue above!
White were your row and breast, O Love!
But I cannot see you now.
Tireless ever the Mission swallow
Dips to meadow and poppied hollow;
Well for her mate that he can follow,
As the buds are on the bough.
By the woods and waters of Carmel, the lark is
glad in the sun.
Harrow! Harrow! Music of God!
Near to your nest her feet have trod
Whose journeyings are done.
Sing, O lover! I cannot sing;
Wild and sad are the thoughts you bring.

Well for you are the skies of spring,
And to me all skies are one ...
On the rocks and beaches of Carmel, the surf
is mighty today.
Breaker and lifting billow call
To the high, blue Silence over all
With the word no heart can say.
Time-to-be, shall I hear it ever?
Time-that-is, with the hands that sever,
Cry all words but the dreadful 'Never!'
And name of her far away.

The Fog- Sea (Excerpts)

The morning is ten thousand miles away.
The winter night surrounds me, vast and cold,
Without a star. The voiceless fog is rolled
From ocean-levels desolate and grey;
But over all the floods of moonlight lay
A glow on those billows that enfold
The muffled sea and forest. Gaunt and old,
The dripping redwoods wait the distant day.
Unknown, above, what silver-dripping waves
Break slowly on the purple reefs of night!
What radiant foam ascends from shadowy
bars,
Or sinks unechoing to soundless caves!
No whisper is upon those tides of light,
Setting in silence toward the risen stars.

The Black Vulture

Aloof upon the day's immeasured dome,
He holds unshared the silence of the sky.
Far down his bleak, relentless eyes descry
The eagle's empire and the falcon's home –
Far down, the galleons of sunset roam;
His hazards on the sea of morning lie;
Serene, he hears the broken tempest sigh
Where cold sierras gleam like scattered foam.
And least of all he holds the human swarm
Unwitting now that envious men prepare
To make their dream and its fulfillment one,
When, poised above the caldrons of the storm,
Their hearts, contemptuous of death, shall

dare
His roads between the thunder and the sun.

This last poem, arguably Sterling's best, seems to anticipate Jeffers' musings to come.

The works of Sterling, like the writings of all these nature Bohemians, attracted others to Carmel, just as artists had been attracted to Monterey by Stevenson's essays.

Fortunately, or unfortunately, depending on one's point of view, these writers served to bring about the very thing they didn't want – influx of what Stevenson had called 'the flaunting caravanserai' and of what Jeffers was later to refer to as 'the spoilers.'

However, Stevenson's stepson-in-law, artist Joe Strong, pre-dated them both when he warned:

"[Monterey is] the most beautiful town in California. But don't tell anybody about it. If it's ever discovered by fashionable people, they'll tear it down to build expensive hotels and fine shops."

Since then, would-be nature Bohemians from many areas have broken away from cities to range on the Big Sur-Monterey coast.

One of the first – following Sterling and London to Carmel -- was Mary Austin who had spent years in New Mexico, Arizona, and California deserts studying Indian lore and the varying moods of nature.

Wallowing in the area's Native American past, her personal invocation became a Navajo chant that expressed her delight with the landscape:

As I walk ... as I walk ...
The universe ... is walking with me ...
Beautifully ... it walks before me ...
Beautifully ... on every side ...
As I walk ... I walk with beauty.

Austin, like Jeffers, was an ecologist long before the word became household. Her concern about the carelessness of humans -- and recognition of the basic wisdom inherent in Native American respect for Nature -- prompted her to write:

Mary Austin

Arnold Genthe's 'Una'

"The cunningest hunter is hunted in turn, and what he leaves of his kill is meat for some other. That is the economy of nature, but with it all there is not sufficient account taken of the works of man. There is no scavenger that

59

eats tin cans, and no wild thing leaves a like disfigurement on the forest floor."

She became aware of her incipient pantheism one day when she had felt particularly encompassed by, and part of, all life. She was overcome with reverence, and a voice inside her spoke, 'God.'

That epiphany led to her belief that she and all living things are part of God's life and to be revered.

In 1905, immediately before joining 'The Bunch' in Carmel, Austin had published Isidro, a novel about life on the Big Sur-Monterey coast that was to lure Big Sur's pioneer artists, Harry Dick and Lillian Bos Ross, to this coast in the 1930's, expanding the seacoast of Bohemia southward.

Another front runner in the exodus of Bohemians to Carmel was Arnold Genthe. He was a raconteur and photographer made famous by his candid shots taken during the San Francisco earthquake, and remembered for a stunning portrait of movie star Greta Garbo. He did the same for Una Jeffers.

Genthe detailed his Carmel experiences in As I Remember. Among other things, he wrote:

"A few miles from Monterey, running in a semi-circle on Carmel Bay, was a peninsula of pine forest, cypressed beach and rolling hill country, which, in 1902, was yet untouched by invasion. Frank Powers, an attorney ... saw it as a perfect setting for a colony of writers, painters and kindred spirits.

" Concentrating his resources, he acquired the whole peninsula and founded there the village of Carmel-by-the-Sea, put up a small hotel, and cut up the land into forest lots, which he sold on long time, easy payments.

"Providing further for extensions and for help in erecting the cottage studios, he made it possible for artists and writers to have homes where they could work, away, from the interruptions of city life.

"One of the first to take advantage of the opportunity was George Sterling. Shortly after, I followed, building the kind of a bungalow I had always wanted to have ... The next to come was Mary Austin, then the MacGowan Cookes, Jimmie Hopper and the Perry Newberrys. Hartley Manners came there to write plays.

There, too, for their summer vacations came professors from Stanford University and the University of California.

"This was the beginning of the Carmel Art Colony ... My particular cronies were George Sterling and Jack London. The latter had no home there – he lived on his ranch in Glendale [Glen Ellen] – but put in many weeks as the guest of Sterling.

"London did considerable writing at Carmel, for he liked to be near Sterling who was his best critic ...

"At a later period in the Carmel days, there came to the colony a tall, gangling young man in his early twenties ... The young man was Sinclair Lewis, and if anyone had told me then that he would be the first American to be awarded the Nobel prize for literature, I should not have been particularly surprised.

"Aside from the inspiration it was to poets and painters, Carmel deserves the credit of the beginning of the little theater movement in this country. There every summer in the Forest Theater, plays of dramatists, past and present, were given intelligent production. If among the actors there were no Julia Marlowes or Edward Sotherns, at least the lines were given sympathetic reading and a real interest in good drama was aroused."

Others artists and writers gradually joined the original 'Bunch' -- Jimmy Hopper, Upton Sinclair, Sinclair Lewis, Herbert Heron, Harry Leon Wilson, Xavier Martinez, the MacGowan sisters, and Harry Lafler.

The Londons, as noted before, frequently left their Glen Ellen ranch to play with the Carmel crowd. And there was the fascinating Nora May French, neurotic love-smitten poet who eventually joined ranks with the suicides.

But -- as with many romantics -- bouts with melancholy were offset by boundless bouts of joy.

When these artists weren't celebrating Nature in Sterling's sacred grove, they were gathering around beach fires for abalone-pounding parties.

They built their own outdoor theater in the Carmel forest, not only to honor Pan but also to celebrate Dionysus, dying and rising savior of the ancient Greeks and regenerative god of drama, wine, and emotions.

Today, Carmelites and tourists alike --

some bringing wine to sip -- gather on wooden benches under stars and pines to watch plays and musicals. Roaring fires on either side of the stage take the nip out of the air on cool nights and provide romantic ambience for picnickers. The theater has outlasted the abalone.

Eventually notables like Robin and Una Jeffers, author Lincoln Steffens (*The Shame of the Cities*) and his journalist wife Ella Winter, Dr. Jaime de Angulo, John Steinbeck, Eric Barker, and Henry Miller would join the ranks of what Steffens described as those who had the good sense to attain Paradise before they die. Said he:

"This Peninsula is a heaven on earth where the wise succeeders in life, wise enough to die before their time, go and live happily ever after."

But the charming aspects of Pan power here were never enough to save these Bohemians from pain any more than they had been able to save the Indians or Spaniards before them. As Jeffers put it, *"This coast, [cries] out for tragedy like all beautiful places."*

The double-dealing Pan is sometimes more kind to solitary individuals like Jeffers than to groups.

Today the wealthy and people who serve them -- intermixed with a few iconoclastic individuals, enterprising artists, and privacy-seeking celebrities – are gradually replacing penniless artists, struggling writers, and dropouts from the darker aspects of the American Dream who sought to live in community with other free spirits.

Nature Bohemians are vanishing in the wake of escalating land prices affordable only by a fortunate few.

Robert Louis Stevenson did indeed prophesy the fate of Monterey, the Peninsula's initial Bohemian colony, when he wrote in 1879:

"Alas for the little town! It is not strong enough to resist the influence of the flaunting caravanserai, and the poor, quaint, penniless native gentlemen of Monterey must perish, like a lower race, before the millionaire vulgarians of the Big Bonanza."

Similarly, Arnold Genthe, years later, would bemoan a similar fate for Carmel:

"It was inevitable that such a place as Carmel, which offered such a variety of superbly beautiful scenery, would in time become too popular and attract a class of people out of touch with those for whom it originally had been intended. But there are things immune to the hand of man. The unique beauty and charm of Carmel will never cease to be an inspiration to painters and writers."

And five decades after the arrival of 'The Bunch' in Carmel, John Steinbeck would lament:

"Carmel, begun by starveling writers and unwanted painters, is now a community of the well-to-do and retired. If Carmel's founders should return, they could not afford to live there, but it wouldn't go that far. They would instantly be picked up as suspicious characters and deported over the city line."

Eventually, Big Sur's most celebrated Bohemian, Henry Miller, would observe: *"Artists never thrive in colonies. Ants do."*

Opposite top-page:
 Mary Austin's Native
American-inspired 'wikiup'
in Carmel-by-the-Sea
Bottom: **George Sterling's
'sacred grove'**

Portrait of Carmel's taciturn Tor House and Hawk Tower self-described
'inhumanist' poet -- Robinson Jeffers as a young man -- by British-born
Utah artist Alvin Gittins in a 1969 portrait done expressly for the author.
Professor Gittins, an ardent 'humanist,' took exception to Jeffers' identification
with the 'hawk image' in himself, magnified by the poet's comment that, except
for the penalties, he'd as soon kill a man as a hawk. The artist admitted that he
softened Jeffers' hawk-like profile to remind the author of the 'softer aspects'
of this poet she admired.

CHAPTER VI

'NOT MAN APART':
THE 'INHUMANISM' OF ROBINSON JEFFERS

Not since the last century B.C. when Lucretius examined man's place in the nature of things, has there been a poet with the ecological fervor of Carmel's Robinson Jeffers.

Jeffers' passion for *'the divine beauty of the universe'* – especially the Big Sur-Monterey coast -- was so intense that he was moved to call himself an *'inhumanist.'* This, to distinguish his attitude from that of traditional humanists who tend to place man's welfare and values above everything else.

In his preface to *The Double Axe*, Jeffers explained 'inhumanism' as *"a shifting of emphasis and significance from man to not-man; the rejection of human solipsism and recognition of the trans-human magnificence."*

For Jeffers, as for Lucretius, man is a part of the natural order of things, not apart from it.

He perceived the world as a single organism – a suffering God full of *'violent strains and conflicts'* – that includes all life and all things. This God is both beautiful and terrifying in its efforts to create, and it must be revered, if not loved.

We identify ourselves with it in moments of mystical religious feeling when opposites – including civil war in our own psyche -- seem to be momentarily reconciled. For Jeffers, God and man alike must suffer, in order to discover and to feel and to create.

Under the spell of this awe-inspiring Central California coast, Jeffers took on the mantle of a 'prophet' in the Biblical sense of that word. His was a 'voice crying in the wilderness' warning of things to come -- if we humans don't change our ways.

He cared enough to spend the rest of his life attempting to jolt us into recognition of our vain anthropocentric -- often egomaniacal and potentially genocidal – attitudes. He urged us to reconnect with our roots in the regenerative cycles of Nature before it is too late.

His views made a lot of readers uncomfortable. But popularity was never his goal. He wrote:

"It seems time [after two world wars and with future wars brewing] that our race began to think as an adult does, rather than like an egocentric baby or insane person.
This manner of thought and feeling is neither misanthropic nor pessimist. It involves no falsehoods, and is a means of maintaining sanity in slippery times; it has objective truth and human value. It offers a reasonable detachment as a rule of conduct, instead of love, hate, and envy. It neutralizes fanaticism and wild hopes; but it provides magnificence for the religious instinct, and satisfies our need to admire greatness and rejoice in beauty."

The longer he lived on this coast, the more intense and muscular his poetry became.

When Dr. Alban D. Winspear wrote: *"For majesty of theme and subject matter, for sustained eloquence of exposition, for acuteness of philosophical insight and argumentation, for poetical imagery and musical cadence, and for the sheer enthusiasm of scientific passion, the Greeks produced nothing to rival Lucretius"* he could also have been speaking of Jeffers.

Jeffers was no stranger to this ancient poet's words -- or to the sheltered garden life of Epicurus, another of the poet's philosophic mentors.

Son of a Presbyterian theologian and devotee of ancient languages, Jeffers was schooled in

Jeffers in 1907 as a rather dreamy-eyed graduate student at University of Southern California following his graduation from Occidental College in Los Angeles

the classics at a very early age, traveling with his family in Europe. Science, medicine, and forestry came later.

He was a quiet man, fated to love his temperamental opposite -- another man's vibrant wife, Una Call Kuster -- while both were both attending university classes in Los Angeles.

After a prolonged ethical struggle, the two gave in to fate and married, ultimately becoming friends and neighbors with Una's ex-husband, Ted Kuster (founder of Carmel's Theatre of the Golden Bough), and his new wife. But not before Robin and Una had spent some time in the state of Washington.

The Jefferses came to Carmel in 1914 and knew at once they had found their niche. Jeffers explained why in an introduction to Selected Poems:

"For the first time in my life I could see people living amid magnificent unspoiled scenery essentially as they did in the idylls, or the sagas, or in Homer's Ithaca. Here was life purged of its ephemeral accretions. Men were riding after cattle, or plowing the headlands, hovered by white seagulls, as they have done for thousands of years, and will for thousands

of years to come. Here was contemporary life that was also permanent life, and not shut from the modern world but conscious of it and related to it, capable of expressing its spirit, but unencumbered by the mass of poetically irrelevant details and complexities that make a civilization."

So the couple decided to abandon city life and live in a log cabin while cultivating a sheltered 'Epicurean Garden' of their own on Carmel Point looking out toward Point Lobos which has been described as the most beautiful meeting of land and sea in the world.

They built a tiny Tudor barn-style house on an outcropping -- a 'tor' -- that had been sacred to the Indians. And Jeffers not only helped his workers haul granite building rocks from the beach below, he also learned the art of *'making stone love stone'*.

By the time Tor House was finished, Jeffers had learned enough about stonemasonry to tackle construction of a W. B. Yeats-inspired medieval tower -- a retreat for Una who adored this Irish poet.

Her husband built it himself, stone by stone, and dubbed it *Hawk Tower* to honor the savagely individualistic bird that had become, for him, a kind of totem.

Hawk Tower occasionally served as a play 'dungeon' for Una and Robin's twin boys, Garth and Donnan. And it didn't hurt at all that Jeffers himself could climb to the top and get a hawk's eye view of the coast.

Except for a tempestuous scene in Taos -- after Jeffers was tempted by 'another woman' – the couple had a storybook marriage, a simple, relatively independent and tranquil lifestyle that few of the nature Bohemians who preceded them in Carmel had been able to achieve.

"My private life," Jeffers wrote, *"is ridiculously happy."* He dreaded any change in it.

Consequently, to enjoy the concord he'd found, he believed he would have to make sacrifices to natural forces of violence on the coast, inventing victims to suffer against the backdrop of *'this coast crying out for tragedy like all beautiful places.'*

Otherwise, he feared, his own flesh might be chosen the agonist, or he might inadvertently martyr some creature to the beauty of the place. He did have disturbing daemons to be delivered through his verse.

JEFFERS WORKING ON HAWK TOWER

'THE DIVINE BEAUTY OF THE UNIVRSE; LOVE
THAT, NOT MAN APART FROM THAT'

TOWER BUILT BY ROBIN FOR UNA
WHO ADMIRED YEATS' IRISH
TOWER

JEFFERS MEDITATING, HAWK
TOWER

UNA, ROBIN, AND HAIG SHORTLY
AFTER COMING TO CARMEL

After all, he explained, *"We write out of our conflicts and excesses. If they were quite reconciled we could afford to keep still."*

Viewed this way, his poetry – the language of his deepest, most primitive feelings -- became therapy. He justified his indulgence In *'Apology for Bad Dreams.* Here is an excerpt:

"Burn sacrifices once a year to magic
Horror away from the house, this little house here
You have built over the ocean with your own hands
Beside the standing boulders; for what are we,
The beast that walks upright, with speaking lips
And little hair, To think we should always be fed,
Sheltered, intact, and self-controlled? We sooner more liable
Than the other animals. Pain and terror, the insanities of desire; not accidents but essential
And crowd up from the core:" I imagined victims for those wolves, I made them phantoms to follow;
They have hunted the phantoms and missed the house ...

Beyond this, he saw himself as another Cassandra, destined to warn of things to come in a time when few would listen.

His friend and publisher, Ward Ritchie, commented about early attitudes toward Jeffers' work:

"The name of Robinson Jeffers was merely a fantasy when I was an undergraduate at Occidental College though he also had been a student there having graduated in the class of 1905. His earlier books, 'Flagons and Apples' and 'Californians' were accessible in the library, but with the publication of 'Tamar' in 1925 and subsequently 'Roan Stallion',['The Women at Point Sur' was yet another] his themes were considered too risqué for our innocent minds. These books were locked beyond the reach of undergraduates and only available to the more mature graduate students. However, by mere chance, I acquired a copy of 'Roan Stallion, Tamar and Other Poems,' which profoundly affected my life as it also did my classmates, Gordon Newell, later to become a well-known sculptor, and Lawrence Clark Powell, librarian and author."

Now, decades after Jeffers' death, readers are more apt to understand the once-strange metaphors that characterized his most controversial narratives, his scathing indictments of politicians and war [e.g. *'The Double Axe'*], his themes of incest, ritual, and violence.

Like John Muir before him, he became increasingly mystical in his outlook and more concerned with what man is doing to his natural environment, long before ecology became a household word.

But Jeffers went further than Muir in getting at the root of the problem -- *explosions of population.*

He wrote, *"You, Death, you watch for these things, these explosions of life: they are your food, they make your feasts."*

Somewhere else he wrote that *'breeding like rabbits'* we hasten to meet our doom. Unfortunately, public dialogue on overpopulation has become 'politically incorrect' -- at least in America -- since the turn of the twenty-first century.

In one of Jeffers' most poignant poems about this problem -- *'The Purse-Seine'* -- he described crowds of fish beating wildly against seine nets, as sardine fishermen pursed the bottom of the nets and hauled in the fish. He compared the scene, not without cynicism, with what he perceived as our perennial urban predicament:

Lately I was looking from a night mountain-top
On a wide city, the colored splendor, galaxies of light: how could I help but recall the seine-net
Gathering the luminous fish? I cannot tell you how beautiful the city appeared, and a little terrible.
I thought, 'We have geared the machines and locked all together into interdependence; we have built the great cities; now
There is no escape. We have gathered vast populations incapable of free survival, insulated
From the strong earth, each person in himself helpless, on all dependent. The circle is closed, and the net
Is being hauled in. They hardly feel the cords drawing, yet they shine already. The inevitable mass disasters
Will not come in our time nor in our children's, but we and our children

Must watch the net draw narrower, government take all powers – or revolution – and the new government
Take more than all, add to kept bodies, kept souls –or anarchy, the mass disasters.
These things are Progress;
Do you marvel our verse is trouble or frowning, while it keeps its reason? Or it lets go, lets the mood flow
In the manner of the recent young men into mere hysteria, splintered gleams, crackled laughter. But they are quite wrong.
There is no reason for amazement: surely one always knew that cultures decay, and life's end is death.

But overpopulation was not his only concern. In the most tender -- and possibly most beloved -- of all his narrative poetry, 'The Loving Shepherdess,' he focused on the fruits of excessive love and pity.

In this story, Clare Walker (an embodiment of what Jeffers saw as saviorism and selfless compassion *carried to the extreme*) makes unfortunate choices that lead to a hopeless pregnancy and a heart-wrenching mystical journey north with beloved sheep that die, one by one.

In describing the long walk from Big Sur to Carmel Valley and beyond -- through majestic landscape that has come to be known as 'Jeffers Country' – the usually tough-minded Jeffers is at his poetic, most tender-minded best.

The trip ends tragically -- in the ancient Greek sense of 'tragedy' which requires that the protagonist become aware that she has been the unwitting cause of her predicament, through some error in judgment.

Clare Walker ultimately realizes how, in confusing love with 'mercy sex', she has not only brought on her own doom but destroyed her unborn child and dear sheep in the process.

Jeffers argues elsewhere that we should be in nothing so moderate as in love of man. But by the time the naïve shepherdess manages to transcend her all-too-human pity and 'fall in love outward' with the whole of life in that fabulous Sur country -- it is too late.

Before death comes, she discovers a truth: *Love and pity are not the same.*

Transcending humanity for the moment, she speaks of cosmic love, love in the most inclusive sense:

"All our pain comes from restraint of love ... the beetle beside my hand in the grass and the little brown bird tilted on a stone, the short sad grass, burnt on the gable of the world near sun and all winds. There was nothing there that I didn't love with my heart ... I looked far over the valley at the patch of oaks at the head of a field ... and loved them ... I'd always been turned to all others, and tired my poor strength confining the joy to few. But now I'd no more reason to confine it, I'd nothing left to lose nor keep back ... I have made peace with death except in my dreams, those can't be denied."

She recognizes that her earlier concept of love, though pure, had been *inefficient*. In the end, she accepts – no, *endures* – her pain and recognizes that she has simply been a willing participant in the *"great river of the blood of life."* She has been yet another of God's dupes, or fools, despite her intention to 'save.'

One admirer of Jeffers, Edward Abbey,

Photo taken from James Shebl's book, *In This Wild Water, Suppressed Poems of Robinson Jeffers*

whom some have called a 'desert Jeffers,' observed in his book, *Desert Solitaire*, that our "idle speculations, feeble and hopeless protests were foreseen nearly a half century ago by the most cold-eyed and clear-eyed of our national poets [Robinson Jeffers], on California's shore, at the end of the open road. 'Shine, perishing republic.'"

And in his introduction to the beautiful *Not Man Apart* volume, published by the Sierra Club (1969), Loren Eiseley would write:

"More than thirty years ago, accompanied by Edward Weston, I met and spoke with Robinson Jeffers on the road beyond his door. The circumstances have long faded from my mind except for the haunting presence of his features, lined and immobile as a Greek mask ...

"The eyes looked at me sidelong as he spoke ... with the remote, almost inhuman animal contemplation that marks his work ... I felt in his presence almost as if I stood before another and nobler species of man whose moods and ways would remain as inscrutable to me as the ways of the invading Cro-Magnons must have seemed dark to the vanishing Neanderthals ... A yearning for that retreat can be felt in Jeffers' work.

"D. H. Lawrence once observed that the essence of poetry 'is stark directness, without a shadow of a lie, or a shadow of deflection anywhere.' No one reading Jeffers can escape the impress of the untamed Pacific environment upon which he brooded. He was its most powerful embodiment – an incarnation of the spirit of place so intense as to epitomize Lawrence's demand that there be no deflection between the poet and what he expresses.

"Jeffers' peculiarly distinctive style ... has the roll of surf and the jaggedness of rocks about it. Something utterly wild had crept into his mind and marked his features. I cannot imagine him as having arisen unchanged in another countryside.

"The sea-beaten coast, the fierce freedom of its hunting hawks, possessed and spoke through him. It was one of the most uncanny and complete relationships between a man and his natural background that I know in literature. It tells us something of the power of the western landscape here at the world's end where the last of the American dream turned inward upon itself ... [Jeffers'] mind was deeply sensitive to those aspects of nature which contribute to the creation and maintenance of human dignity, and which are sadly threatened in our time."

Jeffers' most fervent disciple, however, was William Everson, late poet in residence at the University of California, Santa Cruz. He wrote to Lawrence Clark Powell after Jeffers' death in 1962:

"I have spent the day thinking about him, taking out his books, touching them, looking at his picture ... He was my spiritual father. It was he who broke my own father's agnosticism, and proved to me that there is a God. It was he who taught me how to worship. It was he who woke up my soul, related me to the whole of things. It was he who made me a religious man, gave me the dignity of faith in life and in God. Without him I would probably never have found my voice as a poet. He taught me to write. I mourn the passing of my father. For me it is the end of an epoch, an era of my life and experience. I wish to God I had met him, touched his hands."

In a 1970 talk called 'Earth Poetry,' given during one of four annual tributes to Jeffers[2] sponsored by Monterey Peninsula College to rekindle waning interest in the Tor House poet in his own domain, Everson set the stage by reading Jeffers' prophetic 'Science':

Man, introverted man, having crossed
In passage and but a little with the nature
of things this last century,
Has begot giants; but being taken up Like a maniac with self-love and inward conflicts cannot manage his hybrids.
Being used to deal with edgeless dreams,
Now he's bred knives on nature, turns them also inward; they have thirsty points though;
His mind forebodes his own destruction;
Actaeon who saw the goddess naked among leaves and his hounds tore him.
A little knowledge, a pebble from the shingle,
A drop from the oceans; who would have dreamed this infinitely little too much?

Who indeed, Everson asked, would have believed that so tiny a thing in nature as the human brain could 'unbalance the vastness of nature itself.'

He observed: "This threat to nature from

the mind of man, and the resistance of nature to that threat, find their meeting place in the zone of mystery."

"Anyway," he continued, 'the whole world is beginning to cry 'Hands off!' Man is beginning to recognize that he has converted discovery into knowledge and knowledge into utility, and that utility is strangling not only the earth and its nature, but humanity and its nature as well."

Everson warned that even as we may busy ourselves with betterment, "our concern must end in awe," in what he called 'the ingredient of mystery.' *Wildness.* In order to preserve the world, he said, we must experience the mystery of wildness in itself – and in ourselves.

To illustrate what he meant, he read Jeffers' 'O, Lovely Rock':

William Everson

We stayed the night in the pathless gorge of Ventana Creek, up the east fork.
The rock walls and the mountain ridges hung forest on forest

Above our heads, maple and redwood, laurel, oak, madrone,
Up to the high and slender Santa Lucian firs that stare up the cataracts
of slide-rock
To the star-color precipices and kept a little campfire for warmth.
Past midnight only two or three coals glowed red in the cooling darkness;
I laid a clutch of dead bay-leaves on the ember ends
And felted dry sticks across them and lay down again.
The revived flame lighted my sleeping son's face and his companion's,
And the vertical face of the great gorge-wall across the stream.
Light leaves overhead danced in the fire's breath, tree-trunks were seen;
It was the rock wall that fascinated my eyes and mind.
Nothing strange; light gray diorite with two or three slanting seams in it,
Smooth-polished by the endless attrition of slides and floods; no fern nor lichen, Pure naked rock
… as if I were seeing rock for the first time;
As if I were seeing through the flame-lit surface into the real and bodily and living rock …
I cannot tell you how strange; the silent passion, the deep nobility and childlike loveliness;
This fate going on outside our fates.
It is here in the mountain, like a grave smiling child, I shall die, and my boys will live and die;
Our world will go on through its rapid agonies of change and discovery;
This age will die, and wolves have howled in the snow around a new Bethlehem;
This rock will be here, grave, earnest, not passive;
And I, many packed centuries ago,
Felt its intense reality with love and wonder, this lonely rock.

Both Everson and Jeffers remind us that the mystery of death involves the mystery of renewal, two sides of one existence – God -- to be acknowledged and respected, not feared.

Destruction, death, and 'violence,' as Jeffers put it, 'has been the sire of all the world's values.' It is an element in the process of eternal creation and transformation. Change.

To know this, is to be able to live under

the threat of death and violence, when necessary, without terror, understanding that renewal is the "*real certitude that underlies the horror*," Everson suggested.

He found Jeffers' themes reassuring. He especially liked 'Bixby's Landing' about an abandoned lime kiln on the Big Sur coast, once a blot on the landscape. But nature redecorated it, in time. The poem concludes:

The kilns are cold on the hill but here in the rust of the broken boiler
Quick lizards lighten, and a rattlesnake flows down the cracked masonry, over the crumbled fire-brick.
In the rotting timbers and roofless platforms all the free companies of windy grasses
Have root and make seed;
Wild buckwheat blooms in the fat weather-slacked lime
From the bursted barrels.
Two duck hawks darting in the sky of their cliff-hung nest
Are the voice of the headland.
Wild-hearted solitude, our mother the wilderness.
Men's failures are often as beautiful as men's triumphs, but your returnings
Are even more precious than your first presence.

Meanwhile, there's our individual wildness to be cherished amid distracting, if not destructive, aspects of our stressful lives and narcissistic concerns. Everson read Jeffers' counsel in 'Signpost':

Civilized, crying how to be human again: this will tell you how.
Turn outward, love things, not men turn right away from humanity.
Let that doll lie. Consider if you like how the lilies grow,
Lean on the silent rock until you feel its divinity
Make your veins cold, look at the silent stars, let your eyes
Climb the great ladder out of the pit of yourself and man.
Things are so beautiful, your love will follow your eyes;
Things are the God, you will love God, and not

in vain,
For what we love, we grow to it, we share its nature.
At length you will look back along the stars' rays and see that
Even the poor doll humanity has a place under heaven.
Its qualities repair their mosaic around you, the chips of strength
And sickness; but now you are free, even to become human,
But born of the rock and the air, not of a woman.

And in 'Return' he admonished:

A little too abstract, a little too wise,
It is time for us to kiss the earth again,
It is time to let the leaves rain from the skies,
Let the rich life run to the root again.
I will go down to the lovely Sur Rivers
And dip my arms in them up to the shoulders.
I will find my accounting where the alder leaf quivers
In the ocean wind over the river boulders.
I will touch things and things and no more thoughts,
That breed like mouthless May-flies darkening the sky,
The insect clouds that blind our passionate hawks
So that they cannot strike, hardly can fly;
Things are the hawk's food and noble is the mountain;
Oh noble Pico Blanco, steep sea-wave of marble.

As for troubled humanity in general, Everson offered Jeffers' 'answer':

Then what is the answer? – Not to be deluded by dreams.
To know that great civilizations have broken down into violence,
And their tyrants come, many times before.
When open violence appears, to avoid it with honor or choose the least ugly faction; these evils are essential.
To keep one's own integrity, be merciful and uncorrupted and not wish for evil; And not be duped by dreams of universal justice or happiness;

These dreams will not be fulfilled.
To know this, and know that however ugly the
parts appear the whole remains beautiful.
A severed hand is an ugly thing,
And man dissevered from the earth and stars
and his history -- for contemplation or in fact
-- often appears atrociously ugly.
Integrity is wholeness; the greatest beauty is
organic wholeness,
The wholeness of life and things, the divine
beauty of the universe.
Love that, not man apart from that,
Or else you will share man's pitiful confusions,
or drown in despair when his days darken.

Still, Jeffers would anguish:

"*Dear God, who are the whole*
splendor of things and the sacred
stars, but also the cruelty and greed, the
treacheries and vileness, insanities and filth and
anguish, if you were only waves beating rock,
the wind and the iron-cored earth, the flaming
insolent wildness of sun and stars, with what
a heart I could praise your beauty. You will
not repent, nor cancel life, nor free man from
anguish for many ages to come. You are the one
that tortures himself to discover himself; I am
the one that watches you and discovers you, and
praises you in little parables, idyll or tragedy,
beautiful intolerable God."

If William Everson understood and relished Jeffers' controversial themes, critics and friends of Jeffers urged him to lighten up. But he couldn't do it. Jeffers reasoned:

"*All the prevalent religions think of God*
as blessed or happy, or at least at peace ... If God
is all, he must be suffering, since an unreckoned
part of the universe is always suffering. But
his suffering must be self-inflicted, for he is all;
there is no one outside him to inflict it ... Man
as well as God must suffer in order to discover;
and it is often voluntary, self-inflicted suffering
... what is most disliked in [my] verses remains
most true, unfortunately. If only I could sing
that God is love, or perhaps that social justice
will soon prevail. I can tell lies in prose."

Discussing themes in his poems during a lecture tour across the continent in 1941, Jeffers noted:

"*This divine outer universe is after all*
not at peace with itself, but full of violent strains
and conflicts. The physical world is ruled by
opposing tensions. The world of living things is
formed by perpetual struggle and irreconcilable
desires; and pain is an essential part of life.

"*This is the old dilemma of religions.*
Some of them run away from it, by regarding
the outer world as mere illusion; others explain
it by inventing a devil, Satan or Ahriman, and
the conflict becomes a struggle between good
and evil.

"*But clearly that is not true. The lion*
that kills is not a bit more evil than the lamb that
is killed. The rock that falls on a man's head is
no more evil than the rock he was standing on ...
there is a tortured God in every mythology; and
this seemed to me the fittest symbol to express
something that is most beautiful, and painful,
and true."

In 1956, 350 copies of *Themes in My Poems*, a book based on lectures given by Jeffers during that tour (which included Harvard and The Library of Congress) were published by The Book Club of California, with a preface by Professor B. H. Lehman. [A copy was left in my care by Lehman's grandson, Greg.] This publication is arguably the most comprehensive and *accurate* assessment of Jeffers' intention in his work *because it was written by the poet himself.*

The tour was Jeffers' first attempt to address audiences, reciting his own verses.

"*I have always disliked, and generally refused, to talk about my verses,*" he told his listeners. "*But now I suppose that is what I am here for. So I will try to speak of certain characteristic themes in them, and illustrate with readings.*"

In a voice almost as emotionless as the stones he had grown to love in creating Hawk Tower, he noted that "*one of the simplest and most frequent of [my] themes is the contemplation of death, and of death often desirable, but always to be resisted.*"

He used 'Thurso's Landing' – a story about a courageous man whose back is broken in an accident -- to illustrate.

The man is paralyzed, suffering continual pain, and dreams of death as release but will not acknowledge his desire, even to himself.

His wife, who resented his strength while he was well, is now sympathetic, wishing the pain were her own, not his. Her husband responds:

Point Lobos south beach (Phillip Hyde photo)

Big Sur-Monterey coastal range (Phillip Hyde photo)

Big Sur wilderness

Noble Pico Blanco, Big Sur

Big Sur coast

"He looked in her eyes and smiled, with that bruised look, not hearing, bent inward on his own pain; but after a time he seemed to remember that she spoke of death and said angrily: "Have you death for sale, you talk like a salesman. Every fool knows it's pleasant to rot in peace after long pain but that's not the question. I saw a nigger boxer in Monterey one night, cut all to pieces, sail up on the wind of fists, beaten and blinded, vomiting blood; he needed only let down his knees onto the canvas and be at peace; he wouldn't do it. I say I cared for that man. He was better than a better fighter."

But Jeffers admitted to his audience that he tries 'to take a more equal and less heroic view' of death. He illustrated by reading 'The Bed by the Window':

I chose the bed downstairs by the sea-window
  for a good death bed
When we built the house; it is ready waiting,
Unused, unless by some guest in a twelvemonth,
who hardly suspects
Its latter purpose.
I often regard it, with neither dislike nor
desire;
Rather with both, so equaled that they kill each
other
And a crystalline interest remains alone.
We are safe to finish what we have to finish;
And then it will sound rather like music
When the patient daemon behind the screen of
sea-rock and sky
Thumps with his staff, and calls thrice:
"Come, Jeffers."

One of Jeffers' most interesting notions was his allusion to foreign travel as 'a pleasant temporary death.'

He told his audience that foreign travel "relieves you of responsibilities and familiar scenes and duties. Then, the light and the life in those cloudy islands [Ireland and Great Britain] seem to be keyed so much lower than they are at home; everything appeared dim and soft, mournful and old; and the past, in that year of peace, seemed to a foreigner much more present than the present. So it was easy to imagine myself a dead man in a country of the dead."

In 'The Low Sky,' (Descent to the Dead) he wrote:
"But one to whom mind and imagination sometimes used to seem burdensome is glad to lie down awhile in the tomb. Among stones and quietness the mind dissolves without a sound; the flesh drops into the ground."

And in 'Antrim,' where he wrote about perpetually fighting tribes, he ended the poem by saying:
"I have lain and been humbled in all these graves, and mixed new flesh with the old and filled the hollows of my mouth with maggots and rotten dust and ages of repose. I lie here and plot the agony of resurrection."

Resurrection, discovery, renewal are recurring themes in his poems. But for Jeffers, unlike Lucretius, suicide is never an answer.

He wrote somewhere that he who drinks the wine ought to take the dregs, for even in the bitter lees and sediments, new discovery may lie.

After reflecting on air raid rehearsals in 1936, he lamented, "I wish you could find the secure value, the all-heal I found when a former time hurt me to the heart, the splendor of inhuman things: you would not be looking at each others' throats with your knives."

Later, in a mood involving what he called "a kind of desperate optimism" about the way the world was going, he would write 'The Bloody Sire':

It is not bad. Let them play.
  Let the guns bark and the bombing-plane
Speak his prodigious blasphemies.
It is not bad, it is high time,
Stark violence is still the sire of all the world's
values.
What but the wolf's tooth whittled so fine
The fleet limbs of the antelope?
What but fear winged the birds, and hunger
Jeweled with such eyes the great goshawk's
head?
Violence has been the sire of all the world's
values.
Who would remember Helen's face
Lacking the terrible halo of spears?
Who formed Christ but Herod and Caesar,
The cruel and bloody victories of Caesar?
Violence, the bloody sire of all the world's
values.
Never weep, let them play.
Old violence is not too old to beget new values.

75

Yet another theme for him was culture cycles, what he called 'the patterned rise and decline of one civilization after another.'

He accepted this as nearly as commonplace as death or war and illustrated this theme in 'The Broken Balance' based on an old Etruscan acceptance of such cycles that could mirror our own future:

The People buying and selling, Consuming pleasures, talking in the archways,
Were all suddenly struck quiet
And run from under stone to look up at the sky: so shrill and mournful,
So fierce and final a brazen
Pealing of trumpets   high up in the air, in the summer blue over Tuscany.
They marveled; the soothsayers answered:
"Although the Gods are little troubled toward men, at the end of each period
A sign is declared in heaven
Indicating new times, new customs, a changed people;
The Romans rule, and Etruria is finished;
A wise mariner will trim the sails to the wind."
I heard yesterday
So shrill and mournful a trumpet-blast,
It was hard to be wise …
You must eat change and endure; not be much troubled for the people;
They will have their happiness.
When the republic grows too heavy to endure, then Caesar will carry it;
When life grows hateful, there's power.

Hope? Not much. In 'Hope is Not for the Wise' he suggested to his audience that wise men hope nothing, that the wise are naturally lonely and think November as good as April. They remember that Caesar had heirs, and that men live on.

He reminded them of the 'rich, unplanned life on earth after the foreign wars and the civil wars, the border wars and the barbarians,' yet 'music and religion, honor and mirth' continually renew 'life's lost enchantments.'

And even if life perishes utterly, he insisted, we can still be grateful because we are left with the 'perfect loveliness of earth and heaven.'

Jeffers saw spiritual conflict at the heart of our culture. What he had to tell his audience about this is worth repeating in its entirety:

"The religions and ethics of other civilizations were more or less home-grown; they adapted themselves to the people, and the people to the religions; but Christianity is Oriental and Near-Eastern in origin, and was imposed on the western races rather recently, as history goes; and we have never got used to it. We still hold two sets of ethics, pagan and Christian, simultaneously.

"For instance, we say that we should love our enemies and not resist evil; yet at the same time we believe in justice, and that criminals ought to be punished, and that we should meet force with force, violence with violence. Or another instance: we believe in humility; but we also believe in masculine pride and self-assertion.

"I think that this spiritual conflict creates a strain in our psychology and in the heart of our culture, that has been extremely fruitful both of good and evil, of greatness and intensity, as well as of self-contradiction and hypocrisy and frustration. This theme of spiritual civil war appears often in my verses [as well as] the verses of my betters."

A very important theme in his verses, he went on, is 'religious feeling.' He called it 'pantheism,' although, he said, "I hate to type it with a name."

He described pantheism as "the feeling – I will say the certitude – that the world, the universe, is one being, a single organism, one great life that includes all life and all things; and is so beautiful that it must be loved and reverenced; and in moments of mystical vision we identify ourselves with it."

But the kind of pantheism he accepted was 'the exact opposite of Oriental pantheism.'

He explained that the Hindu mystic finds God in his own soul, holding that the outer world is illusion.

But to Jeffers "the outer world is real and divine; one's own soul might be called an illusion, it is so slight and so transitory."

In his poem 'Orestes,' some of which is written in prose form below, Jeffers tells how the mystically transformed Orestes tries to 'eff' the ineffable to his sister, Electra, explaining how he has 'fallen in love outward':

"I entered the life of the brown forest and the great life of the ancient peaks, the patience of stone" [and felt] the changes in the veins in the throat of the mountain, a grain in many centuries [that have their own time, not

76

human time].

"*I was the stream draining the mountain wood* [and] *I the stag drinking; and I was the stars, boiling with light, wandering alone, each one the lord of his own summit; and I was the darkness outside the stars, I included them, they were a part of me.*

"*I was mankind also, a moving lichen on the cheek of the round stone – they have not made words for it, to go behind things, beyond hours and ages, and be all things in all time, in their returns and passages, in the motionless and timeless center, in the white of the fire'*

"*How can I express the excellence I have found, that has no color but clearness; no honey but ecstasy; nothing wrought nor remembered; no undertone nor silver second murmur that rings in love's voice, I and my loved are one; no desire but fulfilled; no passion but peace, the pure flame and the white, fierier than any passion; no time but spherical eternity: Electra, was that your name before this life dawned?*"

All this, Jeffers explained as '*a protest against human narcissism.*' He continued:

"*If a person spends all his emotion on his own body and states of mind, he is mentally diseased, and the disease is called narcissism. It seems to me, analogously, that the whole human race spends too much emotion on itself. The happiest and freest man is the scientist investigating nature, or the artist admiring it; the person who is interested in things that are not human. Or if he is interested in human things, let him regard them objectively, as a small part of the great music.*

"*Certainly humanity has claims, on all of us; we can best fulfill them by keeping our emotional sanity; and this by seeing beyond and around the human race. This is far from humanism; but it is, in fact, the Christian attitude – to love God with all one heart and soul, and one's neighbor as one's self – as much as that, but as little as that.*"

If, as many maintain, the alternately forgiving and righteously angry Jesus was a model for what men *might* become -- and that he foresaw the end result, if people wouldn't listen to his wise words – it may just be that Jesus and Jeffers were on the same page, despite what organized religions have made of Jesus.

Like the early Church Fathers, who drew on 'the divine Plato' in developing their own theology, Jeffers also drew on this ancient Greek philosopher. At one point in his lecture, he said:

"*I spoke a moment ago of the beauty of the universe, that calls forth our love and reverence. Beauty, like color, is subjective. It is not in the object but in the mind that regards it. Nevertheless, I believe it corresponds to a reality, a real excellence and nobility in the world; just as the color red corresponds to a reality: certain wave-lengths of light, a certain rhythm of vibrations. It was Plato who defined beauty as the effulgence – the shining forth – of truth.*"

Jeffers read '*The Excesses of God*' to express what he was trying to say:

I s it not by his high superfluousness we know
  our God?
For to equal a need is natural, animal, mineral;
But to fling rainbows over the rain,
And beauty over the moon, and secret rainbows
On the domes of deep sea-shells,
And make the necessary embrace of breeding
Beautiful also as fire,
Not even the weeds to multiply without blossom
Nor the birds without music:
There is the great humaneness at the heart of things,
The extravagant kindness, the fountain
Humanity understands, and would flow likewise
If power and desire were perch-mates.

Is God constantly struggling to create and perpetuate such beauty? Jeffers thought so. He introduced the '*self-torturing God*' as another theme in is verses.

After noting that the '*divine outer universe*' is not at peace with itself but '*full of violent strains and conflicts*' -- and that there is a tortured God in every mythology -- he told his audience:

"*The poem called 'At the Birth of an Age' – its action dated in the fifth century -- runs through the struggle between Christianity and paganism, touches Prometheus and Christ and Odin, and comes finally to a vision of the universal God, self-hanged on a mountain far beyond Caucasus. Voices of the world and the people and the stars cry to him, and at last he answers.*"

Then he read '*The Hanged God*' to a riveted audience:

Pain and their endless cries, how they cry to me;
But they are I; let them ask themselves.
I am they, and there is nothing beside. I am alone
and time passes, time also is in me;
The long beat of this unquiet heart, the quick
drip
Of this blood, the whirl and returning waves of
These stars, the course of this thought.
My particles have companions and happy
fulfillments,
Each star as stars to answer him
And hungry night to take his shining and turn it
again and make it a star;
Each beast has food to find and his mating,
And the hostile and helpful world;
Each atom has related atoms, and hungry
emptiness
Around him to take his little shining cry and cry
it back;
But I am all, the emptiness and all, the shining
and the night.
All alone, I alone.
If I were quiet and emptied myself of pain,
Breaking these bonds healing these wounds;
Without strain there is nothing.
Without pressure, without conditions, without
pain is peace;
That's nothing, not-being; the pure night,
The perfect freedom, the black crystal.
I have chosen Being; therefore bonds, limits and
pain;
The crowded mind and the anguished nerves,
experience, and ecstasy. Whatever electron or
atom or flesh or star or universe cries to me, or
endures in shut silence;
It is my cry, my silence;
I am the nerve, I am the agony,
I am the endurance.
I torture myself to discover myself; Trying with a
little or extreme experiment each nerve and fibril,
All forms of being, of life, of cold substance;
All motions and netted complications of event.
  All poisons of desire, love, hatred, joy partial
peace, partial vision.
Discovery is deep and endless, each moment of
being is new;
Therefore I still refrain my 'burning thirst from the
crystal- black water of an end.'

Moving away from these difficult themes,

Jeffers turned, with admitted relief, to what he called 'the simplest and commonest theme of my serve; and that is just the landscape of the Monterey coast-range.'

"This rocky coast," he said, "is not only the scene of my narrative verse, but also the chief actor in it. These mountains rise sheer from the ocean; they are cut by deep gorges and are heavy with brush and forest. Remember, this is Central, not Southern, California. There are no orange groves here, and no oil wells, and Los Angeles is far away.

"These mountains pasture a few cattle and many deer; hawk and vulture, eagle and heron fly here, as well as sea-birds and shore-birds; and there are clouds and sea-fog in summer, and fine storms in winter.

"This coast is described throughout my narrative poems, but I will read a brief piece that notices one special part of it, a mile or two along the coast road ... because the coast here, its pure and simple grandeur, seemed to me too beautiful to be the scene of any narrative of mine. And I have kept the promise I made to it."

The Place For No Story

The coast hills at Soberanes Creek;
No trees, but dark scant pasture drawn thin over
rock shaped like flame;
The old ocean at the land's foot,
The vast gray extension beyond the long
white violence;
A herd of cows and the bull far distant, Hardly
apparent up the dark slope;
And the gray air-haunted with hawks;
This place is the noblest thing I
have ever seen;
No imaginable human presence
here could do anything
But dilute the lonely self-watchful
passion.

When he read the line that took note of 'the gray air haunted with hawks,' he was reminded that birds of prey fly so frequently through his verses 'that hawk and falcon might be called a *characteristic theme in them.'*

He particularly admired the '*savage individualism*' of hawks and, at one point, after telling about having to give the merciful 'lead gift' to a noble, broken-winged hawk he had nursed, he shocked many of his listeners by confessing that, except for the penalties, he'd as soon kill a man as a hawk.

Then he read '*Rock and Hawk.*' The following is an excerpt:

Here is a symbol ...
This gray rock, standing tall
On the headland, where the sea-wind
Lets no tree grow,
Earthquake-proved, and signatured
By ages of storms; on its peak
A falcon has perched.
I think, here is your emblem
To hang in the future sky;
Not the cross, not the hive,
But this; bright power, dark peace;
Fierce consciousness joined with final
Disinterestedness;
Life with calm death; the falcon's
Realist eyes and act
Married to the massive
Mysticism of stone,
Which failure cannot cast down
Nor success make proud.

If Jeffers had a favorite human, it was probably the old man he described in reading '*The Wind-Struck Music*' to his audience. If the poem had been prose, it might have been mistaken for Steinbeck. Here it is, one of the least known and most delightful of all Jeffers' narratives:

Ed Stiles and old Tom Birnam went up to their cattle on the bare hills above Mal Paso;
They'd ridden under the stars' white Death;
When they reached the ridge the huge tiger-lily of a certain cloud-lapped astonishing autumn sunrise opened its petals.
Ed Stiles pulled in his horse,
That flashy palomino he rode – cream color, heavy white mane, white tail, his pride – and said:
"Look, Tom. My God. Ain't that a beautiful sunrise?"
Birnam drew down his mouth, set the hard old chin, and whined:
"Now, Ed, listen here; I haven't an ounce of poetry in all my body. It's cows we're after."
Ed laughed and followed; they began to sort the heifers out of the herd.
One red little deer-legged creature
Rolled her wild eyes and ran away down the hill, the old man hard after her.
She ran through a deep-cut gully,
And Birnam's piebald would have made a clean jump but the clay lip crumbled under his take-off;
He slipped and spilled in the pit, flailed with four hooves and came out scrambling.
Stiles saw them vanish, then the pawing horse and the flapping stirrups.
He rode and looked down and saw the old man in the gully-bottom lat on his back, most grimly gazing up at the sky.
He saw the earth banks, the sparse white grass, the strong dark sea a thousand feet down below, red with reflections of clouds.
He said "My God, Tom, are you hurt?"
Who answered slowly, "No, Ed. I'm only lying here thinking o' my four sons" – biting the words carefully between his lips – "big handsome men, at present lolling in bed in their –silk – pyjamas – and why the devil I keep on working?"
He stood up slowly and wiped the dirt from his cheek, groaned, spat and climbed up the clay bank.
Stiles laughed: "Tom, I can't tell you; I guess you like to -- by God I guess you like the sunrises."
The old man growled in his throat and said, "Catch me my horse."
This old man died last winter, having lived eighty-one years under open sky, Concerned with cattle, horses and hunting, no thought nor emotion that all his ancestors since the ice-age could not have comprehended.
I call that a good life; narrow, but vastly better than most men's lives, and beyond comparison more beautiful;
The wind-struck music man's bones were moulded to be the harp for.

As for the rest of mankind, Jeffers concluded,

quoting from 'The Beaks of Eagles':

"It is good for man to try all changes, progress and corruption, powers, peace and anguish, not to go down the dinosaur's way until all his capacities have been explored; and it is good for him to know that his needs and nature are no more changed in fact in ten thousand years than the beaks of eagles."

If time is running out for humanity, Jeffers is a voice warning of that possibility.

He was, as anthropologist Loren Eisley put it, "deeply sensitive to those aspects of nature which contribute to the creation and maintenance of human dignity, and which are sadly threatened in our time."

His poem 'Birth and Death' ought to be warning enough. But few listen today. It isn't 'politically correct':

I am old and in the ordinary course of nature shall die soon,
But the human race is not old
But rather childish; it is an infant and acts like one.
And now it has captured the keys of the kingdoms of unearthly violence.
Will it use them? It loves destruction you know.
And the earth is too small to feed us, we must have room.
It seems expedient that not as of old one man, but many nations and races die for the people.
Have you noticed meanwhile the population explosion of man on earth, The torrents of new-born babies, the bursting schools?
Astonishing. It saps man's dignity.
We used to be individuals, not populations.
Perhaps we are now preparing for the great slaughter.
No reason to be alarmed; stone-dead is dead;
Breeding like rabbits we hasten to meet the day.

It just may be that the future of humanity, as well as the future of magnificent places like the rugged Big Sur coast, may depend, in part, on heeding the disturbing, ennobling words of this most forceful 'shepherd' of Pan.

Meanwhile, Jeffers offered some comfort by reminding us, as he grew old 'How Beautiful It Is':

How Beautiful It Is

It flows out of mystery into mystery;
there is no beginning;
How could there be? And no end
– how could there be?
The stars shine in the sky like the
spray of a wave
Rushing to meet no shore,
and the great music
Blares on forever,
but to us very soon
It will be blind. Not we nor our
children or the human race
Are destined to live forever, the
breath will fail,
The eyes will break – perhaps of
our own explosive bile
Vented upon each other – or a
stingy peace makes parents fools;
But far greater witnesses
Will take our places.
It is only a little planet, but how
beautiful it is!

Robinson Jeffers shortly before his
death in 'the bed by the window'
in 1962

Man Apart…
(A 'Humanist's' answer to the 'Inhumanism' of Robinson Jeffers)

Tell me, dearest teacher, about
your Jeffers and his lonely rocks;
about the insistent sea and the never-really
yielding sand, and the stones that outlast man!

Tell me how the placid doe drinks the serum of the mountain snows,
and how the eagle wheels and dives in search of food, and why.
Tell me, dearest teacher, about hawks at the headlands brood.
Tell me these and much, much more.

But please answer my nagging questions:
Did the eagle marvel at the majesty of this place
and become inspired to return?
Or was this flight by instinct required?

Man is part of organic wholeness, yes!
But he alone celebrates the rest.
Rock and sea are immutable, but only the soul of man
can cry out for natural beauty and understand.

Yes, man befouls and man destroys.
He poisons and he wastes what
his capacity for love and thought,
and that alone, can immortalize in a Jeffers poem.

"Love that, not nature apart from that,
or else you will share the naturalists' confusions,
or drown in despair when the rocks will not speak
nor the eagle remember."

To Elayne, my dearest teacher,
Bill Duke
7-17-70

CHAPTER VII

JAIME DE ANGULO:
BIG SUR'S FABULOUS OUTLANDER

Jaime De Angulo was Big Sur's brightest and quirkiest outlander. He was lauded by William Carlos Williams as one of the most outstanding writers he had ever encountered and by Ezra Pound who called him the American Ovid.

One day back in 1925, de Angulo threw a Mexican serape over his impressive shoulders, tilted his chin just right to display a carefully trimmed goatee, and strode into Mabel Dodge Luhan's adobe retreat in Taos, New Mexico -- with Dr. Carl Jung in tow -- to make a startling pronouncement that was to become the thesis of his life:

"The white American must preserve the Indian, not as a matter of justice, or even of brotherly charity, but in order to save his own neck. The European can always tie back to his own mother soil and find therein the spiritual pabulum necessary to life. But the American, overburdened with material culture, is threatened with self-destruction unless he can find some way to tie himself to his own mother soil. The Indian holds that key."

The man was brilliant. Controversial. Surreal. Henry Miller, his neighbor on Partington Ridge, described him in *Big Sur and the Oranges of Hieronymus Bosch* as *"definitely the outlaw, a renegade and a reprobate, savage, scholar, man of the world, recluse, idealist, and the very son of Lucifer ... a beloved ... detested, endearing, charming, cantankerous, pesky, devil-worshipping son-of-a-bitch of a man with a proud heart and a defiant soul filled with tenderness and compassion for all humanity ... dear Jaime de Angulo!"*

This 'outlaw' was Basque, born in Paris to aristocratic Spanish expatriates. He was also a disappointed Catholic idealist, renegade from a rigid Jesuit education.

He had expected to experience a sublime transformation during his confirmation. It didn't happen.

Disillusioned with his religious upbringing, but still on quest, he left Paris with some inheritance money In 1905, when he was barely 18, and sailed to America hoping – because he was good with horses -- to make a living as a rancher.

Like D. H. Lawrence, he was a natural seeker. His most passionate desire was to have his own experience of life and God.

Eventually, he believed he had found the uncorrupted religion he sought – a way to 'get at' God – in the pre-Christian primal vitality of our American Indians and spent the rest of his life trying to convince the rest of us that this earth does not belong to us.

Quite the contrary. His view was that we belong to the landscape and that we'd better respect it if we hope to survive.

Along his path of discovery, he worked as a Colorado cowhand and foreman of a road gang in Honduras; helped fight the San Francisco fire after the quake of 1906; won a medical degree from Johns Hopkins, specializing in psychiatry; married a 'hen medic;' became a naturalized citizen; did genetic research with his wife at Stanford; bought a cattle ranch in Alturas and hung out with the Pit River Achumawi Indians; was a maverick professor at UC Berkeley in linguistics, anthropology, psychiatry, astronomy, and mathematics; and an artist/writer who drove a herd of horses 500 miles south to his ranch in Big Sur where he developed dark themes reminiscent of Jeffers and tinged with the lighter touch of Lawrence.

He shelved his writing for awhile in 1917 to join the Army Medical Corp in the first World War, teaching psychiatry to officers at the University of Michigan. When the war ended, he returned to California to develop other talents.

With all this, he managed to introduce Carl Jung, with whom he studied in Zurich, to the Taos Indians, setting the stage for what ultimately came to be known as the Indian Movement in these United States.

Clearly, he was a live one. He quipped somewhere that everything he researched and experienced was just 'for the fun of creating.'

Impatient with solemn scholars who refused to be playful, de Angulo, like Lawrence, had great fun going forth in search of God, following, as Lawrence put it, 'the Holy Ghost and depending on the Holy Ghost within.' (*Phoenix, Posthumous Papers.*)

Yet he was serious in his scholarship. He had a genius for languages and a passionate interest in the psychology of the primitive mind.

Not only did he record Indian languages and myths, including his own subjective impressions in the field, he wrote deep, sometimes surreal, novels. They were 'thought adventures,' like those of Lawrence, that seemed to come from the blood, not just from the mind.

One of his best, *The Lariat*, was about a missionary whose passion was to convert the wild Esselen Indians to Catholicism.

The padre in the tale saw Big Sur as a villainous landscape to be tamed, a view that ended in tragedy.

But to the novel's protagonist – a Spanish deserter who had married an Indian woman and 'gone back wild' – Big Sur was a beautiful and sacred place.

De Angulo was also a great teller of stories about a pre-historic dawn when animals and men in the mountains and plains of this continent weren't as easily distinguished from each other as they are today.

He called these stories *Indian Tales* and read them in his later years to children over KPFA in Berkeley. It became the most popular program in the station's history. My own grandchildren loved the stories and asked me to read them over and over again.

De Angulo described the lives of his California Indians as '*a continuous religious experience.*' He marveled at what he called their "*spirit of wonder, the recognition of life as power, as a mysterious, ubiquitous, concentrated form of nonmaterial energy, of something loose about the world and contained in a more or less condensed degree by every object.*" (*The Californians*)

But he wasn't always so mystical. After befriending the Achumawis in northern California, he would return to these people, time and again, for sustenance, just as he returned to the wilderness in Big Sur.

He said the Indians accepted him because he was Spanish, which, to them, meant 'Mexican.' They considered him 'one of us,' especially when he would drink with them.

However, his overt enthusiasm for their gambling games, their songs, and their 'savage' ways nettled his peers at Berkeley. They admired his work, but they also protested, "*Decent anthropologists don't associate with drunkards who go rolling in ditches with shamans.*"

There's no question that de Angulo was quite off-the-wall at times. Jeffers biographer Melba Bennett repeated a favorite story about the man -- the one where he and the Jefferses meet for the first time on the Carmel beach.

Una was impressed by de Angulo's swashbuckling good looks. He was tall, slender. He dressed like a Spanish vaquero and walked proudly in the company of two Irish wolfhounds.

It was Una who persuaded Robin to accept an impromptu invitation from de Angulo to come to his Carmel cabin and share the Porterhouse steaks, apparently meant for the dogs, he was carrying under his arm.

De Angulo grilled the meat to perfection.

But when the time came to serve it to his guests, he had second thoughts. Guilt, perhaps. On impulse, he tossed it to his wolfhounds, saying, *"It would be a shame for them to go hungry."*

On getting to know this man better, the Jefferses would learn that he held an ancient American Indian belief that animals possess primitive powers superior to our own and ought to be treated with respect -- which would mean that one doesn't give steaks meant for good dogs to strangers.

Far from being put off by this incident, Una gushed to a friend about Jaime and his wife: *"We have the most wildly interesting new friends ... I could go on interminably about them."*

Una noted that Jaime had a commission in the medical corps, that he played the flute and oriental pipes, knew the Chinese language, drew 'clever caricatures,' and cared 'for nothing but living alone far from cities on a homesteaded ranch in Big Sur.'

This is all very interesting, but de Angulo's importance really lies in that startling thesis of his life's work spelled out in *Jaime in Taos*, written by his daughter Gui.

De Angulo believed that the White Man must ultimately recognize what the Red Man knows intuitively -- that *the landscape itself is sacred,* that all nature -- from stones, plants, animals, to human beings or, as Jeffers would put it, to 'the mouse in the wall' -- embodies divinity.

This, of course, is a concept de Angulo shared with all shepherds of Pan, not just with Jeffers whom Mabel hoped would fill the vacancy in her Taos circle after Lawrence's death in 1930.

**Mabel Dodge and Tony Luhan in Taos
(from Mabel Dodge Luhan: New Woman, New Worlds by Lois Palken Rudnick)**

In *Lorenzo in Taos*, the book she addressed to Jeffers to lure him to New Mexico, Mabel described her first encounter with de Angulo while she and her Indian husband, Tony, were visiting Mill Valley:

"One day when Tony and I were lying on the grass outside our house, we heard a shout and a loud 'Hallooo!' We turned and saw a queer fellow coming along to us. He was wearing a long cape, his shirt was open at the neck, and a blue beret clung to the back of his head. He said his name was Jaime de Angulo and that he had heard there was an Indian living on Tamalpais, so he'd walked over from Berkeley to look for him. So began our acquaintance with Jaime! It was he who told me all about Jung, with whom he had been working in Zurich."

I was particularly intrigued by Mabel's reference to Jung because I had met a medicine man in Taos years ago who told me that if I hoped to understand the religion of the American Indian, as well as the wisdom of Lawrence, perhaps even Jeffers, I should read Carl Jung.

The Luhans persuaded de Angulo to drive back to Taos with them to meet Lawrence, largely because Mabel believed Lawrence would share de Angulo's enthusiasm for Jung.

She described de Angulo as being prepared 'to worship Lawrence as a hero.' But when the two men met, she was disappointed. She reported that de Angulo attempted to please the novelist 'in the very way Lawrence couldn't endure!'

For example, Mabel wrote:

"Lawrence himself was outspoken enough ... but he didn't like other people to be so; particularly he disliked uncouth language from other men. So when Jaime called women bitches, Lorenzo just squirmed. And when Jaime tore off his shirt in the dining-room one day after lunch and strutted up and down, showing what fine muscles he had in his back, Lorenzo looked quite pale and sick and ran out of the room."

When the group came together at Manby Hot Springs north of Taos, everyone was delighted by Jaime's theatrics. Everyone but Lawrence.

According to Mabel, as soon as de Angulo entered the hot springs environs he cried, *"I recognize the Power -- the Collective Unconscious!"* Then he closed his eyes, stretched himself out, and began to recite Indian prayers.

Lawrence was indignant: *"A man has no*

business to be so indecent in a nice hot spring like that."

He left in a huff.

It wasn't long before de Angulo became bored with the great man's disdain. He simply passed it off by saying that Lawrence was *'ridiculous, as only an Englishman can be!'* Then he turned his attention to Lawrence's wife who didn't mind at all.

Mabel wrote:

"One night after supper ... Lawrence jumped up from his chair and ran up to Frieda, who was joking with Jaime ... he began to shout invectives at her, calling her a bitch and so on. And he so out-Jaimed Jaime that the latter was speechless for the rest of the evening.

"The next day he told me Lawrence was a red fox, and that, after all, Frieda was much the more important of the two, much more of a person. '[He said] none of you people around here appreciate her. You're all hypnotized by Lawrence. He's nothing but a neurotic!'"

After that, de Angulo stopped trying to impress Lawrence-the-man and began to compete with Lawrence-the- writer.

Mabel reported that "*he produced pounds and pounds of paper, and arranged a writing-table in the wide window of the log cabin ... in plain view of everyone coming or going. There he sat [writing] all day long for days.*"

De Angulo didn't stay long on that first trip to Taos in 1924. But he was to return, shortly, for some meaty encounters with the Indians. In a letter to his wife about the pending trip, he admitted:

"*I don't intend to work -- just loaf. I may never find anything of interest to my special line of research among the Pueblo Indians. I feel that they are too civilized, almost as much as the Aztecs, or the early Greeks. My Indians are the California tribes, real primitives with the 'wonder stuff' loose and free on tap. Still you can't tell. Deep in my heart there is an ambition that I may be able to reach that group of old men, the Keepers of the Faith ... I feel it in my bones that they know a great deal about the translation of certain powerful elemental forces into safe symbols.*"

He did get to those Keepers of the Faith, thanks to Tony Luhan. Tony took a liking to Jaime, just as he would take a liking to Jeffers in 1930.

In fact he liked Jaime, trusted him so much that he broke with his rule of ignoring white men who were curious about Indian secrets.

He not only put de Angulo in touch with Antonio Mirabal, the Indian known as Mountain Lake, he introduced him to other important Pueblo elders.

In 1925, both the Pueblos and de Angulo would benefit from Tony's decision. De Angulo wrote to Mabel about a trip to Taos with Carl Jung:

"*You can imagine my excitement. I made up my mind that I would kidnap [Jung] if necessary and take him to Taos.*

"[When we arrived] *it was a revelation to him, the whole thing. Of course I had prepared Mountain Lake. He and Jung made contact immediately and had a long talk on religion. Jung said that I was perfectly right in all that I intuited about their psychological condition ...*

"*The trip was an immense success all around. Jung got a great deal out of it. I got a great deal out of Jung, both about philosophy and about my own work. I needed his confirmation of all the stuff I have been working out by my own lonely self and against all anthropological precedent.*

"*I got [the Americans who accompanied us] interested in the Indian question. They saw my thesis ... and they solemnly promised me that they would not forget it but would use their energy and their influence towards some sort of steady campaign ... Maybe the dream of my life is on its way!*"

Jung himself would write, after the trip with de Angulo, "*I was able to talk with [Mountain Lake] as I have rarely been able to talk with a European [and discovered] new approaches to age-old knowledge that has been almost forgotten.*"

He told in Memories, Dreams, and Reflections how the Indian had complained, "*[Whites] are always uneasy and restless. We do not understand them. We think that they are mad. They say that they think with their heads.*"

"*Why of course,*" Jung answered. "*What do you think with?*"

"*We think here,*" Mountain Lake replied,

ABOVE: MABEL DODGE LUHAN'S HOUSE, DON
QUIXOTE TILE ON THE LUHAN PORCH, TAOS
PUEBLO, D. H. LAWRENCE RANCH, AND DHL GRAVE
NEAR TAOS

indicating his heart, and his eyes filled with tears.

After a long silence, he continued, *"The Americans want to stamp out our religion. Why can they not let us alone? What we do, we do not only for ourselves but for the Americans also. Yes, we do it for the whole world. Everyone benefits by it."*

Jung asked how.

The Indian explained that the Pueblos are a people who live on the roof of the world, nearest to God and the sky. So they are quite specially *"the sons of Father Sun."*

With their religion, he said, Indians help their Father go across the sky. Everything is interconnected, he reminded. To maintain balance, the Great Spirit needs humans to do their part.

"We do [ceremonies] not only for ourselves," Mountain Lake explained, *"but for the whole world. If we were to cease practicing our religion, in ten years the sun would no longer rise. Then it would be night forever."*

"I then realized," Jung wrote, *"on what the 'dignity,' the tranquil composure of the individual Indian, was founded. It springs from his being a son of the sun; his life is cosmologically meaningful, for he helps the father and preserver of all life in his daily rise and descent.*

"If we set against this our own self-justification, the meaning of our own lives as it is formulated by our reason, we cannot help but see our poverty. Out of sheer envy we are obliged to smile at the Indians' naiveté and to plume ourselves on our cleverness ... knowledge does not enrich us; it removes us more and more from the mythic world in which we were once at home by right of birth."

He pointed out that the Christian religion *"is [also] permeated by the idea that special acts or a special kind of action can influence God -- for example, through certain rites or by prayer, or by a morality pleasing to the Divinity ... Our [Christian] prayers are all directed to asking favors of God; the Indian has far more dignity, for he thinks with his heart and wishes to give as well as receive."*

The Indians, he said, speak a mythological language, much nearer to the primal vitality, the archetypal world of the unconscious.

"The decisive question for man," he wrote, *"is: 'Am I related to something infinite or not?'"*

The Indian not only has this relationship, Jung concluded, he has all the dignity and peace of soul which it brings.

Then he shared an incident that occurred as he stood alone, looking up at the Pueblos' sacred mountain. An old Indian materialized noiselessly beside him and asked *"in a deep voice vibrant with emotion ... 'Do you not think that all life comes from the mountain?'"*

Jung interpreted this as a synchronistic message and answered: *"Everyone can see that you speak the truth."*

When Jung came to America he couldn't help noticing what he called the 'Indianizing' of whites who had settled on this foreign-to-them soil.

On returning to Switzerland, ,Jung made use of Jaime's thesis -- that white Americans must preserve the Indian *'in order to save our own necks.'*

He even went so far as to warn his students that when they analyze an American about his 'shadow,' they must be much more careful than when they analyze a European.

Why?

"[Because] when the American opens a ... door in his psychology, there is a dangerous open gap, dropping hundreds of feet, and in those cases where he can negotiate the drop, he will then be faced with an Indian ... shadow, whereas [it] is safer for the European to open the door because [he] finds a shadow of his own race."

One result of Jung's trip to Taos was that he joined the ranks of all the prophetic voices who have understood the importance of Indian symbols and rites, as well as the necessity of convincing white Americans that our own religions must eventually relate back to the earth, that the sacred landscape must dominate and structure our culture -- not the other way around -- if we are to survive our own population explosions and uprooted technological cleverness.

Back in 1909, when, Jung accompanied Freud to America to receive honorary doctorates from Clark University, he made a telling comment in a letter to his wife:

"We have seen things here that inspire enthusiastic admiration, and things that make one ponder social evolution deeply. As far as technological culture is concerned, we lag miles behind America. But all that is frightfully costly and already carries the germ of the end

in itself."

This, when the rest of the world was looking forward to an era of unprecedented social and economic progress.

Jung, like Jeffers, was already in touch with the primal shadow that stalks all human enlightenment.

Visiting Taos on his second trip to America, Jung became as convinced as any Indian that the sacred Blue Lake area must be restored to the people of the Taos Pueblo, if only to avert environmental catastrophe.

The Blue Lake controversy encapsulated the whole distinction between Indians and non-Indians, a distinction spelled out so clearly in the now-famous letter sent in 1854 by **Chief Seattle** from the state of Washington to the Great White Chief in Washington D.C.

It seems important to quote the letter in its entirety because neither Mountain Lake, nor de Angulo, *nor even Jung himself, has ever spelled the message out so clearly and movingly:*

Above: The Hopi's humpbacked flute-playing Pan symbol. Below: Hopi migration symbol. (Drawings by Oswald White Bear Fredericks)

"HOW CAN YOU BUY OR SELL THE SKY, THE WARMTH OF THE LAND? *The idea is strange to us. If we do not own the freshness of the air and the sparkle of the water, how can ou buy them?*

Eery part of this earth is sacred to my people. Every shining pine needle, every sandy shore, every mist in the dark woods, every clearing and humming insect is holy in the memory and experience of my people. The sap which courses through the trees carries the memories of the red man.

"The white man's dead forget the country of their birth when they go walk among the stars. Our dead never forest this beautiful earth, for it is the mother of the red man. We are part of the earth and it is part of us. The perfumed flowers are our sisters; the deer, the horse, the great eagle, these are our brothers. The rocky crests, the juices in the meadows, the body heat of the pony, and man – all belong to the same family.

"So, when the Great Chief in Washington sends word that he wishes to buy our land, he asks much of us. The Great Chief sends word he will reserve us a place so that we can live comfortably to ourselves. He will be our father and we will be his children. So we will consider your offer to buy our land. But it will not be easy. For this land is sacred to us.

This shining water that moves in the streams and rivers is not just water but the blood of our ancestors. If we sell you land, you must remember that it is sacred, and you must teach your children that it is sacred and that each ghostly reflection in the clear water of the lakes tells of events and memories in the life of my people. The water's murmur is the voice of my father's father.

The rivers are our brothers, they quench our thirst. The rivers carry our canoes, and feed our children. If we sell you our land, you must remember and teach your children, that the rivers are our brothers and yours and you must henceforth give the rivers the kindness you would give any brother.

"WE KNOW THAT THE WHITE MAN DOES NOT UNDERSTAND OUR WAYS. One portion of land is the same to him as the next, for he is a stranger who comes in the night and takes from the land whatever he needs. The earth is not his brother, but his enemy, and when he

has conquered it, he moves on. He leaves his fathers' graves behind and he does not care. His fathers' graves and his children's birthright are forgotten. He treats his mother, the earth, and is brother, the sky as things to be bought, plundered, sold like sheep or bright beads. His appetite will devour the earth and leave behind only desert.

"There is no quiet place in the white man's cities. No place to hear the unfurling of leaves in spring or the rustle of an insect's wings. But perhaps it is because I am a savage and do not understand. The clatter only seems to insult the ears. And what is there to life if a man cannot hear the lonely cry of the whippoorwill or the arguments of the frogs around a pond at night? I am a red man and do not understand. The Indian prefers the soft sound of the wind darting over the face of a pond, and the smell of the wind itself, cleansed by a midday rain, or scented with the pinon pine.

"The air is precious to the red man, for all things share the same breath – the beast, the tree, the man, they all share the same breath. The white man does not seem to notice the air he breathes. Like a man dying for many days, he is numb to the stench. But if we sell you our land, you must remember that the air is precious to us, that the air shares its spirit with all the life it supports. The wind that gave our grandfather his first breath also receives his last sigh. And if we sell you our land you must keep it apart and sacred as a place where even the white man can go to taste the wind that is sweetened by the meadow's flowers.

"SO WE WILL CONSIDER YOUR OFFER TO BUY OUR LAND. If we decide to accept, I will make one condition: The white man must treat the beasts of this land as his brothers. I am a savage and I do not understand any other way. I have seen a thousand rotting buffaloes n the prairie, left by the white man who shot them from a passing train. I am a savage and I do not understand how the smoking iron horse can be more important than the buffalo that we kill only to stay alive.

"What is man without the beasts? If all the beats were gone man would die from a great loneliness of spirit. For whatever happens to the beasts soon happens to man. All things are connected.

"You must teach your children that the ground beneath their feet is the ashes of our grandfathers. So that they will respect the land, tell your children that the earth is rich with the lives of our kin. Teach your children what we have taught our children – that the earth is our mother. Whatever befalls the earth befalls the sons of the earth. If men spit upon the ground, they spit upon themselves.

"WHATEVER BEFALLS THE EARTH BEFALLS THE SONS OF THE EARTH. Man did not weave the web of life; he is merely a strand in it. Whatever he does to the web, he does to himself.

"Even the white man whose God walks and talks with him as friend to friend, cannot be exempt from the common destiny. We may be brothers after all. We shall see. One thing we know, which the white man may one day discover, our God is the same God. You may think now that you own Him as you wish to own our land; but you cannot. He is the God of man, and His compassion is equal for the red man and the white. This earth is precious in Him and to harm the earth is to heap contempt on its Creator. The whites too shall pass; perhaps sooner than all other tribes. Contaminate your bed and you will one night suffocate in your own waste.

"But in your perishing you will sine brightly, fired by the strength of God who brought you to this land and for some special purpose gave you dominion over this land and over the red man. That destiny is a mystery to us, for we do not understand when the buffalo are all slaughtered, the wild horses are tamed, the secret corners of the forest heavy with scent of many men, and the view of the ripe hills blotted by talking wires. Where is the thicket? Gone. Where is the eagle? Gone. The end of living and the beginning of survival."

Despite such pleas – and there were many after it -- the Department of Agriculture fought hard to retain the Blue Lake area's valuable timber for future industrial profit. But in 1970, President Nixon signed the bill to get their Blue Lake shrine returned to the Taos people. The bill also guaranteed that Indian's religious practices would be given equal respect along with Christian ceremonies.

This happened after a five-year groundswell among grass roots Americans moved by their admiration for the Indians' refusal to take money for their sacred ground.

Perhaps it was no accident that the Indian Movement of the 1960's paralleled another grass roots movement in ecology that sparked new interest in Jeffers and prepared the way for Edward Abbey's controversial book, The Monkey Wrench Gang, about what we would refer to as 'eco-terrorists' today.

Had they lived to see this, Jung (who died in 1961) and de Angulo (1950) would have been delighted, not only for the Indian's right to his land and ceremonies, but for the rest of us as well.

Back in 1925, de Angulo wrote an impassioned letter (quoted in Jaime in Taos) to Ruth Benedict, assistant to anthropologist Frank Boas, who had sought his help in getting an "informant" to reveal secrets of the Taos Indians:

"Oh, God! Ruth ... do you realize that it is just that sort of thing that kills the Indians? I mean it seriously. It kills them spiritually first, and, as in their life the spiritual and the physical element are much more interdependent than in our own stage of culture, they soon die of it physically. They just lie down and die.

"That's what you anthropologists with your infernal curiosity and your thirst for scientific data bring about ... Of course if you promised that you would never publish the actual secrets, I would tell you a lot myself about the meaning of the whole thing. It is all right to talk about it in a general way, with ... the necessary care that must be always used in handling all esoteric knowledge. It is as powerful and dangerous as the lightning. Look at all the harm that raw psychoanalysts do to their patients ... But the actual details of ceremonies, that must never be told ... You wouldn't inveigle my child into telling you the secrets of my home."

Then he spelled out his thesis for her:

"Don't you see the meaning of it all? In Europe we can go back to our mother the earth through the spirits of our own ancestors. They inhabit the soil, the trees, the rocks. In America the soil is teeming with the ghosts of Indians. Americans will never find spiritual stability until they learn to recognize the Indians as their spiritual ancestors. [But] you would lose [their legacy] by killing the Indian off before that message has been comprehended by the white

Americans. And you kill the Indian as surely by disorganizing his spiritual social life as you do with guns."

As de Angulo suspected, it would be a natural leap for Jung, dedicated as he was to the God-image in the human psyche, to recognize the Collective Unconscious in the Indian's concept of the primal source of generative energy underlying cosmic diversity.

Every school child knows it as the 'Great Spirit' or 'Mighty Something.' Jamake Highwater calls it 'Primal Mind;' the ancient Greeks mythologized it as Pan-power, Alan Watts referred to it as 'It,' and Robinson Jeffers saw it as the 'divine beauty of the universe.' God.

Lawrence, yet another fierce advocate for the primal mind, perceived it as 'the Holy Ghost within.' For him, the primal consciousness of the Indian was akin to what he saw as a pre-mental 'blood consciousness' that charges all life. From the standpoint of human ethics, it isn't always beautiful, as Lawrence knew. But for him, as for the Indians, it was to be trusted, religiously.

He wrote in 'Pan in America':

"It was a vast old religion, greater than anything we know: more darkly and nakedly religious. There is no God, no conception of a god. All is god. But it is not the pantheism we are accustomed to, which expresses itself as 'God is everywhere, God is in everything.' In this Indian religion everything is alive, not supernaturally but naturally alive."

It should come as no surprise, then, that Lawrence was hugging trees, literally, on his Kiowa Ranch here. Especially a big pine tree that *'rises like a guardian spirit'* in front of the cabin where he lived.

Living at the ranch, he had his first *'permanent feeling of religion'* after questing around the world. He wrote (Phoenix):

"[In New Mexico], a vast old religion which once swayed the earth lingers in unbroken practice... older, perhaps, than anything in the world save Australian aboriginal taboo and totem, and that is not yet religion ... "I have become conscious of the tree, and of its interpenetration into my life. Long ago, the Indians must have been even more acutely conscious of it, when they blazed it to leave their mark on it. I am conscious that it helps to change me, vitally. I am even conscious that shivers of energy cross my living plasm, from the tree, and I become a

degree more like unto the tree, more bristling and turpentiney, in Pan. And the tree gets a certain shade and alertness of my life, within itself."

He echoes Jeffers when he describes the 'splendid silent terror and vast far-and-wide magnificence' of this place that was 'the greatest experience from the outside world that I have ever had … It changed me forever.'

However, neither Lawrence nor de Angulo idealized the Indians. Nor did Jeffers. Lawrence rightly observed in 'Pan in America' that, in time, even the Indian 'will kill Pan with his own hands, for the sake of a motor car.'' But he concluded with a modicum of hope:

"Whether we are a store-clerk or a bus-conductor we can still choose between the living universe of Pan, and the mechanical conquered universe of modern humanity. The machine has no windows. But even the most mechanized human being has only got his windows nailed up, or bricked in."

De Angulo would complain in *Indians in Overalls*, not without some admiration mingled with affection for his Indians:

"My God, think of it, to pass in one lifetime from the stone ax to wireless telegraphy! Indians in overalls; no, there was nothing picturesque about these Indians, no feather headdresses or beaded moccasins, nothing to delight the tourists about these 'digger Indians' in their battered hats and cheap calicos, picking the offal of the whites on the garbage dumps at the edge of town. My Indians in overalls!"

AS FOR JEFFERS, who wrote just one poem about his Taos experience, he stopped only a little short of cynicism:

I watch the Indians dancing to help the young corn at Taos pueblo;
The old men squat in a ring and make the song; the young women with fat, bare arms, and a few shame-faced young men, shuffle the dance.
The lean-muscled young men are naked to the narrow loins, their breasts and backs daubed with white clay;
Two eagle-feathers plume the black heads.
They dance with reluctance, they are growing civilized; the old men persuade them.
Only the drum is confident, it thinks the world has not changed; the beating heart, the simplest of rhythms,
It thinks the world has not changed at all; it is only a dreamer, a brainless heart, the drum has no eyes.
These tourists have eyes, the hundred watching the dance, white Americans, hungrily too, with reverence, not laughter;
Pilgrims from civilization, anxiously seeking beauty, religion, poetry; pilgrims from the vacuum.
People from cities, anxious to be human again.
Poor show how they suck you empty! The Indians are emptied,
And certainly there was never religion enough, nor beauty nor poetry here -- to fill Americans.
Only the drum is confident, it thinks the world has not changed.
Apparently only myself and the strong see that civilization is a transient
sickness.
Tribal drum and the rock head of Taos mountain remember.

De Angulo may have been disappointed that he wasn't able to connect on a friendly basis with Lawrence, but he did connect deeply with Jeffers. Jeffers seemed to be his alter ego. They shared common interests. They even spoke to each other in French and debated the merits of ancient and modern Greek pronunciation.

More often, however, they absorbed each other's energy, a little like Lawrence's interaction with his pine tree.

Evidence?

When the Robinson Jeffers supplement to 'The Carmelite' was published in Carmel in 1928, de Angulo was asked about his friendship with Jeffers. His answer was wonderfully child-like and primal:

"I couldn't tell you anything about Jeffers. That man is a mystery to me and has always been. I don't know what he is thinking about, or how he thinks, as I have never read any of his books … I like him because he is good looking.

He never talked with me. I did all the talking.

I don't know whether he ever understood a word of what I said. But that didn't matter.

"On the contrary, that was the beauty of it; to talk to a man, and to know that he is not listening to your words. It's like carrying on a conversation with yourself. You talk and talk and say anything you feel like saying without any regard for the contradictions, and all the while you have a feeling that the fellow is thinking about something else, something inside of him.

"You are perhaps walking with him along the road by the beach. There is the stunted chaparral, and the sand, the beach, the breakers booming. We both see all that. I talk. He is dreaming away.

"The stunted chaparral, the breakers, the glistening sand colour my talk. They colour his dreaming. Somehow or other his dreaming gets inside of me and my words get inside of him.

"He built himself a house, with his own hands. Enormous boulders, mortar, half of cement, walls as thick as half the room inside.

"Why did he do it? He doesn't know himself. But I could tell him. It was all for the sake of that little window, that tiny little window upstairs where you lie on your stomach and peep at the stormy sea outside!"

Post card showing Jeffers' Tor House and Hawk Tower in Carmel and that *'tiny little window where you lie on your stomach and peep at the stormy sea outside'* described by Jaime de Angulo

With the advent of the Atomic Age, Jaime de Angulo returned to a more primitive way of life in Big Sur. He chopped a smoke hole in the roof of his house on Partington Ridge, had all the trappings of civilization hauled away and squatted by the fire hole -- built in cement under the roof hole -- to cook his food, Indian style. He called himself the 'Old Coyote of Los Pesares.' Here he talks with writer Linda Sargent. (Photo by George Cain, courtesy of Marjorie Van Peski)

INDIAN PRAYER

O' GREAT SPIRIT,
Whose voice I hear in the winds,
And whose breath gives life to all the world,
Hear me? I am small and weak. I need your
strength and wisdom.

LET ME WALK IN BEAUTY, and make my eyes
ever behold the red and purple sunset.

MAKE MY HANDS respect the things you have
made and my ears sharp to hear your voice.

MAKE ME WISE so that I may understand the
things you have taught my people.

LET ME LEARN the lessons you have hidden
in every leaf and rock.

I SEEK STRENGTH, not to be greater than my
brother, but to fight my greatest enemy – myself.

MAKE ME ALWAYS READY to come to you with
clean hands and straight eyes.

SO WHEN LIFE FADES, as the fading sunset,
my spirit may come to you without shame.

Red Cloud Indian School
Pine Ridge, South Dakota

CHAPTER VIII

BIOLOGY AND CHIVALRY:
JOHN STEINBECK

W*hen you collect marine animals there are certain flat worms so delicate that they are almost impossible to capture whole, for they break and tatter under the touch. You must let them ooze and crawl of their own will onto a knife blade and then lift them gently into your bottle of sea water. And perhaps that might be the way to write this book – to open the page and to let the stories crawl in by themselves.*

This is how John Steinbeck wrote *Cannery Row*. It's the way he wrote most of his stories while his marine biologist friend, Ed 'Doc' Ricketts, was alive. He would just let them 'ooze and crawl' like that worm.

There was an ease about Steinbeck and his writing then. A laid back biological way of looking at things.

His characters were people who just seemed to merge with their habitat, like Ricketts himself.

Consequently, his societal ne'er do wells in *Cannery Row* were not so much to be pitied or blamed as accepted. Everyone – and everything -- has a role in the 'suchness' of things.

Steinbeck saw his motley bunch not only as '*whores, pimps, gamblers, and sons of bitches*' but also as '*saints and angels and martyrs and holy men.*' Two poles of the same Truth.

Like Ricketts, Steinbeck was a nature mystic, grounded in science. He attended classes in marine biology and English at Stanford University -- when he got around to them – and saw himself as 'a sort of biologist.'

But instead of seeking prestige as a Stanford graduate, he chose to drop out of school and get more life experience. He wanted to *know* what he was writing about.

This Salinas-born writer supported himself by doing manual labor during the Great Depression, sometimes by road work, sometimes as a farm hand.

One result was *The Grapes of Wrath*. This

Ed 'Doc' Ricketts

99

novel -- which won him a Pulitzer in 1939 -- gave voice to the plight of migrant workers in America -- and to working poor all over the world. The story left them with a glimmer of hope for bettering their lives if they would stand together, like the Joad family.

Steinbeck was a realist. He had no illusions about humans or the 'beautiful, intolerable' ways of amoral nature.

But he was somewhat of an idealist when it came to human potential. He was not only concerned about individuals, he opted for widespread social concern among humans, if we are to survive.

Simultaneous tones of bitterness and possibility permeate his writing. His characters may feel utterly defeated, but on the brink of despair they can still opt for the good, as Rose of Sharon did when she offered milk from her breast to a starving man.

Somewhere Steinbeck wrote:

"The writers of today, even I, have a tendency to celebrate the destruction of the spirit, and God knows it is destroyed often enough. But the beacon thing is that sometimes it is not. And I think I can take time right now to say that. There will be great sneers from the neurosis belt of the south, from the hard-boiled writers, but I believe that the great ones, [together with] Plato, Lao Tze, Buddha, Christ, Paul, and the great Hebrew prophets are not remembered for negation or denial.

"Not that it is necessary to be remembered, but there is one purpose in writing that I can see, beyond simply doing it interestingly. It is the duty of the writer to lift up, to extend, to encourage. If the written word has contributed anything at all to our developing species and our half-developed culture, it is this: Great writing has been a staff to lean on, a mother to consult, a wisdom to pick up stumbling folly, a strength in weakness and a courage to support sick cowardice. And how any negative or despairing approach can pretend to be literature I do not know.

"It is true that we are weak and sick and ugly and quarrelsome but if that is all we ever were, we would millenniums ago have disappeared from the face of the earth, and a few remnants of fossilized jaw bones, a few teeth in strata of limestone would be the only mark our species would have left on the earth."

Like other shepherds of Pan, Steinbeck was a seeker who had tapped into the *Perennial Philosophy* – the common, eternal, intuitive wisdom underlying naturalistic philosophies and mystical streams in all religions and mythologies. Here was the recurring understanding that lives and minds are all connected, that we have come from an all-encompassing Source, to which we shall return, and that we mirror the nature of a psycho-physical Reality.

This experiential wisdom, Steinbeck believed, is the goal of human beings in touch with their deepest and best instincts. Its pursuit and development are the purpose of our existence. It is the metaphorical 'Holy Grail' sought by the noble knights of King Arthur's court who had obsessed Steinbeck since boyhood.

Grabbed by these tales early on, Steinbeck was ever 'on quest.' His searching is evident in all his writings.

One of his earliest was a short novel, *To a God Unknown* (1933), a cautionary tale that, like the short story 'Flight,' reflected his affinity with Robinson Jeffers. (*"I hardly dare to meet Jeffers,"* he said once, *"because his poetry is perfect to me, and I don't think one should get the man mixed up with his work."*)

Steinbeck had no illusions that this novel would ever become a popular book in America. It was one of those stories that just 'oozed' out from his unconscious, leaving a few careful readers, then and now, to ponder its message.

He used an ancient *Hindu Veda* -- 'To A God Unknown' -- to set the stage:

He is the giver of breath, and strength is
his gift.
The high Gods revere his commandments.
His shadow is life, his shadow is death;
Who is He to whom we shall offer our
sacrifice?

Through His might He became lord of the
living and glittering world,
And he rules the world and the men and the
beasts.
Who is He to whom we shall offer our
sacrifice?

From His strength the mountains take being,
and the sea, they say, and the distant river;
And these are his body and his two arms.
Who is He to whom we shall offer our
sacrifice?

He made the sky and the earth, and His will
fixed their places, yet they look to Him and
tremble.
The risen sun shines forth over Him.
Who is He to whom we shall offer our
sacrifice?

He looked over the waters which stored His
power and gendered the sacrifice.
He is God over Gods.
Who is He to whom we shall offer our
sacrifice?

May He not hurt us, He who made earth.
Who made the sky and the shining sea?
Who is the God to whom we shall offer
sacrifice?

The story is about young Joseph Wayne
who travels from Vermont to a fertile valley in
Central California where he comes to revere
a magnificent live oak on his new ranch as the
embodiment of his dead father's spirit: "… and
the great tree stirred to life under the wind. Joseph
raised his head and looked at its old, wrinkled limbs.
His eyes lighted with recognition and welcome, for his
father's strong and simple being, which had dwelt in
his youth like a cloud of peace, had entered the tree."
Exploring his environment, Joseph
becomes "timid and yet eager, as a young man
is who slips out to a rendezvous with a wise and
beautiful woman. He was half-drugged and
overwhelmed by the forest of Our Lady. There
was a curious femaleness about the interlacing
boughs and twigs, about the long green cavern
cut by the river through the trees and the
brilliant underbrush. The endless green halls
and aisles and alcoves seemed to have meanings
as obscure and promising as the symbols of an
ancient religion."
But he is momentarily alarmed about his
strong feeling for this land. He had been warned
about pagan excesses, yet he knew, instinctively
that he "could never lose the feeling for the land."
He experiences a kind of epiphany. It is as if he
had been asleep before and was now awakened.
Steinbeck describes how Joseph is grabbed
by atavistic instincts that may, at first, seem to
belie his early Christian indoctrination about
stewardship – the teaching that men are stewards
over nature and that nature had been created
solely for human use:
"Joseph's horse raised its head and
sniffed the air. On top of the ridge stood a
clump of giant madrone trees, and Joseph saw
with wonder how nearly they resembled meat
and muscles. They thrust up muscular limbs
as red as flayed flesh and twisted like bodies
on the rack. Joseph laid his hand on one of
the branches as he rode by, and it was cold and
sleek and hard. But the leaves at the ends of
the horrible limbs were bright green and shiny.
Pitiless and terrible trees, the madrones. They
cried with pain when burned.
"Joseph gained the ridge-top and looked
down on the grass lands of his new homestead
where the wild oats moved in silver waves under
a little wind, where the patches of blue lupins
lay like shadows in a clear lucent night, and the
poppies on the side hills were broad rays of sun.
He drew up to look at the long grassy meadows
in which clumps of live oaks stood like perpetual
senates ruling over the land. The river with its
mask of trees cut a twisting path down through
the valley. Two miles away he could see, beside
a gigantic lonely oak, the white speck of his tent
pitched and left while he went to record his
homestead.
"A long time he sat there. As he looked
into the valley, Joseph felt his body flushing

with a hot fluid of love. 'This is mine,' he said simply, and his eyes sparkled with tears and his brain was filled with wonder that this should be his. There was pity in him for the grass and the flowers; he felt that the trees were his children and the land his child. For a moment he seemed to float high in the air and to look down upon it. 'It's mine,' he said again, 'and I must take care of it ..."

Here, a patriarchal feeling of stewardship *over* the land appears to have won out over a more primal feeling of oneness, or fellow feeling, *with* the land.

View of Joseph's grassy meadows
(Photo from Steve Crouch's Steinbeck Country)

"'It's mine,' he chanted, 'Down deep it's mine, right to the center of the world.' He stamped his feet into the soft earth. Then the exultance grew to be a sharp pain of desire that ran through his body in a hot river. He flung himself face downward on the grass and pressed his cheek against the wet stems. His fingers gripped the wet grass and tore it out, and gripped again. His thighs beat heavily on the earth. The fury left him and he was cold and bewildered and frightened at himself. He sat up and wiped the mud from his lips and beard. 'What was it?' he asked himself. 'What came over me then? Can I have a need that great?' He tried to remember exactly what had happened. For a moment the land had been his wife.'"

One of his brothers, terrified by what he perceives as Joseph's growing pagan excesses, kills the tree that Joseph believes to embody the spirit of their father. Drought ensues, and his brothers do the reasonable thing. They search for greener pastures.

But Joseph stays behind obsessed with the belief that it is his duty – and therefore within his power -- to *save* the land – vindictive as it now seemed. So he barricades himself near what he perceives as a power place (a rock in a glade near a scant stream) and tries to fight against the natural course of events by moistening what little greenery remains.

But the green continues to turn brown. In desperation, he asks a village priest to use his power and pray for rain. But the padre explains that he can only pray for souls. Revealing his own somewhat heretical trust in the spirit of nature, the padre tries to assure Joseph that rain will come in due time because '*the land does not die.*'

When Joseph leaves, the padre not only prays for his soul, he relents and prays for rain. Returning to the glade, Joseph discovers that the stream has dried up.

Then, distraught and beyond reasoning, Joseph does the unspeakable. He 'sins' against life – the holy spirit -- by sacrificing his own.

Steinbeck wrote that when he "*gently opened the vessels of his wrist ... his body grew huge and light. It arose into the sky and out of it came the streaking rain. 'I should have known,' he whispered, 'I am the rain' ... 'I am the land ... and I am the rain. The grass will grow out of me in a little while.'*"

Whether seen as a mystic recognition or self delusion, Joseph's death is reminiscent of some Jeffers' themes involving hubris and errant saviorism [e.g. *The Loving Shepherdess*, *The Women at Point Sur*, *Dear Judas*].

Readers are left to wonder: Did Joseph kill himself just before the natural cycle of rain would have come of its own accord? Did prayer – or the sacrifice -- 'work'? Can one revere nature and feel that one has power over it at the same time? Ought we to simply accept nature as it is and work with it toward harmony and survival of the good, as Joseph's brothers did?

Joseph came very close to holistic thinking. Did he fall short because he couldn't fully accept the pragmatic impersonal ways of nature?

His belief in human stewardship over the land led him to feel that if he prayed hard enough – or made the right sacrifice – he had *power* to *make* something happen.

Perhaps his lack of humility did him in. Perhaps he failed to see that the non-teleological cycles of nature, alternately catastrophic and beautiful, are to be accepted and endured and celebrated, not manipulated?

Ricketts and Steinbeck wallowed in discussions provoked by such stories. During their 1940 journey together to study marine life in Mexico's Sea of Cortez, they played a game called 'speculative metaphysics.'

Ricketts called his way of thinking 'non-teleological.' Here was the idea that nothing is ever finished or complete -- that everything is in process, *'one thing growing on and out of another'* -- yet another way of expressing the *Perennial Philosophy*.

Steinbeck noted that when he and Ricketts put their heads together, the result was always a joint effort:

"I do not now know in some cases who started which line of speculation since the end thought was the product of both minds."

Steinbeck described a typical 'Doc' analysis:

"You know, at first view you would think the rattlesnake and the kangaroo rat were the greatest of enemies since the snake hunts and feeds on the rat. But in a larger sense they must be the best of friends. The rat feeds the snake and the snake selects out the slow and weak and generally thins the rat people so that both species can survive. It is quite possible that neither species could exist without the other."

He explained that *such "non-teleological thinking concerns itself primarily not with what should be, or could be, or might be, but rather with what actually IS – attempting at most to answer the already sufficiently difficult questions 'what' or 'how,' instead of 'why'."*

'Fears' served as an example. *"If you have fears, they are. They are real things and to be considered. Whether or not they're foolish is beside the point. 'What' they are is unimportant alongside the 'that' they are."*

With non-teleological thinking, he went on, *"there is only the love and understanding of instant acceptance; after that fundamental has been achieved, the next step, if any should be necessary, can be considered more sensibly. The whole picture is portrayed by 'is,' the deepest word of deep ultimate reality, not shallow or partial as reasons are, but deeper and participating, possibly encompassing the oriental concept of 'being.'"*

With non-teleological thinking, the propensity to blame gives way to acceptive understanding, the inclusive way of the all-god Pan.

Steinbeck recognized the Pan god in Ricketts from the beginning. In his tribute to Doc in the introduction to *The Log From the Sea of Cortez*, he wrote:

"[Ricketts] was half-Christ and half-goat. He was a great teacher and a great lecher – an immortal who loved women. Surely he was an original and his character was unique, but in such a way that everyone was related to him, one in this way and another in some different way. He was gentle but capable of ferocity, small and slight but strong as an ox, loyal and yet untrustworthy, generous but gave little and received much. His thinking was paradoxical as his life. He thought in mystical terms and hated and distrusted mysticism.

"He was an individualist who studied colonial animals with satisfaction ... [He] had no religion in the sense of creed or dogma. In fact he distrusted all formal religions, suspecting them of having been fouled with economics and power and politics. He did not believe in any God as recognized by any group or cult. Probably his God could have been expressed by the mathematical symbol for an expanding universe. Surely he did not believe in an afterlife in any sense other than chemical. He was suspicious of promises of an afterlife, believing them to be sops to our fear or hope artificially supplied."

Steinbeck said that *"knowing Ed Ricketts was instant. After the first moment I knew him [1930], and for the next eighteen years, I knew him better than I knew anyone, and perhaps I did not know him at all. Maybe it was that way with all of his friends. He was different from anyone and yet so alike that everyone found himself in Ed, and that might be one of the reasons his death had such an impact. It wasn't Ed who had died but a large and important part of oneself."*

After Ricketts' death in 1948 (he was crushed by a train that collided with his car on Cannery Row), Steinbeck found it difficult to maintain the dynamic balance in his fiction that his association with Ricketts had inspired.

That his first wife, Carol, would grow to resent his camaraderie with Ricketts was inevitable. She had been his best friend as well as secretary and critic and no doubt felt demoted after John encountered Doc.

But his second wife, Gwyn, who gave him his only children -- and expected even more from him than Carol required -- was livid about the relationship. When Ricketts died, she struck hard: *"Now your public will see you as you really are. Without [Doc] you are nothing. You will now be the failure you were before you met him, and I don't want to be married to a failure!"*

After that – and when he was forced to write for money to support a growing family -- it's no wonder he broke, for a time, with non-teleological 'acceptance.' He even took an all-too-human swipe at women:

"Part man, part politician, they have the minds of whores and vaginas of Presbyterians. They are trained by their mothers in a contempt for men ... The American girl makes a servant of her husband and then finds him contemptible for being a servant. American married life is the doormat to the whorehouse. Eventually they will succeed in creating a race of homosexuals."

Fortunately, he was less vituperative with his third wife, Elaine Scott. After marriage, they moved to Sag Harbor where he could wean himself away from 'Steinbeck Country' that had both formed -- and transformed him -- and from the memories of Ricketts it evoked.

But his writing, though great (he was ultimately awarded a Nobel prize) was never quite as great as when Ricketts was around.

He devoted his later years to writing a book he had been incubating most of his life – a novel called The Acts of King Arthur and his Noble Knights.

It was based on his own sense of kinship with Sir Lancelot who had fallen short of discovering the Holy Grail because of a chink in his armor – his fatal vulnerability to the charms of Queen Guinevere.

Steinbeck said he had discovered in the stories of Arthur *"all the vices that ever were – and courage and sadness and frustration, but particularly gallantry – perhaps the only single quality of man that the West has invented. I think my sense of right and wrong, my feeling of noblesse oblige, and any thought I may have against the oppressor and for the oppressed, came from this secret book."*

He explained further that these tales didn't *"outrage my sensibilities as nearly all the children's books did. It did not seem strange to me that Uther Pendragon wanted the wife of his vassal and took her by trickery. I was not frightened to find that there were evil knights, as well as noble ones. In my own town there were men who wore the clothes of virtue whom I knew to be bad ... Children are violent and cruel – and good – and I was all of these – and all of these were in the secret book.*

"If I could not choose my way at the crossroads of love and loyalty, neither could Lancelot. I could understand the darkness of Mordred because he was in me too; and there was some Galahad in me, but perhaps not enough. The Grail feeling was there, however, deep-planted, and perhaps always will be."

Steinbeck believed that these stories were not only alive in him. They are also alive *'even in those of us who have not read them.'* So he wanted to re-tell them *'in plain present-day speech for my own young sons, and for other sons not so young.'*

He recounted the rules of chivalry for future questers: Never use violence without good purpose; never fall to murder or treason; be merciful when mercy is asked; protect damsels, ladies, gentlewomen, and widows; enforce their rights to choice and never enforce lust on them; never fight in an unjust cause; never fight for personal gain only.

On quest, he directed, we should take any adventure that falls to us. After questing, there are marvelous stories to tell. And if we prove ourselves brave and honorable, we will be of The Round Table, a fellowship of courage and courtesy and honor. Yet Steinbeck was quick to observe that *'in the combat between wisdom and feeling, wisdom seldom wins.'*

Steinbeck researched and wrote *The Acts of King Arthur and His Noble Knights* when he wasn't cultivating his lettuce garden in a cottage he and Elaine rented together in Somerset, England, near Glastonbury and Avalon -- environs of the legendary Arthur.

His avowed purpose in writing was to put the acts of Arthur *"into a language which is understandable and acceptable to a modern-day reader ... since these stories form, with the New Testament, the basis of most modern English literature.*

"But if you change Indians or outlaws for Saxons and Picts and Danes, you have exactly the same story. You have the cult of the horse, the cult of the knight. The application with the present is very close, and also the present day with its uncertainties very closely parallels the uncertainties of the fifteenth century. It is actually a kind of nostalgic return to the good old days.

And it can be shown and will be shown that the inherent part of the so-called 'Western' with which television is filled at the present time – same characters, same methods, same stories, only slightly different weapons and certainly a different topography.

"I think Malory did it, and I think our writers for television are doing it – exactly the same thing and, oddly enough, finding exactly the same symbols and methods ... Malory lived in as rough and ruthless and corrupt an age as the world has ever produced.

" In 'The Morte de Arthur' he in no way

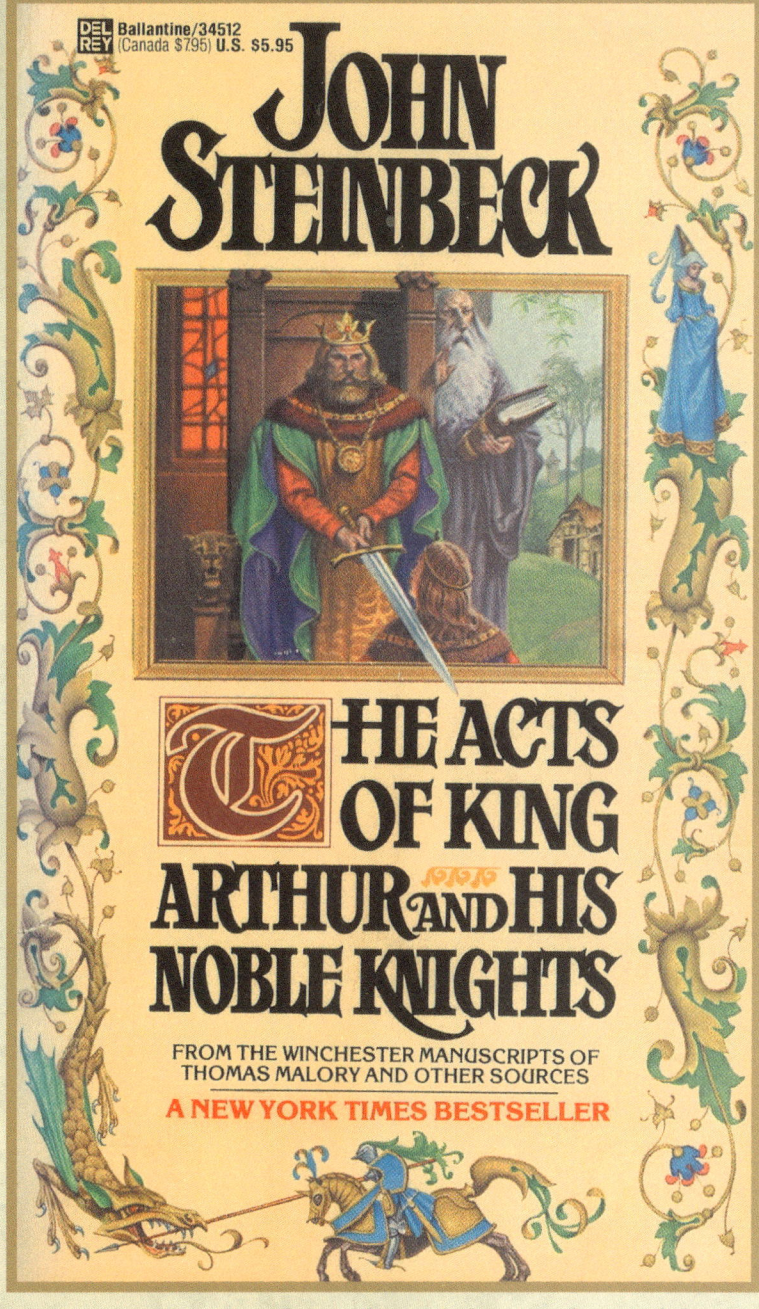

minimizes these things, the cruelty and lust, murder and childlike self-interest. They are all here. But he does not let them put out the sun. Side by side with them are generosity and courage and greatness and the huge sadness of tragedy rather than the little meanness of frustration ... no matter how brilliantly one part of life is painted, if the sun goes out, that man has not seen the whole world. Day and night both exist. To ignore the one or the other is to split time in two and to choose one like the short stick in a match game ... An artist should be open on all sides to every kind of light and darkness.*

But he never finished the book. It was

published posthumously by Elaine Scott Steinbeck -- and became a New York Times bestseller -- several years after the massive heart attack that ended his life in 1968.

His avowed purpose in writing had been to put the acts of Arthur "into a language which is understandable and acceptable to a modern-day reader ... since these stories form, with the New Testament, the basis of most modern English literature.

"But if you change Indians or outlaws for Saxons and Picts and Danes, you have exactly the same story. You have the cult of the horse, the cult of the knight. The application with the present is very close, and also the present day with its uncertainties very closely parallels the uncertainties of the fifteenth century. It is actually a kind of nostalgic return to the good old days.

"And it can be shown and will be shown that the inherent part of the so-called 'Western' with which television is filled at the present time – same characters, same methods, same stories, only slightly different weapons and certainly a different topography.

Maybe he had really said all that he needed to say and knew it. Shortly before his death he would write, *"I have nothing I can or want to communicate – dry as dust, worked-out feeling."*

Like Jack London before him, Steinbeck may have burned himself out pursuing 'success' and fallen short of attaining his own integrative philosophy without that goat-man Doc Ricketts around to keep him on course.

But there was a time when he did feel as whole and connected as any 'shepherd' of Pan. Toward the end of *The Log from the Sea of Cortez*, Steinbeck wrote:

"The shape of the trip was an integrated nucleus from which weak strings of thought stretched into every reachable reality, and a reality which reached into us through our perceptive nerve trunks.

"The laws of thought seemed really one with the laws of things. There was some quality of music here, perhaps not to be communicated, but sounding clear and huge in our minds

" ... The real picture of how it had been there and how we had been there was in our minds, bright with sun and wet with sea water and blue or burned ,   and the whole Crusted over with exploring thought.

"Here was no service to science, no naming of unknown animals, but rather – we simply liked it. We liked it very much.

"The brown Indians and the gardens of the sea, and the beer and the work, they were all one thing and we were that one thing too."

Surely one can imagine all this as contentment enough to last a lifetime.

'King Arthur territory:' the Somerset, England cottage occupied by Steinbeck and his wife while he worked on his King Arthur novel.

The King Arthur Cross

The leaden plate in the form of a Cross found in King Arthur's grave at Glastonbury Abbey in the reign of King Henry II.

The inscription reads: Hic jacet sepultus inclytus Rex Arthurus in Insula Avalonia ("Here lies interred in the Isle of Avalon the renowned King Arthur.")

To believe in immortality is one thing,
but it is first needful to believe in life.

... ROBERT LOUIS STEVENSON

ly Wizard of Oz? Or Puck? Or Pan? I like
im immediately. Big Sur's best-known live
n poet, Eric Barker, may have had the lo
nd arrogance
f a wizard but... with a childlike imp
shness... tened a touch
aught
romi
wa... rggly eyebrow
tron... the baldi
ead
y a... and i was e
ited by... half at any momen
e might
orns, grow... ull out pan pip
nd lead... woods.
e did t
ometi... ng of
j... enough red wine,
... ful with words,
... ecn... mmons... transport
... rs,

The
The... ve
... he

... en
mont

CHAPTER IX

BIG SUR PIPINGS:
ERIC BARKER, A PERSONAL PORTRAIT

He looked like a leprechaun. Or was it the wily Wizard of Oz? Or Puck? Or Pan? I liked him immediately. Big Sur's best-known live-in poet, Eric Barker, may have had the look and arrogance of a wizard, but there was a childlike impishness about him that softened a touch of haughtiness and promised fun, treasure to come.

I was impressed by the straggly eyebrows, strong nose, piquant face and the balding head haloed by a horseshoe of wiry hair. And I was excited by the possibility that, at any moment, he might sprout horns, grow cloven hooves, pull out pan pipes and lead me through the redwoods.

He did this – in his poems.

Sometimes, after an evening of lively dialogue and just enough red wine, the clever wizard, so careful with words, would turn to the commons and transport us to a Cockney pub in Blackfriars, carelessly reciting bawdy limericks.

Eric was born British, in Thames Ditton, Surrey, in 1905. This could have accounted for the held-high chin. But the eyes danced with Dionysus, that maverick in the Greek pantheon.

He died in 1973, victim of an apparent valve failure occurring about six months after a heart operation. The surgery was intended to correct a weakness so he could travel to the land of Pan and Dionysus to pay homage to those revelers in life. He didn't get there.

Oddly, just three years before Eric's death, his wife, Madelynne Greene, had died of heart failure as they were planning a trip to Greece.

They had been married 34 years, each keeping a separate residence to accommodate differing vocations. Madelynne was head of the International Dance Theater of San Francisco. Eric

Caricature of the impish Eric Barker from the cover of a remembrance distributed at the scattering of his ashes at Point Lobos …

was poet-gardener at Coastlands estate in Big Sur.

But they spent weekends and holidays together, traveled together. When Madelynne hosted dance camps, Eric was poet-in-residence. When Madelynne came to Big Sur, she was Nepenthe's folk dancer-in-residence.

When she died, there was a funeral in San Francisco. Afterward, Eric brought her ashes to Point Lobos, scattering them in fertile crevices in rocks at the edge of Cypress Grove, where his own ashes would ultimately be strewn.

When Eric died, there was no funeral. But there was a picnic. A few close friends – bringing bread, wine, and cheese – gathered at Point Lobos to celebrate his life. Carmel Highlands artist Ephraim Doner had put Eric's ashes in a Greek vase for the occasion.

As the solemn little group read poetry, played guitar music and ate the sacramental meal, a capricious chipmunk nibbled at Doner's bread, coaxing laughter, not to mention speculation, about the whereabouts of Eric's spirit. It would have been like him to take over the body of the chipmunk to liven up the party.

Even the weather was appropriate. There was rain when the picnickers arrived at Point Lobos. But the sun broke through for the celebration, retreating behind clouds after Eric's ashes were scattered by a lady called Gypsy.

[Years later – in 1993 – the Big Sur Land Trust, Carmel's Cherry Foundation for the Arts, and Monterey Peninsula College would cooperate to establish The Eric Barker Scholarship for Creative Writing.]

It was Tom Broadbent who first introduced me to Eric, back in 1969. Tom was British – a woodworker who lived in Carmel. He and Eric were buddies who drank 'black and tan' -- Guiness beer and ale – together on weekends.

An admirer of the poetry of Robinson Jeffers, I had come from the University of Utah to work with Jeffers scholar Dr. John Brophy in organizing the first tribute to Carmel's then-neglected Tor House poet at Monterey Peninsula College. I suggested to Tom that Eric might like to read at the celebration because the two poets liked – and echoed -- each other. Jeffers had written:

"[Eric's] poems please me more than any others that are being written at this time. They are natural and quiet, very far removed from the exhibitionist nonsense that afflicts poetry magazines. Barker's verses go straight, and he has a great theme in the coast range mountains above Big Sur. There is nothing artificial, no tricks, no self conscious vanity, but the natural man speaking beautifully."

Eric declined the invitation to read, but we did become friends. When he went to Carmel Valley on weekends to visit Tom at his Valley Hills atelier, Eric spoke of hippies and the Vietnam war, coyotes and hawks. He spoke of Jeffers – how Jeffers would have understood the flower children and the bitterness of returned Vietnam soldiers.

When Eric wrote about the hippies – 'Though some are dirty, they are much cleaner than the Establishment' – I thought about Clare Walker in *The Loving Shepherdess*, Jeffers' own tragic prototype of the all-pitying, all-loving flower child.

When I returned to Carmel the following summer to teach Philosophy at MPC, Tom, Eric and I would go to the wharf pub on Friday nights for fish and chips and British beer. Sometimes we would visit artist Wah Chang [a sculptor who is best remembered for creating the Pillsbury doughboy] or meet friends at Gordon Newell's old Sculpture Center on Cannery Row.

Occasionally, I would visit Eric's cottage in Big Sur. He was a gardener who lived in a tool house transformed into a studio about the size of a trailer. But it had everything he needed – refrigerator, stove, teapot, clothes, bed, table, writing tablets, pencils, and space for pictures, poems and posters. There was even a friendly cat. Outside, he cultivated a delicious garden. He could even catch a glimpse of the sea from the garden path.

The year of his heart operation, Eric was excited about the remodeling of the garage above his studio. It was to become an expanded living area for him – gift of a grateful landlord – complete with fireplace and new furniture. He had just begun to enjoy his new home when the technology in his heart failed.

I was back at my then-home in Utah when Eric died.

Tom wrote to me about Eric's last day. He had driven into Carmel in the little white Valiant that his wife had given him. He joined Dick Irwin and the two drank beer and ate hamburgers

The Anghelaki-Rookes with the author in Big Sur

together at a favorite haunt, the Red Lion pub. Then they walked around Point Lobos. Going there, for Eric, always meant being near Madelynne.

When they returned to the Irwin place in Carmel, they played Scrabble. Tom said Eric had come up with the name of a bird, the existence of which Irwin questioned, so he consulted a bird dictionary.

Irwin found the name (Tom couldn't recall what species) and said, "You're right! There is such a bird."

Triumphant, Eric replied, "I knew I was right!"

Death punctuated that sentence.

Eric had lived fully all of his 68 years. In spite of that knowledge, I was saddened because I shared his love of things Greek, and I realized his life had been cut off before he could make his own odyssey there.

Yet, I rationalised, fate may have softened the severance. Hadn't a taste of Greece come to him just a few months before in the person of Katerina Anghelaki-Rooke, Greek poet and only godchild of Nikos Kazantzakis who wrote *Zorba the Greek?*

Katerina was in the States on a Ford Foundation grant, traveling around reading her poetry. I want to San Francisco to see her (we'd met two years before in Athens). Then I took her to Big Sur for a retsina wine and feta cheese-and-bread picnic with Gordon and Eleanor Newell at Helmut Deetjen's house in Castro Canyon,l the occupied by sculptor Jim Hunolt

Later, we all went to the old Thunderbird Bookstore in Carmel Valley for dinner. There, Katerina and Eric met and talked about Greece, poetry and the likeness of this coast to the Greek landscape. They spoke of the passions of people in such ruggedly beautiful places. And they talked about Zorba, another lovable scamp.

This encounter was the next best thing to a visit to Greece for Eric because no one, short of Zorba himself reflected the double-edged Greek spirit more than Katerina, who had been permanently lamed in a childhood accident.

Translator of both Kazantzakis and Anghalak-Rooke, Imon Friar wrote of Katerina:

"Spiritually, Kazantzakis bequeathed to Anghalaki-Rooke a fierce desire to participate in the joys of life and love, a worship of natural beauty, and, at the same time, a despair that often

113

reaches beyond ... nihilism and knocks on death's door ... Only those who have a fine palate and are therefore capable of tasting the great joys of life are also capable of great despair."

If such capability is the essence of Greekness that Kazantzakis, her teacher, bequeathed to Katerina, the same spirit had also touched Eric.

But with all their capacity for extremes of joy and despair, Greeks have a special virtue, playfulness, and Eric was, above all, playful.

For example, after Dame Judith Anderson came to the outdoor Forest Theater to read Jeffers' 'Medea,' there was a reception in her honor at The Lodge at Pebble Beach. Eric, writer Bill Brandon, and I attended the theater together, then debated which car we should take to Pebble Beach – my Firebird, Eric's Valiant, or Bill's 'Sad Eyes' – an old green camper-truck that had bumped over too many back roads on Indian reservations. (Bill authored the great American Heritage book about Indians.)

Eric suggested that it would be fun to drive up to the front door of the elegant Lodge in the much-less-than-elegant 'Sad Eyes.' That we did, Eric flashing his most impish smile as we were helped out of our chariot by a very gracious doorman.

Of all the tributes paid Eric in his lifetime, perhaps the words of another Greek-souled Big Sur resident, Henry Miller, best get at the essence of this charmer who is missed.

Miller wrote that Eric was *"British to the core – the Shropshire lad with the bloom still on his cheek and a dewy twinkle in his eyes. Perhaps I associate him in my mind with the masters of the haiku because I see in him the connection between the poet and poetry which is so markedly missing in most modern poets, to be honest. Eric Barker lived as a poet should live, that is, in a constant state of awareness of the animate and inanimate world about him.*

"Superbly without ambition, thoroughly unconcerned with politics, he does as little as possible to keep alive. He makes no stir, in other words. He simply breathes, you might say. And this he does through his gills rather than through his lungs. An amphibian who has also cultivated wings. The result of doing things effortlessly, possibly.

"That he will never get anywhere is certain. Never will he be anything more than a poet. What a marvelous future! What a luxury! ... He lives blithely and serenely, floating rather than walking, dreaming rather than doing, singing rather than talking. The job which keeps him is one which even a boy could hold down. It keeps his pipe filled and gives him his cup of tea. There is no promotion in store for him. Just more verse, more idle rambling, more seashore, more mushrooms, more abalone, more rejection slips.

"Who could ask for a better life ... Who has the courage any more to live the simple life, the life which is always there to be lived, the life which is based on doing without, on biding one's time, and relying solely on one's native intelligence." Not surprisingly, the faith of this Big Sur poet-gardener was always in the earth to which he knew he would return. Eric explained his attachment in a poem:

Faith In The Earth

Transmitted though wood and stone
To my feeling hands, the rough enduring symbols
Outlasting human love, the roots deeper,
The fibres tougher, the grave grey heads
Wearing under both skies
Their deep and full acceptance, like the sea.
On the grooved and lichened skies my hand moves,
Spelling like the blind the cycles of dead seasons;
The rages and the calms,
Voices of wind and rain,

The white and summer silences;
In the full-leafed singing shadows
The green love returning under more suns
Than have wakened the oldest of men.
Birds in the leaves do not remember
The full throats brimming round rings
Of old years in their green shade song.
But my hand remembers –
Tapping through wood and stone
The waters of the aged and ageless springs –
The faith at the fire's center
Burning before birdsong or tree.
The changes in the blood toiling
Through salt streams to the cloud-loved hill;
The tidemarks blind with grass in the growing sun,
And lichen, linked to memories of the sea.

ERIC BARKER AT THE PEBBLE BEACH LODGE
COCKTAIL PARTY

Painting of Henry Miller by Big Sur-Carmel artist Shell Fisher

CHAPTER X

HENRY MILLER TRANSFORMED:
GREECE TO BIG SUR

That rogue elephant of American literature, Henry Valentine Miller -- remembered by the hoi polloi for **Tropic of Cancer** and **Tropic of Capricorn** -- romped with nymphs and satyrs in Brooklyn and Paris before embracing less populous playgrounds of Pan in Greece and Big Sur.

Miller had always savored landscapes praised by artists and poets. And he did understand Pan as a powerful metaphor conceived by the imaginative Greeks to explain the mysteries of creation -- to comprehend, as he put it, *'a reality which was too great for their human comprehension.'*

But he had never experienced, firsthand, the transforming power of the capricious defender of things wild and pastoral, until he traveled to Greece. To him, Greece was *'what you expect the earth to look like given a fair chance.'*

The man was not only charmed by the Greek landscape, he was delighted with the country's inquisitive, playful, highly individualistic people.

Their forebears had not only spawned western civilization but inspired respect for the divinity that permeates all nature, Pan.

Miller's praise of the Greeks was characteristically candid and effusive:

"The Ancient Greek ... lived amidst brutal clarities which tormented and maddened the spirit. He was at war with everyone, including himself. Out of this fiery anarchy came the lucid, healing metaphysical speculations which even today enthrall the world ...

"Marvelous things happen to one in Greece – marvelous good things which can happen to one nowhere else on earth. Somehow, almost as if He were nodding, Greece still remains under the protection of the Creator.

"Men may go about their puny, ineffectual bedevilment, even in Greece, but God's magic is still at work and, no matter what the race of man may do or try to do, Greece is still a sacred precinct – and my belief is it will remain so until the end of time."

As he basked in the extraordinary light of Attica that, for him, expunged all ugliness, Miller came to believe that the happiest people on earth are like ordinary Greeks who live simply and naturally, with faith in themselves.

Even being poor, he observed, doesn't seem to degrade and befoul the Greek as it does the poor in other countries.

After exposing himself to the power of the sacred in a land that *'opened my eyes, penetrated my pores, expanded my whole being,'* Miller was ready to live the rest of his life among its ebullient people.

But events leading up to World War II in 1939 forced him to return to America.

Back in the states, he consoled himself by writing about the land that had sparked a spiritual transformation. The result was **The Colossus of Maroussi**, in which he not only praised Greece but immortalized a Zorbatic fellow called Katsimbalis.

That finished, he teamed up with a friend who had a car and motored across America's Southwest searching for men and women of spirit and vision to write about. He was largely disappointed.

What he did discover was recorded in **The Air Conditioned Nightmare**, a book that expressed little optimism for America's future.

He feared that the future will belong to *machines and robots* that have nothing to do with man's real nature. And he perceived the plethora of mechanical devices, not as saviors of mankind but as traps baited by Death.

Only when he arrived in the Indian territories that had so vividly impressed D. H. Lawrence two decades earlier, did he begin to smile.

He liked the traditional Indian's reverent attitude toward the land because it was so much like the Greek's.

At one point, he even visualized America's indigenous people rising up to take back their country as the usurpers grew soft and degenerate.

Beyond that, the trip brought him close to despair:

"THIS WORLD WHICH IS IN THE MAKING FILLS ME WITH DREAD ... It is not a world I want to live in ... It is a world cluttered with useless objects which men and women, in order to be exploited and degraded, are taught to regard as useful. The dreamer whose dreams are non-utilitarian has no place in this world. Whatever does not lend itself to being bought and sold, whether in the realm of things, ideas, principles, dreams, or hopes, is debarred."

Miller settled in Los Angeles for awhile, still smarting from what he called "the false, restricted life of the city man." He longed for things Greek.

Then, in 1943, an exuberant Greek expatriate came to his rescue. His name was Janko Varda.

Varda introduced him to Big Sur, another Pan-blessed landscape. Only then did Miller begin to change his mind about America.

He was so smitten by the magnificence of this coastal wilderness and the independent spirit of its people that he was moved to 'never mind' about Greece and announce:

"The only place in the world thus far that I can think of as home is Big Sur. It is American in the best sense of the word, which is what makes it so unlike the rest of the country."

Here, in a climate that was very close to Mediterranean, he found sanctuary for nearly two decades. During this period, he arrived at what he called 'a state of wisdom, a mystic way of life' that had been seeded in Greece.

His maturing nature mysticism enabled him to transform what had been a near-manic preoccupation in cities with *'impulsive urges that were wholly beyond control'* into a transcending love affair with the divinity in all life that was to satisfy his spiritual aspirations for the rest of his life.

Even before his sojourn in Greece, Miller's soul had been 'properly prepared' for what he would discover in Greece and Big Sur by three great writers: America's Transcendentalist poet, **Walt Whitman** (who had had also inspired Robert Louis Stevenson); English novelist **D. H. Lawrence** (whose essay, 'Pan in America,' set the stage for this book); and Carmel's Tor House poet, **Robinson Jeffers** (whose controversial narrative poetry had been admired by Miller in Paris).

Imbibing all this literature had set him up for a kind of metamorphosis he likened to that of a lowly caterpillar turning into a butterfly. He longed to *evolve*.

Change began to happen for him in Paris in 1931 when he met diarist **Anais Nin**, the only woman he ever considered his match and his mentor.

Nin was intensely interested in the philosophy of Lawrence -- particularly in his biology-based ideas on relations between the sexes developed under the influence of depth psychologist, **Dr. Trigant Burrow**. Burrow had suggested in *The Social Basis of Consciousness*, a book approvingly reviewed by Lawrence:

"We ourselves are the subjective expression of the same organic sequence which we observe objectively in the world about us ... As our give and take expressions among our fellows develop into activities that are reciprocally creative, in the same measure, our obsessive drive toward the satisfactions of sexuality, whether repressed or indulged, will cease to dominate human personality."

In getting to know Miller, Nin perceived that he and Lawrence, different as they were personally, had similar ideas that were essentially *religious*, in the best sense of that word.

A major goal for both was to get what Lawrence had called the *'dirty little secret'* out of Victorian closets so that sex could be openly acknowledged as the necessary act of procreative nature that it is, and spiritually transformed.

Miller's initial response to her insistence that he, a street-wise writer from Brooklyn, had something in common with the pallid professor from Nottingham who had titillated the English-speaking world with *Lady Chatterley's Lover*, was vitriolic.

L awrence, he retorted, was no more than *"a little runt, a nasty devil, a dry thoroughly English type. I despise his workingman's (no, it was bourgeois) attitude about things -- scrubbing floors, cooking, laundering, etc. And his being alone crap! Not sensitiveness, but timidity, lack of guts, lack of humanity ... remark the sickly letters [he] wrote [to Mabel Dodge Luhan] ... How could he have fallen into the clutches of such a woman? There was something feeble about him -- despite his glorious language."*

Nin tried to persuade him that, despite their differences in approach (Miller's characters *'fucked with a cold heart,'* Lawrence's *'fucked with a warm heart'*), he and Lawrence had much in common. But he only became more rigid.

He set out to prove to her -- and to their literary peers in Paris -- that Lawrence was a wimp. He planned to attack him from *"every possible angle."* He would accumulate *"all the facts and interpretations possible. I may never refer to him again in my life. Must wash myself clean of him."*

M iller inundated himself in Lawrence's writings. But after devouring a collection of essays in a book called *Death of a Porcupine* -- and one essay in particular, 'The Crown' -- he did an about face.

Deep and difficult piece that it is, 'The Crown' convinced him that Anais had been right all along. The man. He concluded, can be faulted for many things but never for intellectual dishonesty. It was time for an apology:

"I feel I have said unkind, unjust things about Lawrence. He is far greater than I ever dreamt ... He stands out like a rock. He bides his time. I was practically ignorant of Lawrence when I began this study. Now I appreciate him deeply ... I feel humble and chastened. But I am more now than ever I was before."

He vowed to change course and critique Lawrence as a visionary:

"[His] language is matchless – reminiscent of the best in the Bible. The thought is superior to any of Jesus' sayings, in my opinion. It is like a new Revelation. It is based on Spengler ... And it goes beyond Spengler ... The seed of all Lawrence's writing is here -- and more than just seed. It is the mystic at his most mystical. I am in love with it."

The works of Lawrence had become a kind of manifesto for Miller expressing what he had been trying to put into words for months.

Far from being his opponent, Lawrence was a kindred spirit. It impressed him that Lawrence *'embraced everything.'* Like Whitman.

Early on, Miller's typical guilt-encumbered pubescent feelings had been liberated by Whitman's 'Native Moments' -- so liberated that he passed the poem out to friends with a self-important notation:

"For a complete and unequivocal understanding of the undersigned [himself] the rendition below is absolutely prerequisite."
NATIVE MOMENTS! *When you come upon me – Ah you are here now!*
Give me now libidinous joys only!

Left: Henry Miller in his Partington Ridge studio; Anais Nin looks over his shoulder in upper right photo ... (Photograph by Joseph Whitnah, 1946) Below: Miller at home of his neighbor, pioneer artist of Big Sur, Harrydick Ross.

Give me the drench of my passions! Give me life coarse and rank!
Today, I go consort with nature's darling – tonight too;
I am for those who believe in loose delight – I share the midnight orgies of young men;
I dance with the dancers and drink with the drinkers;
The echoes ring with our indecent calls;
I take for my love some prostitute – I pick out some low person for my dearest friend,
He shall be lawless, rude, illiterate – he shall be one condemn'd by others for deeds done;
I will play a part no longer – Why should I exile myself from my companions?
O you shunn'd persons! I at least do not shun you,
I come forthwith in your midst – I will be your poet,
I will be more to you than to any of the rest.

Miller's unbridled enthusiasm for this poem surprises no one who has read his once-banned books which are intellectual banquets dotted with raw sex.

It wasn't until he revised a philosophical treatise called *The World of Sex* while living in Big Sur that he came up with a recipe for transforming those compelling 'native moments':

"One may succeed in repressing ugly, 'sinful' thoughts and desires, impulses and urges, but the results are patently disastrous. (Between being a saint and being a criminal there is little to choose.) To live out one's desires and, in so doing, subtly alter their nature, is the aim of every individual who aspires to evolve."

Live them out he did. He married five times. What he didn't live out, he conjured up in best sellers that were banned in his own country for nearly three decades.

Through it all, Lawrence was his man. He felt more respect for Lawrence than for any other writer.

So -- the only fitting way to pay tribute to such a mentor, he said, was "to give another creation. Not explain him – but prove by writing about him that one has caught the flame he tried to pass on."

With Anais Nin's help – and against the wishes of his publisher who preferred that he concentrate on *Tropic of Cancer* – Miller focused on writing a book in praise of Lawrence.

He went about this just as eagerly as any disciple ever extolled and elucidated the wise words of Jesus. Now Miller wanted to shed light on Lawrence's *meaning* rather than write a sensational critique exposing the other writer as a fool. He was seeking *truth*, not notoriety.

In a letter to his agent, Miller explained his radically altered outlook:

"As I see it, people have not changed, nor is there much likelihood they will. The world grows grayer, drearier, deader. And as it does I grow brighter, gayer, harder. I will not change. I will not compromise. If yesterday I was willing to cut out phrases and lines, paragraphs even, tomorrow I will not change a word, not a word. The word may be trite, cliché, inartistic, wrong even ... I will not alter it! I am going to have my say even if it kills me. And what does it matter to me, in the long run, whether I am published now or after my death? I don't give a fuck about posterity – get that straight. Nor about humanity. I care about my own integrity – that means everything to me. There I will not concede an inch, not a millimeter.

"Sad news for Kahane [his publisher who expected to publish a marketable tirade against Lawrence], perhaps, and all the rest who look forward to feeding on the dead body of the artist ... Who is Kahane or Knopf or anybody else in this world to tell me what I am to say or what not to say? ... They can deny me, refuse to listen to me. That's their outlook, not mine. I go my way ... I am so beastly sick of the lily-livered bastards who are feeding the public with the muck and garbage of literature today.

"In defending Lawrence, in championing this corpse, I am waging war against his eternal enemies, my eternal enemies. Never was there an age which a man could be less proud of than *this. It is a crime to have been born. And every new child born of this age is a crime against God.*

"Is that going too far? That's nothing. I have much worse to say. Perhaps you won't stick when you hear the rest. All right, don't! ... I am for a complete fanatical and religious revolution ... I wouldn't mind if half the earth were depopulated, if there sprang up a plague that strewed the earth with cadavers so that the very heavens stank.

"I think it would be a relief to have a genuine stench, a putrescent stench and not just the stench of SHIT.

"I think, if you will permit me the delicacy, that Joyce is such a stench. As much as I have championed Lawrence so much and more will I attack Joyce. I should like by the end of this year to get Joyce and Lawrence and Proust, and the whole thesis of my brochure done with, for good and all. Let that be my philosophy. It was humiliating to me to sit in your office and be requested to write a little brochure about this man or that man in order to introduce myself. I didn't want any introduction.

"I wanted simply to stand up and let go – be knocked over for it or lauded for it. But not apologize, not explain myself ...

"Kahane will never accept my Lawrence book, I feel quite confident of it. Nor the 'brochure' ... Nor my 'Tropic of Capricorn' ... I feel that at bottom he doesn't give a damn about me, about what I stand for. He doesn't know what I stand for. And perhaps it's that that galls me.

"But before this year's out it will be known what I stand for ... I am hoping that you will always remain one of the friends. Even when you disagree with me – mostly then. That is all."

Naturally his agent was more concerned about the monetary bottom line to all this. If this explosive American writer -- whose words were, as Anais Nin had put it, *'like hearing wild drums in the midst of the Tuileries Gardens'* -- was now in agreement with the more gentile D. H. Lawrence, would a public, hungry for sensation, *buy his books?*

What would happen to sales if he went soft, identifying not only with Lawrence's vitality and phoenix-like response to death, but with his underlying belief that *"there is only one thing that a man really wants to do all his life and that is to find his way to his God, his Morning Star, and be alone there. Then, afterwards, in the Morning Star, salute his fellow-men, and enjoy the woman who has come the long way with him"?*

Ignoring publishers' concerns, Miller continued to work on *The World of Lawrence* 'like one possessed' in the summer of 1933.

Ultimately, of course, it would dawn on him that in so doing he was also shedding light on himself. He finally admitted, *"It's not Lawrence – it's myself I'm making a place for!"*

Unfortunately, but not surprisingly, he had immersed himself so deeply in the voluminous Lawrence that he lost perspective. He couldn't distance himself enough to think or write clearly.

Near despair, he complained to Nin: *"The great need I have, with the terrific mass of data in my head, is to see it before my eyes, to see it in some order."*

He worked on the book intermittently through publication of his eventual best-sellers -- *Tropic of Cancer, Black Spring, Tropic of Capricorn,* even *Quiet Days in Clichy.*

All the while he insisted that after the Lawrence book was finished, he would retire and have nothing more to write.

He published a few sections of the Lawrence manuscript between 1938 and the early 1940s. And, in 1952, he recalled in a preface to an essay from his manuscript called 'The Universe of Death:' *"Never did I work so hard and so assiduously, only to end up in utter confusion."*

Eventually, he gave up entirely on finishing the Lawrence material for publication in book form, explaining, once again near despair:

"NOT EVEN A LAWRENCE WAS ABLE TO EXERCISE ANY VISIBLE INFLUENCE UPON THE WORLD. THE TIMES ARE STRONGER THAN THE MEN

WHO ARE THROWN UP. *We are in a dead-lock. We have a choice, but we are unable to make it. It was the realization of this which impelled me to end my long introduction to 'The World of Lawrence,' of which this is the final section, with the title 'The Universe of Death.'"*

In 'The Universe of Death,' Miller pointed to a pervasive *cultural fear of life* which, he believed, has created an empire of neurosis to which we are becoming increasingly accustomed. He wrote:

"The function of the psychologist, who is the priest of life today, comes more and more to resolve itself to this – that, instead of aiding man to go crazy under the crazy system by which we live, instead of urging man to revolt, to upset the system, or at least, to alter the external pattern, all his efforts tend rather toward adjusting him to an impossible condition of things. With the result that what was once regarded as disease becomes the norm."

One answer, of course, to the stresses of mainstream living, short of revolt, is to slow down and break with the norm for awhile to think, to feel, to wonder -- to open up to who we essentially are. How? Miller's man, Whitman, had an answer for that, too:

"I loaf, and invite my soul."

Miller resolved to do just that in Big Sur. He would pay more attention to his psyche. He aspired to put into practice what Whitman, Lawrence, Jeffers and a host of other wise individuals through the ages – including St. Francis of Assisi, one of the world's most famous drop outs -- had been preaching.

In Big Sur, he not only felt at peace with nature's God, he believed he had come close to attaining his own Morning Star.

Here, he could say with conviction, *"I AM"* surrounded by landscape that had *"a prehistoric a look. The look of always. Nature smiling at herself in the mirror of eternity."*

He was so stunned by this magnificent coastal landscape in which '*the masculine and feminine elements are perfectly blended*' that he was moved to declare:

"How wonderful is the earth and the creatures which inhabit it! This is Heaven enough. Why ask for more!"

For the first time in his life, he felt at home. He was convinced that we humans could be well and happy *if we just knew how to live in accord with Nature.*

Not only was he able to 'salute his fellow men' in his Big Sur paradise, he found in **Emil White** the type of male friend Lawrence had considered as essential to happiness as finding a woman to enjoy for the long haul.

It's true that Miller was unlucky in love in Big Sur, for reasons outlined elsewhere (i.e. **Doing It With the Cosmos: Henry Miller's Big Sur Struggle for Love Beyond Sex**).

But, with customary candor, he admitted his marital shortcomings:

"I created a monstrous character in my books and I gave him my name, Henry Miller. He's a demon, a rogue, a scoundrel. He fancies himself the playboy of the western world; he thinks he's a great lover, when, in reality, he's a shitty lover! He's always too preoccupied with his own needs and desire to open himself up to the woman's needs."

But through it all there was Anais Nin. Even though Nin had refused to leave her husband and marry him, she remained his friend until the day she died.

Apropos of all this, living the good life in Big Sur was so important to Miller that he shouted, almost desperately:

"One can live joyously – one must! – in the midst of a world peopled with sorrowing suffering creatures. What other world is there in which to enjoy life? ... After all, the world we inhabit is only the reflected image of our inner chaos [but] given only half a chance, men will express the best that is in them."

Miller had been given a chance to do just that. He expressed the best in himself, not only through writing but through experimenting with delightful, childlike watercolors.

"To paint," he announced, *"is to love again"* – to fall in love outward with what one is painting and see through the eyes of a child again.

Just as Mexico and the Southwest had impacted Lawrence, Big Sur struck Miller as **'the face of the world as the Creator intended it to look.'**

He was not only open here to expressing the best in himself through writing and painting, he knew what it meant to feel born again.

Mother Nature was providing the unconditional love he'd sought – and failed to find – in women, beginning with his own mother.

He was so overwhelmed by the majesty of Sur country that his sexual appetites seemed relatively unimportant – only a minor aspect of what he called *'the greater drama perpetually enacted in the soul of man.'*

He was 'doing it' now with the cosmos just as intensely as any saint ever felt communion with his God.

He had convinced himself that when a person like himself matures *'the sex problem falls*

'Clear and Bright' a 1952 Miller watercolor from copy number 3 of the 1960 Special Edition of his book To Paint is to Love Again, dedicated to his then-wife Eve and given to the author by Harry Dick Ross, pioneer artist of Big Sur and Miller's next door neighbor who ultimately married Eve.

into its proper perspective. The genitals are impressed, so to speak, into the service of the whole being. Then one can fuck, not only with heart and soul, as we say, but as a new being."

Whether his wives in Big Sur benefited from any 'heart and soul' love-making is subject matter of another book.

Suffice it to say that much of his writing now – like Whitman's *'Song of Myself'* – was intended as therapy. Miller wrote:

"Maybe it will do you good as well as me, for whatever itches me must itch you too. None of us is exempt. We are all one substance, one problem, one solution … We don't have to make [this earth] a Paradise – it IS one. We have only to make ourselves fit to inhabit it … Whatever happens to this earth is man's doing. Man has demonstrated that he is master of everything – except his own nature.'

How he worked on making himself fit! He was having great fun *"following the Holy Ghost within."* Lawrence taught him to do that.

Every morning in *Big Sur* became a spiritual high. In *Big Sur and the Oranges of Hieronymus Bosch*, he wrote:

"I'd get up with a smile on my lips. I'd walk out the front door and take in the surroundings. Then I'd bless everything as a kind of ritual. I blessed the ocean, the trees, flowers, birds, even the poison oak! Then I would bless every person in the world – man, woman, and child. I even blessed my enemies. I said a prayer for the Germans and the Japanese with whom we were at war. In a place that is virtually a paradise one can't help but feel a sense of humanity, and a connectedness to everything and everyone alive and moving on the face of the earth."

This was extraordinarily like his illumination in Greece. In *The Colossus of Maroussi* he described an experience in Crete. After climbing a bluff at Phaestos and exclaiming, *'God, it's incredible!'* he felt impelled to *'give prodigally and indiscriminately of all I possessed."*

So he gave from his soul:

I sent out a benediction in every direction – to old and young, to the neglected savages in the forgotten parts of the earth, to wild as well as domesticated animals, to the birds of the air, to creeping things, to trees and plants and flowers, to rocks and lakes and mountains. This is the first day of my life, said I to myself, that I have included everybody and everything on this earth in one thought. I bless the world, every inch of it, every living atom, and it is all alive, breathing like myself, and conscious through and through."

He had no inkling then that five years later he would be giving advice from a mountain top in Big Sur:

"The world being what it is, I give it as my candid opinion that anyone who knows how to work with his two hands, anyone who is willing to give a fair day's work for a fair day's pay, would be better off to abandon his art and settle down to a humdrum life in an out-of-the-way place like this rather than a celebrity in a world which has lost all sense of values."

Of course dropping out isn't for everyone. As usual, he agreed with Lawrence's insight:

"When you cut off a man and isolate him in his own pure and wonderful individuality, you haven't got the man at all, you've only got the dreary fag-end of him … In absolute isolation, I doubt if any individual amounts to much; or if any soul is worth saving, or even having …

"So that everything, even individuality itself, depends on relationship … Strip us of our human contacts and of our contact with the living earth and the sun, and we are almost bladders of emptiness. Our individuality means nothing."

But, to Lawrence, the opposite was also true. "The most vital thing in life," he wrote, "… is to learn to live alone … I profoundly believe that a single individual may prove to be of more worth than the whole generation of men in which he has lived."

It was this quixotic yearning for the seemingly impossible -- the all-too-human need to satisfy equally compelling desires to be alone as well as to be connected -- that made Lawrence interesting to Miller. The conflicting desires of creatives for both solitude and company is probably a strictly human quirk.

As Lawrence observed in 'Pan in America,'

Miller's 'Banjo Self-Portrait' from the Limited Edition of To Paint is to Love Again, done in 1944 for his friend Emil White

"My individualism is really an illusion. I am part of the great whole, and I can never escape. But I can deny my connections, break them, and become a fragment. Then I am wretched. What we want is to destroy our false, inorganic connections, especially those related to money, and re-establish the living organic connections with the cosmos, the sun and earth, with mankind and nation and family."

Miller understood Lawrence as a naturally 'bi-polar' man, like himself.

This, because Lawrence recognized opposing, but complementary, states of consciousness -- "the utter futility and frustration of life" and the ecstatic "union and dissolution of the mystic who, for a moment, becomes one with the universe."

He went on to explain:

"Lawrence tried to give us what he had experienced which is impossible, since each man must experience it for himself and most of us never do. He knew that the eternal harmony, the attainment of the One and Absolute, could be experienced only through the *annihilation of the self. When one comes face to face with this enigma one must realize also that there is no solution, except death, that this is the wheel upon which one is broken."*

At one point, Miller attempted to 'eff' his own ineffable mystical experience for others in a metaphorical tale he called *The Smile at the Foot of the Ladder.*

It's about an earnest clown named Auguste who longed to give his audiences a lot more than fleeting laughter when he dared to fabricate the miracle of ascension in a circus ring.

His intention was noble. By feigning ecstasy on the top run of a 'ladder to the moon,' he hoped to impart to his audience a peak experience, *'a joy which would prove imperishable.'*

Audiences loved his act.

But one night he failed to 'come back' from what had always been a simulated trance. In opening himself up to ecstasy by acting 'as if,' on this particular occasion, he actually experienced himself the very joy he had tried to transmit to his audience.

Fans jeered. It was entertainment they wanted, not *truth.*

Disappointed in his fans, yet *strangely at peace with himself* because he clarly had been touched and transformed, Auguste shed his clown clothes, left the act he loved and attempted to live an ordinary life, but with tragic results that were not to be repeated by Miller when he made a similar move.

He reluctantly quit Big Sur for Los Angeles in 1962 for practical reasons.

His fourth wife, Eve, was divorcing him and moving in with Harry Dick Ross, his next door neighbor; he wanted to be closer to his children who were living in LA with their mother; and he needed to be closer to publishers who wanted to exploit him – and make money for everyone concerned -- now that bans had been lifted on his early books.

In abandoning his life in Big Sur, he lamented, *"I walked out of my true paradise – and now, like the hero of 'Lost Horizon,' I am fucked!"*

'Really the Blues,'a 1955 watercolor, from the Special Edition of To Paint is to Love Again

But not entirely. His mettle was severely tested in LA. But there, he discovered that, although he could still clown and 'act as if' to please fans, his inner transformation was permanent.

He came to believe that, in the process of following his bliss in Big Sur, he actually had evolved into the kind of transfigured, joyful man that Lawrence too might have become had he been allotted more time to live.

Ultimately, for Miller, heroic shepherd of Pan that he was, art was the key to happiness after leaving his home in Big Sur. He wrote:

"The return to art is the only solution life offers, for art ... is the imaginative resolution of the inner conflict, the deep lying mask of illusion through which we can at once face the cruel enigma and bear with it ...

"The artist is he who carries in his soul the cruel mysteries, who gives expression to them, not in order to divest them of terror and insolubility, but to sustain the heroic image of himself through and by which he has empowered himself to play the God.

"For if it is true, as Lawrence says, that all his life the one thing he wanted to do was to find his way to his God, his Morning Star, let it be understood also that by God he means himself. The authority he wishes to serve is the authority which he has vested in himself and ... he finds it difficult to believe in himself, to say simply I Am and let that suffice.

"If it was weak and human of Lawrence to have wanted a woman in the Morning Star and a man, a friend, it was also very weak and human of God to have created a world of men and women instead of existing alone in his own absolute void."

And whether one feels victorious or defeated in 'finding himself' -- following his natural bliss instead of blindly following the trends and 'norms' of society -- Miller believed, with the mythical Sisyphus, that *"the important thing for the man, for the artist is the struggle."*

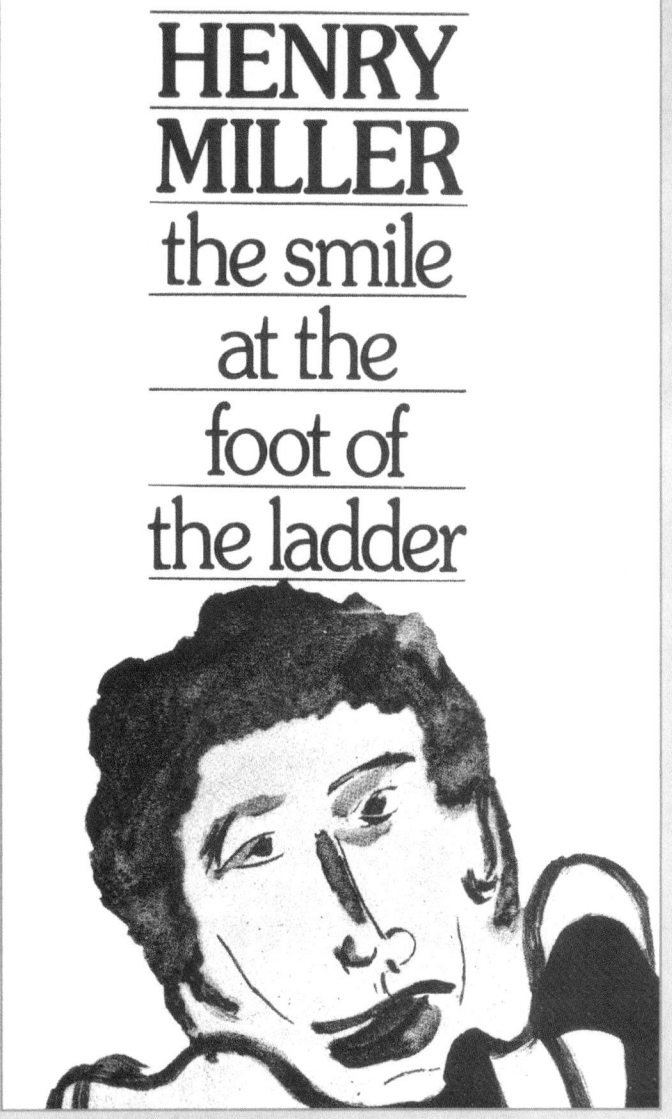

HENRY MILLER
the smile at the foot of the ladder

Miller's own struggle and subsequent transformation is a good example of Carl Jung's observation in *Modern Man in Search of a Soul* that *"the living spirit grows and even outgrows its earlier forms of expression [and] freely chooses the men in whom it lives and who proclaim it."*

That Miller believed himself to be one of the 'chosen' is evident from his declaration:

"I do think that I'm an innocent, even though I've committed crimes in my innocence. I'm guilty of the worst behavior — treachery, disloyalty, unfaithfulness — and still I think I'm one of God's chosen ones. I think I have a guardian angel looking after me."

No doubt he believed that Lawrence had

been among 'the chosen' too.

Unfortunately, from Miller's point of view, Lawrence was chosen to point the way without ever arriving at his own Morning Star.

"There is evidence for believing," Miller wrote, *"that had it been given him to enjoy the normal span of life, he would have arrived at a state of wisdom, a mystic way of life, in which the artist and the human being would have been reconciled."*

That Miller believed he had arrived at that state of wisdom himself, seems evident. Nothing to brag about, hoever. The 'powers that be' had simply allotted him more time to follow his bliss and share his experience by means of his art.

Just one work was left unfinished as he neared the end of his life: the book on Lawrence.

He had been obsessed with it for fifty years. But the unpublished manuscript -- the one he considered the most important writing of his life, despite the fact that he saw it as both 'confused and inspired' -- was still gathering dust on a shelf.

Only when he knew his time was running out did he give the go ahead to two tenacious professors from Canada's University of Manitoba -- Evelyn J. Hinz and John J. Teunissen -- to edit the manuscript for publication.

Their avowed aim – encouraged by Miller -- was to preserve the 'violent integrity' which characterized his confrontation with Lawrence's work.

Work accomplished, Miller's long time friend, **Noel Young** of Capra Press, published **The World of Lawrence: A Passionate Appreciation** in June, 1980, as a fulfilled Miller was quietly dissolving into the cosmos -- six months away from what would have been his ninetieth birthday and fifty years after Lawrence's death.

Miller's parting shot from *The World of Lawrence* is worth repeating:

"To surpass himself man does not, or should not, become God, but more a man, more Man. Towards the end Lawrence caught on to this, but then it was too late. The books written on his death-bed are a paean to the earthly life of man, the life he had forsaken in his quest of a beyond. But this earthly life, though he himself was not to experience it, was a transfigured life which is open to all of us to know and to enjoy. It is as impressive to me now, when I contemplate Lawrence, as it was to the disciples when they contemplated Christ. It is the desire at the bottom of every man's heart when he is truly alone with his own soul."

Miller's children scattered his ashes below Partington Ridge in Big Sur.

CHAPTER XI

MILLER'S MYSTIC COUNTERPART:
D. H. LAWRENCE

[A talk given by Fitzpatrick in Santa Fe, NM, at the 10th Annual International D.H. Lawrence Conference]

Approaching literature, as I do, with lusty philosophic curiosity and a journalist's craving for truth, I have mixed feelings about addressing D. H. Lawrence scholars here today.

On the one hand, I feel like an impertinent yellow daisy poking up in a field of lavender. This, because whenever I mention Henry Miller's book, **The World of Lawrence: A Passionate Appreciation**, scholars generally raise their eyebrows and dismiss the book, even if they haven't read it, in three words:

"Miller misunderstood Lawrence."

I do understand their hasty conclusion. After all, this street wise American writer from Brooklyn had originally dispensed with his professorial counterpart from Nottingham as "a little runt, a nasty devil, a dry thoroughly English type."

In 1932, while living in Paris, Miller sent a vitriolic letter to Anais Nin, the only female he ever considered his match as well as his mentor. (But she had the good sense not to marry him).

Nin had published an insightful treatise on Lawrence that had inspired Miller to learn more about this writer his enamorata so admired.

In this letter, he protested:

"I despise [Lawrence's] workingman's (no, it was bourgeois) attitude about things -- scrubbing floors, cooking, laundering, etc. And his being alone crap! Not sensitiveness, but timidity, lack of guts, lack of humanity ... remark the sickly letters [he] wrote [to Mabel Dodge Luhan] ... How could he have fallen into the clutches of such a woman? There was something feeble about him -- despite his glorious language."

Outbursts like this -- plus the likelihood that the author of *Tropic of Cancer*, whose cavalier protagonist repeatedly "fucked with a cold heart," could in no way relate to *Lady Chatterley's* gamekeeper who "fucked with a warm heart" -- might cause any Lawrence aficionado to conclude that these two were worlds apart.

During his early encounter with Lawrence's work, Miller would have agreed. At first, he, too, regarded the gap between them as unbridgeable.

His original critique of Lawrence was defiant. Wanting to attack him from "every possible angle" in order to put him in his place, Miller inundated himself in Lawrence's writings.

But instead of destroying Lawrence, he was seduced by the other writer. In 1933, he wrote, after reading "The Crown":

"I feel I have said unkind, unjust things about Lawrence. He is far greater than I ever dreamt ... He stands out like a rock. He bides his time. I was practically ignorant of Lawrence when I began this study. Now I appreciate him deeply ... I feel humble and chastened. But I am more now than ever I was before."

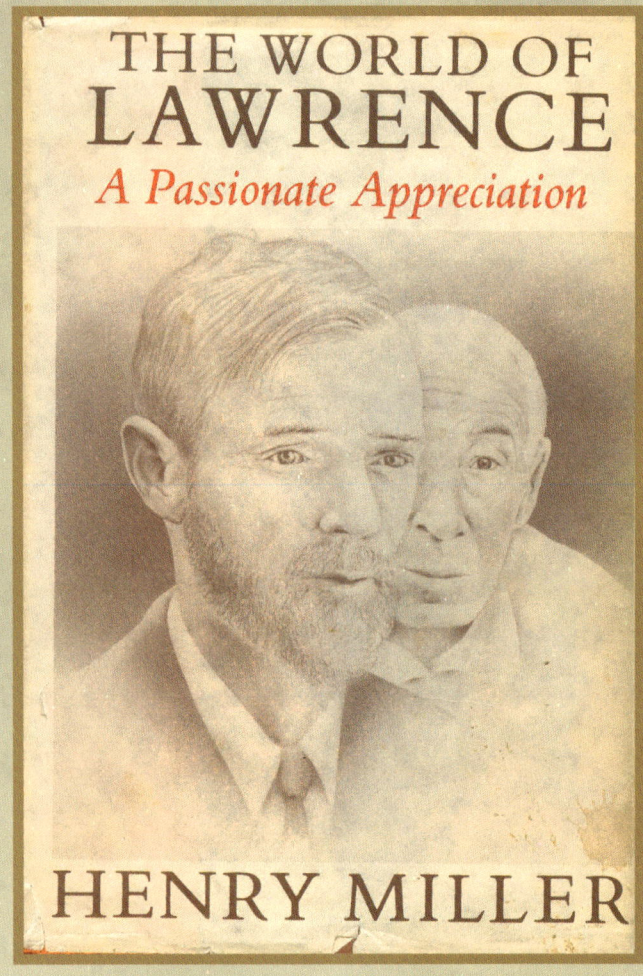

THE WORLD OF LAWRENCE

A Passionate Appreciation

HENRY MILLER

Now he was praising Lawrence as a visionary:

"[His] language is matchless – reminiscent of the best in the Bible. The thought is superior to any of Jesus' sayings, in my opinion. It is like a new Revelation … The seed of all Lawrence's writing is here -- and more than just seed. It is the mystic at his most mystical. I am in love with it."

Quite an about face in attitude for a budding cynic who had written a best seller in Paris which he'd described as "a prolonged insult, a gob of spit in the face of Art, a kick in the pants to God, Man, Destiny, Time, Love, Beauty …"

One of those scholars who believes that Miller misunderstood Lawrence – is our own conference chairman, Virginia Hyde.

However, on hearing the title of my own book, ***Doing It With the Cosmos: Henry Miller's Big Sur Struggle for Love Beyond Sex***, she backed off a bit, allowing, in an exchange of e-mails, that they had something in common.

"Both writers," she wrote, *"did have a cosmic concept of love and interrelationship that went far beyond the usual idea of sex."*

Because of that exchange, here I am, like the 'yellow daisy' I mentioned earlier, a bit timid but delighted to be with all of you fellow 'thought-adventurers,' described by DHL as those of us willing to risk 'going forth to meet life in the body' then face the results in our minds.

It can indeed be great fun "following the Holy Ghost within" wherever it leads. Lawrence taught me that.

Then Miller egged me on in ***Big Sur and the Oranges of Hieronymus Bosch*** when he wrote:

"It may indeed be the highest wisdom to elect to be a nobody in a relative paradise such as this rather than a celebrity in a world which has lost all sense of values … In simplifying our lives, everything acquires a significance hitherto unknown. When we are one with ourselves the most insignificant blade of grass assumes its proper place in the universe. Or a piece of manure, for that matter."

I acted on this wisdom years ago because it resonated with what I believed to be my own deepest and best instincts.

When my children were grown, I left an urban ant heap to re-root in a coastal paradise -- a place once described by one of America's first great muckrakers, Lincoln Steffens (*Shame of the Cities*), as "a heaven on earth to which the wise succeeders in life, wise enough to die before their time, go and live on happily ever after."

He was referring to the same Big Sur-Monterey coast that was to cast its spell on Henry Miller for seventeen years. (It's true, there did come a time when Miller felt it necessary to desert Big Sur for the sprawl of Los Angeles -- for reasons I reveal in my own book about him *Doing It With the*

Cosmos.

But in so doing, he lamented, "It's almost as if, in quitting Big Sur, I walked out of my true paradise -- and now, like the hero of *Lost Horizon*, I am fucked!")

Miller's involvement with Lawrence's nature mysticism had already been enriched during a sojourn in Greece which he told about in *The Colossus of Maroussi*.

He echoed some Lawrencian moments in *The Air Conditioned Nightmare* during ensuing travels in our American Southwest en route to California.

For example: He deplored what he perceived as the rift between man and Nature in America and had little hope that most of us would be able to escape the treadmill we have created for ourselves.

Like Lawrence, he was moved by the reverent Native American attitude toward the land and saw himself now as communing with Nature on what others would erroneously call 'a low level of life.'

He even expressed hope that some of the hardiest among America's indigenous people, the Navajos, for example, might rise up and reclaim their land -- should the rest of us continue to grow soft and degenerate.

But when he discovered Big Sur in 1943, he was ecstatic and emphatic:

The only place in the world thus far that I can think of as home is Big Sur … It is American in the best sense of the word which is what makes it so unlike the rest of the country."

Just as Mexico and the Southwest had impacted Lawrence, Big Sur struck Miller as "the face of the world as the Creator intended it to look."

Now he was not only open to expressing the best in himself through writing and painting, he was 'doing it' with the cosmos just as intensely as any saint ever felt communion with God.

Few scholars seem to have paid much attention to the fact that all the things Miller had to say about his attempt to live the life of a 'natural man' in Big Sur were imbued with the same atavistic spirit that had motivated Lawrence.

Fact is, Miller obsessed about Lawrence

for the last fifty of his 88 years. He was working on a book that was not intended to be a critique but, in his words, 'an appreciation, passionate and prejudiced, an emotional document, which I consider the only kind of criticism worthwhile."

Unfortunately, he identified so closely with the other writer's frustrations and resulting melioristic philosophy that he couldn't distance himself enough from his material in the beginning to write without confusion. Consequently, he was unable to organize his material to his own satisfaction.

Only when he knew he was on the doorstep of death did he give the go ahead to allow this work he considered both 'confused and inspired' to be edited and published by two Canadian professors at the University of Manitoba -- Evelyn J. Hinz and John J. Teunissen.

Their avowed aim was to preserve the "violent integrity" which characterized Miller's confrontation with Lawrence's work. It was published as he lay dying in June, 1980, fiftieth anniversary of Lawrence's death.

Why did he wait so long? Partly, I believe, to own up to his indebtedness to Lawrence and to pass along the torch he had carried for so long.

I also believe there was some real guilt involved. He hadn't just put off *finishing* the Lawrence tribute, he had *shrugged it off* long ago, despairing, "Not even a Lawrence was able to exercise any visible influence upon the world. The times are stronger than the men who are thrown up."

But there may also have been a more practical motive in abandoning the book. Miller needed money to live in Paris. And his publishers had shown little interest in what he had to say about Lawrence, insisting that sales of *Tropic of Cancer* could be hurt if his fans were to discover that this explosive American writer -- whose words were, as Anais Nin put it, "like hearing wild drums in the midst of the Tuileries Gardens" -- was now in agreement with the more gentile D. H. Lawrence who suggested in *The Plumed Serpent*, something that really didn't seem to fit the Miller image:

"There is only one thing that a man really wants to do all his life and that is to find his way to his God, his Morning Star, and be alone there. Then, afterwards, in the Morning

Star, salute his fellow-men, and enjoy the woman who has come the long way with him."

It was just this quixotic yearning for the seemingly impossible -- the need to have it all -- to satisfy equally compelling desires to be alone and to be connected -- that made Lawrence interesting to Miller. And to me. For Miller, writing was not only an art that required solitude, it was also a way of connecting. He wrote:

"Maybe [my writing] will do you good as well as me, for whatever itches me must itch you too. None of us is exempt. We are all one substance, one problem, one solution."

Miller understood Lawrence as a man who recognized "the utter futility and frustration of life," as well as one who experienced "the union and dissolution of the mystic who, for a moment, becomes one with the universe."

He explained:

"Lawrence tried to give us what he had experienced [as Miller himself tried to do in The Smile At The Foot of the Ladder], which is impossible, since each man must experience it for himself and most of us never do.

"He knew that the eternal harmony, the attainment of the One and Absolute, could be experienced only through the annihilation of the self. When one comes face to face with this enigma one must realize also that there is no solution, except death, that this is the wheel upon which one is broken."

Is there any solution to this seemingly tragic predicament spelled out years before by Schopenhauer? Miller answers in the affirmative, echoing not only Lawrence but Frederick Nietzsche's answer to philosophy's most famous pessimist. Miller wrote:

"The return to art is the only solution life offers, for art ... is the imaginative resolution of the inner conflict, the deep lying mask of illusion through which we can at once face the cruel enigma and bear with it ...

"The artist is he who carries in his soul the cruel mysteries, who gives expression to them, not in order to divest them of terror and insolubility, but to sustain the heroic image of himself through and by which he has empowered himself to play the God.

"For if it is true, as Lawrence says, that all his life the one thing he wanted to do was to find his way to his God, his Morning Star, let it be understood also that by God he means himself. The authority he wishes to serve is the authority which he has vested in himself and ... he finds it difficult to believe in himself, to say simply I Am and let that suffice.

"If it was weak and human of Lawrence to have wanted a woman in the Morning Star and a man, a friend, it was also very weak and human of God to have created a world of men and women instead of existing alone in his own absolute void."

This is what I like about Miller and Lawrence. They put into words what many of us only think and keep to ourselves, especially such thoughts about God.

Miller felt at peace with his God on the soft and violent Big Sur-Monterey coast. Here, he attained his own Morning Star. He was able to say "I AM" in a landscape he described as having "a prehistoric a look. The look of always. Nature smiling at herself in the mirror of eternity."

What's more, he also managed to acquire Emil White as a good male friend and attain the love of a woman [well, two wives who didn't exactly go 'the long way with him' as he had hoped, but you can read about that in my book].

He shouted his gospel from Partington Ridge:

"One can live joyously – one must! In the midst of a world peopled with sorrowing suffering creatures what other world is there in which to enjoy life? ... After all, the world we inhabit is only the reflected image of our inner chaos [but] given only half a chance, men will express the best that is in them."

But the difficulty is that artistic creation requires periodic isolation, being alone with one's creative spirit. Surely Lawrence would have understood the feelings of Miller's wives who became irked by their husband's preoccupation with solitude, not to mention his male friend, in Big Sur. Lawrence himself had observed:

"When you cut off a man and isolate him in his own pure and wonderful individuality, you haven't got the man at all, you've only got the dreary fag-end of him ... In absolute isolation, I doubt if any individual amounts to much; or if any soul is worth saving, or even having ... So that everything, even individuality itself, depends on relationship ... Strip us of our human contacts and of our contact with the living earth and the sun, and we are almost bladders of emptiness. Our individuality means nothing."

Still, he continued to insist that *"the most vital thing in life ... is to learn to live alone ... I profoundly believe that a single individual may prove to be of more worth than the whole generation of men in which he has lived."*

But the conflicting desires of creatives for both solitude and company may be a strictly human quirk. *"My individualism,"* Lawrence wrote in 'Pan in America,' *"is really an illusion. I am part of the great whole, and I can never escape. But I can deny my connections, break them, and become a fragment. Then I am wretched. What we want is to destroy our false, inorganic connections, especially those related to money, and re-establish the living organic connections with the cosmos, the sun and earth, with mankind and nation and family."*

But whether one feels victorious or defeated in striving for his personal Morning Star, Miller would add, *"The important thing for the man, for the artist, is the struggle."*

It seems to me that Miller's personal struggle and subsequent transformation was a prime example of Carl Jung's observation in *Modern Man in Search of a Soul* that "the living spirit grows and even outgrows its earlier forms of expression [and] freely chooses the men in whom it lives and who proclaim it."

That Miller believed himself to be one of the chosen is evident from his declaration:

"I do think that I'm an innocent, even though I've committed crimes in my innocence. I'm guilty of the worst behavior — treachery, disloyalty, unfaithfulness — and still I think I'm one of God's chosen ones. I think I have a guardian angel looking after me."

He regarded Lawrence as among 'the chosen' too. But Lawrence seemed fated to point the way without ever arriving at his own Morning Star himself.

Miller wrote:

"There is evidence for believing that had it been given him to enjoy the normal span of life, [Lawrence] would have arrived at a state of wisdom, a mystic way of life, in which the artist and the human being would have been reconciled."

I have little doubt that in his old age Miller was convinced that, despite his crude beginnings, he himself had evolved into the kind of transfigured, joyful man that Lawrence might have become had Lawrence lived longer.

Miller's message: *"We don't have to make this earth a paradise, it is one. We have only to make ourselves fit to inhabit it."*

Yet some hardheaded fans still prefer to think of him as the incorrigible "King of Smut," living out a Playboy mentality. Fact is, Miller grew to despise that image, even though he occasionally played the game in his old age -- to sell books. So I'll rest my case with Miller's parting words in *The World of Lawrence: A Passionate Appreciation:*

"To surpass himself man does not, or should not, become God, but more a man, more Man. Towards the end Lawrence caught on to this, but then it was too late. The books written on his death-bed are a paean to the earthly life of man, the life he had forsaken in his quest of a beyond. But this earthly life, though he himself was not to experience it, was a transfigured life which is open to all of us to know and to enjoy. It is as impressive to me now, when I contemplate Lawrence, as it was to the disciples when they contemplated Christ. It is the desire at the bottom of every man's heart when he is truly alone with his own soul."

Did Miller misunderstand Lawrence? I don't think so.

CHAPTER XII

ON BEING A SUNNY CYNIC:
THE AUTHOR'S SEASONED OUTLOOK FROM CARMEL VALLEY

Old age is an interesting season. Having 'been there, done that,' I'm content to be living a pastoral, self-styled poetic life, alone but far from lonely. It's as if I've returned to the metaphorical Garden of Eden or entered the Kingdom of Heaven by becoming a blessed child again.

I see myself these days as a Cynic, but not a spoilsport or peevish naysayer in the modern sense of the word. I'm a *sunny* Cynic, in tune with a minor school of Socratic philosophy made famous by Diogenes, that legendary dropout from Athenian society who practiced voluntary simplicity.

Diogenes was a curious old fellow. He scorned city life, aspiring to live more virtuously in harmony with Nature. We're told that he threw a coarse cloak over his shoulders, carried a bag of necessities, and wandered around the countryside with staff and lantern, searching for an honest man.

Some say he lingered for awhile around Corinth and lived alfresco in a tub. He became so famous for his independent spirit and haughty humility that when Alexander the Great marched into Corinth, he insisted on meeting this Cynic. When he found the venerable philosopher sunning in his tub, Alexander asked what service he might render. Diogenes replied, *"Stand from between me and the sun."*

"If I weren't Alexander," the great one laughed, *"I would want to be Diogenes!"*

Well now, I love my Carmel Valley sunshine, but I'm certainly no Diogenes. Fact is, I feel more kinship with Socrates who chided the Cynics: *"Why so ostentatious? Through your rags I see your vanity."*

What I do admire about these Cynics, however, is their reverence for Nature and their belief that *ethics is the only subject that really matters in philosophy.* They weren't stuffy scholars.

They were quipsters, preferring satire and an occasional diatribe to formal philosophic dialogue. *They taught by example, no matter how often they were mocked.*

City folks jeered them for living like *kynikos*, a Greek word meaning dog. But the Cynics only smiled. What was intended as an insult they accepted as a compliment.

The masses simply didn't know about the revered white canine that symbolized their reconciliation with the forces of nature. It had always been the dog's privilege, during sacrificial feasts, to carry off to the gods a portion of the meat.

I like these Cynics. I emulated them, in a way. I, too, dropped out of urban ant heaps and mainstream happenings to live more simply. It seems to me that anyone who aspires to grow old gracefully without acknowledging the native wisdom of the Cynics must be living with the three little monkeys.

My 'sunny' take on their philosophy means, among other things, that since moving to the country, creating a little world of my own and dubbing it 'Capricorn Brae', I've preferred boots and blue jeans to dresses.

I delight in simple pleasures like stretching in the morning sun or listening to afternoon winds blowing through the pines.

On summer evenings, I scrunch down in feather pillows and smile while crickets sing outside my bedroom window. When rain comes, I hardly ever avert my face and run for cover, unless I'm wearing suede …

When I'm not glued to this computer, I like to observe the goings and comings of bugs and lizards and birds, just like a little kid. Sometimes I toot on a tin whistle or beat on the elk hide drum I bought from Indians at the Taos Pueblo.

On cold nights, I can wallow in books and music in front of a roaring fire. And when I write nowadays -- or 'teach' -- I expound only on subjects that excite me.

I'm deliciously free to care for myself, to jolt the mind of an occasional student, to drive my car on back roads instead of freeways, and to use credit card awards to fly to exotic landscapes still unsullied by human developers.

I can pretty much do as I please now, despite increasing dangers along the narrowing road to *Whatever*.

It's not that I'm without responsibilities. I have an active conscience directed by an intuitive voice I'm inclined to interpret as my 'God spot.' I answer to that inner monitor and dote on welcome duties such as maintaining the little redwood house I created from scratch on a genesta-dotted acre. I tidy it up joyfully.

I bring hay and water to a couple of mischievous goats who play with me and provide fertilizer for my gardens in exchange for grain and carrots. A puckish Sheltie looks to me for nurturing, and I look to him for true devotion and steadfast shepherding activities.

Plants rely on my attention. And I rely on them for sustenance and color. Grapevines and fruit trees look to me for pruning and thank me at harvest time.

Family members -- and a few friends still interested enough to put up with me – occasionally seek me out for companionship.

Sometimes I'm not so 'sunny.' I get sad, even grumpy -- especially during periods of unrelenting rain. That's when I tend to reflect on how inept we humans are with each other -- and how we are messing up our earth.

Still, in those dark periods when I abandon hope on stage, I find courage and compassion waiting in the wings. Then Zorba goads me to dance. Sisyphus prompts me to laugh. And I manage to assume an attitude of joyful resigned resistance to forces that would break my spirit.

The older I get the more Cynically playful I feel, given *'what fools we mortals be.'* I have become more opinionated, more discerning, and, occasionally,

downright misanthropic. But I'm more *smilingly* so.

I'm grateful too. I feel gratitude for kindred spirits and for the divine beauty of Nature, despite its 'tooth and claw' underpinnings.

Yes, it bothers me that everything must kill to live. I grow things in my garden for the sole purpose of eating them.

Worse, I have to decide which baby carrots to abort so others can grow big for better eating. If I don't do it, Nature will. The stronger carrots simply stunt the growth of the weak.

I don't like that, but it's Nature's way. I may try to expiate my guilt by tossing the tiny carrots into a salad. It may sound silly, but I eat them with gratitude, inviting them to live on through me so they won't have died in vain.

When I reflect on such things, I question the existence of any humanized deity, worthy of worship, who, if personal and caring, would so arrange life that it would depend on the mutual killing and ingestion of various species. No *ethical* entity would set life up that way if it had the power to do otherwise.

The Biblical concept of original sin is hardly a satisfying explanation anymore. It seems to me that the humanized God of the Eden story, being omniscient, must have known that curious Mother Eve would bite the apple of awareness long before He told her not to. So where is the freedom? Where is the justice in punishment?

Truth may be less complicated.

Living here in my valley, it's easy to feel that the creative, all-encompassing divinity of Nature is kinder to those who reconnect with the earth -- kinder to those who try to live more simply and creatively in the tension between life's essential polarities. It's just easier here to be a *sunny* Cynic.

... Elayne Wareing Fitzpatrick

Capricorn Brae and the original
'four-footed gang', Carmel Valley

Work keeps us from three great evils:
boredom, vice, and poverty ...
We must cultivate our garden.
(Voltaire's Candide)

*I*ntegrity is wholeness.
The greatest beauty is organic wholeness,
The wholeness of life and things,
The divine beauty of the universe.
Love that, not man apart from that,
Or else you will share man's pitiful confusions,
Or drown in despair when his days darken.

                                 ... *Robinson Jeffers*

Pertinent Postscripts

BACKDROP FOR SOJOURNERS:

A BRIEF ROMANTIC HISTORY OF CARMEL

*This Peninsula is a heaven on earth to which the wise succeeders in life,
wise enough to die before their time, go and live on happily ever after.*

Lincoln Steffens, author, *The Shame of the Cities*
('The Villager,' Vol. 1 No. 2, Carmel, August, 1933)

CARMEL-BY-THE-SEA, with its dazzling white beach guarded by wind-twisted cypresses and granite headlands, was America's first nature Bohemia and one of the earth's few lyrical places actually *enhanced* by constructs of developers.

In 1902, a sentimental lawyer and a visionary realtor with strong feelings for the Big Sur-Monterey coast ~ Frank Powers and James Franklin Devendorf ~ formed the Carmel Development Company on the premise that contact with nature is a fundamental human need.

Like coastal natives who came before them, these men believed that the land requires respect and that human communities should be designed to harmonize with nature, not replace it.

This, even if roads had to be curved around existing trees and groves of new trees had to be planted to guard against erosion. They fought intrusion of any industry or mainstream business that didn't suit their romantic vision.

When asked, early on, about Carmel's resulting eccentricities, Devendorf[1] quipped:

"I might have been a millionaire, but I'm glad I sold the land cheap [$10 down and $5 a month] to poets and painters who were glad to plant my trees. I didn't know Carmel was going to be quite like this, but I'm glad it is, and I'm rooting for the poets against the business men to keep it so."

The man was a rare bird – a *sensitive* developer – who regarded the profit motive – obsession with monetary security and consequent repression of cultural and spiritual dimensions ~ as the fatal flaw of contemporary society.

The traditional resistance of Carmelites to mainstream standards is not unlike the Bohemian mentality in the Monterey art colony that hosted Robert Louis Stevenson in 1879.

[1] Today Devendorf's great grandson, Jack Galante, carries on the family's nature-oriented philosophy in his operation of a 700-acre working cattle ranch and vineyard in the Cachagua area of upper Carmel Valley, and he has opened Carmel-by-the-Sea's first wine-tasting room. He carries on the family's 'poetic' tradition by hosting weekend tours and wine-tasting picnics for sojourners at the vineyard.

Even then, RLS lamented that the little town wasn't strong enough to resist the influence of what he called *"the flaunting caravanserai."*

He rightly predicted that *"the poor, quaint, penniless native gentlemen of Monterey must perish, like a lower race, before the millionaire vulgarians of the Big Bonanza."*

Carmel, as it turned out, was more fortunate.

When the San Francisco earthquake and fire of April 1906 left two-thirds of the population homeless, Carmel was ready to receive the city's Bohemian refugees.

That's because the previous year poet George Sterling, an Oakland realtor who hung out on San Francisco's Barbary Coast with his buddy Jack London, had become disenchanted with what he called *"the somewhat cruel atmosphere of all great cities"* and built a house in the woods in Carmel.

He moved there with his wife, Carrie, hoping to simplify his life and avoid "temptations to folly and luxury."

At thirty-eight, Sterling wanted to change his life. Carmel seemed to be a place where he could escape to fish for his dinner, hunt game freely, grow his own food, run and swim naked, wander alone in forests and on beaches ~ and be free to write in peace in a land where it was always springtime.

Friends followed: novelist Mary Austin and photographer Arnold Genthe. Even London and his 'mate-woman,' Charmian Kittredge.

Later, Sterling befriended Tor House poet Robinson Jeffers who went on to become Carmel's most famous genus loci.

After the quake, more artists - mostly eccentrics from elite college backgrounds ~ fled to Carmel and formed a bohemian community that revolved around Sterling. They built cheap board-and-batten shelters or rented a house for $6 a month.

Calling themselves 'The Bunch,' they disavowed traditional Christianity in favor of nature mysticism, a form of pantheism inspired by this gentle-yet-powerful landscape.

Often called the most beautiful meeting

of land and sea in the world, this coast activates a latent sense of awe and wonder that artists and philosophers alike have connected with Divinity.

When they weren't meeting in the pagan grove Sterling had sanctified by nailing cow skulls to trees, they were prying abalone off rocks and pounding the meat to tenderize it as they sang 'abalone songs' around a driftwood fire.

The first verses, invented by Sterling, went this way:

> *Oh! Some folks boast of quail on toast,*
> *Because they think it's tony;*
> *But I'm content to owe my rent*
> *And live on abalone.*
> *Some say that God is fat*
> *Others say he's bony;*
> *But as for me I disagree*
> *He resembles abalone*

'The Bunch' grew. Ultimately, their Nature Bohemia and this coastal paradise stretching down to Big Sur, attracted others away from cities both here and abroad – just plain interesting individuals as well as luminaries.

The list grew to include such interesting people as:

Ambrose Bierce, Sinclair Lewis, Upton Sinclair, Jimmy Hopper, Xavier Martinez, William Rose Benet, Harry Lafler, Nora May French, Bert Heron, Harry Leon Wilson, Vernon Kellogg, David Starr Jordan, William Ritschel, Edward Kuster, Charles Sumner Greene, Martin Flavin, Hugh Comstock, Lincoln Steffens, Ella Winter, Perry Newberry, M. J. 'Rock' Murphy, Samuel F. B. Morse, Gloria Vanderbilt, Lillian Bos and Harrydick Ross, Nicholas Roosevelt, Nathaniel Owings, Philip Johnson, Ansel Adams, Edward Weston, Jaime de Angulo, Ed "Doc" Ricketts, John Steinbeck, Bruce Ariss, Jean Varda, Emil White, Henry Miller, Michael Murphy, Richard Price, Jack Kerouac, Joan Baez, Fritz Perles, Emil Norman, Eric Berne, Benjamin Spock, Kim Novak, Allen Funt, Ted Turner, David Packard, Jeff Norman, Ephraim Doner, Eric Barker, Alex and Marian Weygers, Wah Chang, Gordon Newell, Poco Ferro, William Brandon, John Thodos, Erma Bombeck, William Giles, Morley Baer,

Barclay Ferguson, Donald Teague, Hank Ketchum, Charles Schulz, Eldon Dedini, Gus Ariola, Shell Fisher, Bill Fassett, Peter Meckel, Magnus Toren, Dr. Linus Pauling, Betty White and Alan Ludden, Merv Griffin, Taelen Thomas, Bill Minor, Joseph Cloonan, Doris Day, and Clint Eastwood.

Many, after settling here, worked hard to fight 'improvements' considered important to mainstream America: grassy lawns, street numbers, factories, mail delivery, street lights, sidewalks, even paved roads.

They detested any form of business that wasn't essential ~ or artistic. Small was beautiful.

Inevitably, the area attracted business people motivated more by profit than aesthetics, and the original art types' slogan, *"Don't Boost, Keep Carmel off the Map,"* produced an effect quite opposite to the publicists' intention.

Even area bohemians, in order to survive, eventually acquiesced to a proliferation of tea rooms, restaurants, inns, and shops, with one caveat:

"If we must grow, let us grow along our original lines."

By 1961, however, John Steinbeck would visit his family retreat in Pacific Grove and observe:

"Carmel, begun by starveling writers and unwanted painters is now a community of the well-to-do and the retired. If Carmel's founders should return they could not afford to live there, but it wouldn't go that far. They would be instantly picked up as suspicious characters and deported over the city line."

Carmel has never been a place to get rich monetarily. An old real estate folder admitted quite frankly:

"For those who seek a place to vent their enterprise in money-making, Carmel is perhaps the most unfortunate choice on the Pacific Coast that could be made. For those who 'come west' for a job in California climate, there is little opportunity in Carmel except for the domestic servant or perhaps for some artisan of the

building trades that construct the houses in which Carmel villagers live."

That's still true for the most part. Today Carmel and its neighbors generally attract retirees and haven-seekers who have made their money elsewhere, along with the creative folks who serve them – from artists, educators, and dog-walkers to enterprising inn-keepers, clever restauranteurs, poetic architects, and meticulous contractors, not to mention a plethora of realtors, doctors, lawyers and small business owners.

But Carmel-by-the-Sea, with its beguiling spirit of rarity, had a lasting effect on its neighbors ~ Carmel Valley, Carmel Highlands, Big Sur, Monterey, Pebble Beach, and Pacific Grove.

The original Carmelites created a new model of what life might become for the disaffected offspring of middle-class Americans, then and now, who tend to regard mainstream culture as a blight on sensibility, truth, adventure, romance, humanity – even life itself.

It's a given that in every generation there has been some form of *romantic resistance* by children of the so-called bourgeoisie.

At best, they have aspired to refine the middle class so it might become its promise: *a combination of the venturesome liberty of artists with the enterprising pragmatism of science, technology, and business in order to form a more soul-satisfying protoculture in each new century.*

Gustave Flaubert explained it this way: *"Every bourgeois in the flush of his youth, were it for but a day, a moment, has believed himself capable of immense passion, of lofty enterprises … Every accountant bears within him the debris of a poet."*

The Monterey Peninsula, perhaps more than any other place in America today, remains essentially poetic. It is a wildly picturesque haven enhanced by dreamers and only slightly altered by human excess. A consummate blending of sea and land, fog and sun, shadows and light, storm and quiet, it evokes a gamut of emotions and continues to invite the uncommon.

Elayne Wareing Fitzpatrick

THE RACONTEUR AND THE POET
|Elayne Wareing Fitzpatrick

[The following essay, published in *"Jeffers Studies"* (Winter, 1999), was prompted by Dr. Robert Brophy's comment in the ***"Robinson Jeffers Newsletter"*** (Winter, 1996): ***"For the most part [Henry] Miller seems only coincidentally interested in landscape, as a backdrop and contributing mood for human dramatics; Jeffers is almost entirely immersed in landscape."*** It took me three years to get around to quibbling over this with my long-time friend, Professor Brophy, partly because I was absorbed in finishing my 2001 book on Miller, ***Doing It With the Cosmos***.]

Henry Miller and Robinson Jeffers. Two Capricorns. The first, a glib raconteur. The other, a taciturn poet. On the surface, no two humans seemed less alike. Inwardly, they were kindred souls. Both were touched deeply by the nobility of the primordial in Greece and Big Sur. Both fell in love outward with the divine beauty of the cosmos.

Interacting in Big Sur with what he described as the landscape's hoary "look of always" (*BIG SUR*, 8), Miller felt "a connectedness to everything and everyone alive and moving on the face of the earth." (*REFLECTIONS*, 84)

Paraphrasing in "*Picodiribibi*" the dying words of another mentor, D. H. Lawrence, who wrote "For man, as for flower, beast and bird, the supreme triumph is to be most vividly, most perfectly, alive," Miller pleaded: "Let us become fully alive, that is what I have been trying to say." (*READER*, 94)

Then, he would add, "When you have expressed yourself to the fullest, then and only then will it dawn upon you that everything has already been expressed, not in words alone but in deed, and that all you need really do is say Amen!" (*BIG SUR*, 32)

The result, for Miller, was a heightened sense of the import of his own humanity in the life process, if only as one of God's dupes.

Jeffers, on the other hand, was less enthusiastic about the importance of humanity in the total scheme of things. He was drawn to the *primacy* of the non-human ~ mountains, oceans, rocks, water, birds, beasts, trees. "Their beauty has more meaning," he insisted, "than the whole human race" (*SHINING*, 232).

Humans were only symbolic interpreters, not to be loved apart from "the wholeness of life and things, the divine beauty of the universe" ("The Answer," *SELECTED POETRY*, 594).

Despite their differing priorities, both men were pantheists. Miller looked forward to reincarnation, Jeffers to transmutation.

The Raconteur didn't mince words. During a 1961 interview in London, he maintained: "Of course you don't die, nobody dies; death doesn't exist; you only reach a new level of vision, a new realm of consciousness, a new and unknown world. Just as you don't know where you came from, so you don't know where you're going. But that there is something there, before and after, I firmly believe." (*WRITERS*, 189)

And just before his death in 1980, he confessed in "*On Death*" that although he didn't have memories of past lives, he did believe he was "a very old soul." He went on: 'Seeing how I didn't learn much from my experiences this time around, I most likely will return again. I go back and forth on this ... But if I should happen back this way once more, if given the choice, I'd like not to live the life of the artist, or the writer. I'd like more than anything, to be a man who grows flowers. It seems to me that the life of the horticulturist is the cleanest, the purest, the most natural life of all. The man who tends a garden is the man most directly in touch with God." (*REFLECTIONS*, 125)

Conversely, the Poet, feeling vulnerable after the death of his mate, waxed sentimental in his cosmotheism:

Y ou have gone up with the flame to the high air; and that
         pitiful bone-ash,
              Not buried deeply, lives in bright flowers
In the garden you loved. –
As for the precious human consciousness –
(Yours was most precious to me not mine, nor theirs)–
I think it is taken into the great dream of the earth
For this dark planet
Has its own consciousness, from which yours came,
And now returns, as the Earth's consciousness,
Half-separate for a time, will return at length
To the whole galaxy; and when that perishes
To the whole endless universe – that is, to God,
Who will make all things new.

("Whom Should I Write For")

Miller imbibed Jeffers in the 1930's while living in Paris under the wing of his inamorata, Anais Nin. Nin was a Lawrence aficionado, and references to Jeffers and Lawrence in their letters suggest that both writers helped prepare Miller for his impassioned encounters with landscape in Greece (1939) and in Big Sur (1944-1962).

Corresponding with Nin in 1944, he announced, "I am offered a cottage for awhile in Big Sur, which is a site I find magnificent (just as Robinson Jeffers describes it)." (NIN, 3.310)

Later, he would tell her, "I am living with nature more and more, and this Big Sur country ... is truly tremendous ... Back from the coast over the mountains, there is an absolute emptiness. It is almost as forbidding as Tibet, and it fascinates me. I should like to go back in there and live for a time quite alone." (NIN, 4.6)

As for Jeffers' tragic narratives, he told her he understood that they were written because the poet had rediscovered in Big Sur the atmosphere of the gods and fates that obsessed the ancient Greeks. He compared the light, the hills, and the autonomous people in Big Sur with the ancient Greeks and saw Jeffers as the voice of the pioneers who had settled there.

He explained, "I knew of Point Sur because I'd read Robinson Jeffers. I read his WOMEN AT POINT SUR in the Cafe Rotonde in Paris – I'll never forget it." (WRITERS, 179)

Asked "Isn't it surprising that you should have gone out to nature that way, since you'd always been a city man?" Miller replied, "Well, you see, I have a Chinese nature. You know, in ancient China, when the artist or the philosopher began to get old, he retired to the country to live and meditate in peace ... I fell in love with Big Sur. I had no desire to resume my Paris life, it was finished." (179)

In REMEMBER TO REMEMBER, he compared Jeffers with Janko Varda, a Greek collage artist who had encouraged Miller to settle in Big Sur: "I thought of THE WOMEN AT POINT SUR and that lighthouse endlessly throwing out its revolving beams. Two poets living on the very edge of the Western World; one somber, prophetical and keen as a hawk, the other gay, full of wisdom, and endlessly rearranging the world. "(8)

When he arrived in Big Sur, Miller knew what it meant to feel born again. He was "doing it" with the cosmos just as intensely as any saint ever communed with God. Every morning became a spiritually orgasmic experience.

In "Introduction to Big Sur," he noted:

"I'd get up with a smile on my lips. I'd walk out the front door and take in the surroundings. Then I'd bless everything as a kind of ritual. I blessed the ocean, the trees, flowers, birds, even the poison oak! Then I would bless every person in the world – man, woman, and child. I even blessed my enemies. I said a prayer for the Germans and the Japanese with whom we were at war. In a place that is virtually a paradise one can't help but feel a sense of humanity, and a connectedness to everything and everyone alive and moving on the face of the earth." (*REFLECTIONS*, 84)

But humans are only part of the act, he warned, not the actor. "Mentally, morally, spiritually," he charged, "we are fettered." What have we achieved, he asked, in "mowing down mountain ranges, harnessing the energy of mighty rivers, or moving whole populations about like chess pieces, if we ourselves remain the same restless, miserable, frustrated creatures we were before?" (*SEX*, 112)

Echoing Jeffers' own cynicism, he continued, "To call such activity progress is utter delusion. We may succeed in altering the face of the earth until it is unrecognizable even to the Creator, but if we are unaffected wherein lies the meaning?" (112)

Like Lawrence ~ and not unlike Jeffers ~ Miller sought a revolution in consciousness, rediscovery of the sacred in the natural at every level of being. He referred to himself as "a deeply religious man without a religion" adding, "I feel that life and everything in it is holy ... God is within you." (*REFLECTIONS*, 123)

In an article written for his friend Emil White's "Big Sur Guide," Miller warned of dangers in trying to settle in Big Sur:

"Think twice about it before you try it. Or read Robinson Jeffers first. He described it all before it ever happened. He saw it as a poet would see it. Jeffers didn't make it attractive. He made it dramatic, violent, awesome. And that's what Big Sur is even today. But you won't discover that until you live there awhile." (*From unpublished tape*)

Clearly, Henry Miller was more than coincidentally interested in landscape in Big Sur. He was smitten. Immersed. God-intoxicated. His great attention-getter, sex, was merely the bottom rung of a mystic ladder leading toward his "doing it" spiritually with the cosmos.

"Many are attracted to Big Sur," Miller wrote in his Preface to Lillian Bos Ross' novel *THE STRANGER*, "but few remain. It looks inviting but it demands sterling qualities to root oneself here ... it seeks to remain unspoiled, uninhabited by man. It has to be wooed, like a bride ... Often I say to myself ... 'this is the face of the world as the Creator intended it to look ... This is Heaven enough. Why ask for more?'" ("*What's Doing*," 22)

When circumstances forced him to leave the Sur coast after seventeen fruitful years, Miller lamented (*A LIFE*, 342), "It's almost as if, in quitting Big Sur, I walked out of my true paradise ~ and now, like the hero of '*Lost Horizon*,' I am fucked!"

Jeffers, it seems, was more fortunate.

WORKS CITED:

Beilke, Marlan. *Shining Clarity*. Amador City, CA, Quintessence Publications, 1977.

Brophy, Robert. "*Henry Miller Meets Robinson Jeffers*." Robinson Jeffers Newsletter, Winter, 1996.

Ferguson, Robert. *Henry Miller, A Life*. New York and London, W. W. Norton, 1991.

Jeffers, Robinson. *Selected Poetry*. New York, Random House, 1959.

Jeffers, Robinson. "*Whom Should I Write For.*" Laguna, CA, Laguna Verde Press, 1979; printed on Albion hand press by Ward Ritchie for Tor House Foundation.

Miller, Henry. *Big Sur and the Oranges of Hieronymus Bosch*. New York, New Directions, 1957.

Miller, Henry *Reflections*. Santa Barbara, CA, Capra Press, 1981.

Miller, Henry. *Remember to Remember*. New York, New Directions, 1941.

Miller, Henry. *The Henry Miller Reader*. New York, New Directions, 1969.

Miller, Henry *The World of Sex*. New York, Grove Press, Inc., 1965.

Miller, Henry. "*A Preface to The Stranger*". published in "*What's Doing*," Vol. 3, No. 2., Monterey, CA, May, 1948.

Nin, Anais. *Diary of Anais Nin*, Volumes 3 and 4. New York, N. Y., Harcourt Brace Jovanovich, Inc., 1969, 1971.

Unpublished taped interview with Emil White. Miller quote from "*Big Sur Guide*" plates owned by White and read by White during Fitzpatrick interview, omitting dates and pages, 1980.

Wicks, George. "*Henry Miller.*" *Writers at Work*, "*The Paris Review Interviews*," Second Series, edited by George Plimpton. New York, Penguin Books, 1977.

***

IS LIFE WORTH LIVING?
THE 'ORGANIC' WISDOM OF WILLIAM JAMES

An external creator and his institutions may still be verbally confessed at Church in formulas that linger by their mere inertia, but the life is out of them, we avoid dwelling on them, the sincere heart of us is elsewhere ... [The only opinions] quite worthy of arresting our attention [fall under] the pantheistic field of vision [which sees God as the] indwelling divine rather than the external creator, and of human life as part and parcel of the deep reality.

WILLIAM JAMES
(A Pluralistic Universe, 1910)

THIS POSTSCRIPT is a chapter from *Existential Aspects of William James' Philosophy,* a thesis submitted to the faculty of the University of Utah as a requirement for the author's Master of Science degree in the Department of Philosophy, August 18, 1968.[11] It is included here, for kindred spirits who not only delight in dabbling in metaphysics but are also inveterate 'seekers.'

My subject is William James (1842-1910), America's most widely read -- and most beloved -- philosopher who was also a trained scientist. His naturalistic, pragmatic attitude toward living is the gospel I want to pass on to my own children, grandchildren,   and students.   His 'organic' wisdom is the common sense psychology underlying all 'shepherds' of Pan.

James grew up on the East Coast in the bailiwick of 'mystical' Transcendentalists like Emerson, Thoreau, and Whitman.[12] He experienced California only once. This, when he left his teaching post at Harvard to become a visiting professor at Leland Stanford University five years before his death. But his impression of California is noteworthy.

Like his mentor Robert Louis Stevenson, who preceded him on this coast, James saw California back then as **'a utopian wilderness'** which not only gave him and his wife, Alice, an opportunity to enjoy **'the simple life,'** it also allowed them **'honeymoon picnic time.'**

James described his new environment as *"really a miracle; and so simple the life and so benign the elements, that for a young ambitious professor who wishes to leave his mark on Pacific civilization while it is most plastic -- or for anyone who wants to teach and work under the most perfect conditions for eight or nine months, and who is able to get to the East, or Europe, for the remaining three -- I can't imagine anything finer. It is Utopian. Perfection of   weather. Cold nights, though above freezing. Fire pleasant   until   10 o'clock, then unpleasant. In short, the 'simple life' with all the essential higher elements thrown in as communal possessions. The drawback is, of course, the great surrounding human vacuum ... and the social insipidity ... [Yet] the students, though rustic, are very earnest and wholesome."*

But his enchantment ended abruptly on April 18, 1906 when the hibernating San Andreas fault began to rumble. This violent act of previously pacific Nature sent the Jameses packing. They took the next train to the East and never came back.

As a philosopher, James is best remembered for the personal twist he gave to Pragmatism, a term first used by an American logician, Charles S. Peirce, to cover his method of treating *nonspeculative* facts with special reference to causes and effects, utility and workability. James expanded Peirce's pragmatic method to include analysis of the usefulness or meaning of *belief*.

He discovered, through personal experience, that even though a metaphysical theory may not be scientifically verifiable as either 'true' or 'false' in this lifetime, acting on belief in it – *if it is a genuine* option -- can be *meaningful* to the life of an individual. The importance of an *authentic* hypothesis could be determined by observing the fruits of *acting* as if it were true. Thus, in addressing common spiritual concerns of ordinary people, James avoided the 'ivory tower' label so often associated with the 'either-or' thinking of strictly rational logicians.

More traditional colleagues at Harvard were amused, if not bemused, by his obsession with intuitive, non-rational suppositions. For example, George Santayana acknowledged his genius and respected him as a man, but regarded him as *"a sort of 'raider' of the philosophical garden. Residence on the premises was not native to his disposition. Philosophy, to him was rather like maze in which he happened to find himself wandering, and what he was looking for was the way out. In the presence of theories of any sort he was attentive, puzzled, suspicious, with a certain inner prompting to disregard them. He lived all his life among them, as a child lives among grown-up people."*

Because of his dramatic explorations into human consciousness -- and his lackluster about technical manipulation, complicated explanations, and the efficacy of reason to cure men's ills -- James did seem to belong more to Literature and Psychology than to Philosophy.

He was passionately concerned with the 'here and now' possibilities of life and intent on getting at the heart of things that matter to everyday living. He cared deeply about character development and the spiritual suffering[13] of real people. This, because his own *authentic* life had begun on the other side of despair after a long period of unresolved conflict.

Here's what happened:

While living with his family[14] in Europe, James was attracted to science, the humanities, and art. He gave up the idea of becoming an artist -- and living a bohemian life – in favor of what seemed to be a more practical career in science and medicine, discounting the joy he experienced while delving into Literature and Philosophy.

Needless to say, his father was pleased when William enrolled in Harvard's Lawrence Scientific School and School of Medicine and later accompanied naturalist Louis Agassiz on an exploration of the Amazon.

But when James returned to medical school and his studies, he not only began to suffer eye strain and back problems, he became severely depressed. Was there any relationship between possible misgivings about the 'sensible' career path he had chosen and his psycho/physical health? He attempted to find an answer to that question by taking a year off in Europe. In today's vernacular, he hoped to 'find himself.' Who was he really in his deepest, most demanding Self?

"There is no more miserable human being than one in whom nothing is habitual but indecision," he would write in retrospect, *"[just as there is] nothing so fatiguing as the eternal hanging on of an uncompleted task."*

On arriving in Berlin, he enrolled in the university and threw himself into studying Physiology to discover more about the mechanical functioning of his body. He satisfied his mental and spiritual needs by reading works of great philosophers and poets.

The abrupt decision to go abroad was explained to his father in a letter from Berlin in 1867:

"Although I cannot exactly say that I got low-spirited, yet thoughts of the pistol, the dagger and the bowl began to usurp an unduly large part of my attention, and I began to think that some change, even if a hazardous one, was necessary."

When he returned to Harvard, he felt sufficiently composed to complete his studies and attain his medical degree. But when it came time to actually *practice* medicine, he froze. The profession he had chosen seemed like sterile drudgery.

Instead of feeling pleased with himself because he had successfully reached his goal and was about to embark on an important career, he found himself questioning whether he really wanted to dedicate his life to curing people's physical ailments. Worse, he suffered from a debilitating sense of purposelessness and meaninglessness. He described a panic attack[15] in his notebook:

"Whilst in this state of philosophic pessimism ... there fell upon me without warning, just as if it came out of the darkness, a horrible fear of my own existence. [I would awake with] a horrible dread at the pit of my stomach, and with a sense of the insecurity of life that I never knew before, and that I have never felt since ... It was like a revelation; and although the immediate feelings passed away, the experience has made me sympathetic with the morbid feelings of others ever since ... In general I dreaded to be left alone. I remember wondering how other people could live, how I myself had ever lived, so unconscious of that pit of insecurity beneath the surface of life."

His use of the word '*revelation*,' is interesting. It seems to suggest that some indwelling 'voice' was trying to get his attention. Consequently, he began foraging among philosophers for answers. One day in 1870, his efforts paid off:

"I think that yesterday was a crisis in my life. I finished the first part of Renouvier's[16] second 'essais' and see no reason why his definition of Free Will – 'the sustaining of a thought because I choose to, when I might have other thoughts' – need be the definition of
an illusion. At any rate, I will assume for the present – until next year – that it is no illusion. My first act of free will shall be to believe in free will."*

He decided to shelve recurring thoughts about suicide.[17] With a more positive intention, he would become his own guinea pig, deliberately choosing thoughts that promoted free will over thoughts to the contrary. He would pit his good will against a depression so deep and so dark that he had been moved to ask the fundamental question of philosophy:

Is this precarious life worth living?

He vowed to stop doing what delighted him most[18] -- weighing pros and cons of theories incapable of scientific proof, issues about freedom versus determinism, the existence of God, immortality of the soul, and moral values.

Now, instead of struggling with conflicting 'answers' to unanswerable questions, he would focus on reading books[19] favorable to the idea that, as a fully conscious person of sound mind, he was not only free to choose but had a 'right' to choose one particular idea among a stream[20] of alternate thoughts in order to experiment. He would *act as if* each chosen thought were true in order to determine, as a result of experienced consequences, whether his belief would make any positive difference in his zest for living.

So -- after committing to the idea that he was a free agent, he went on to affirm that his life was important, against a shadowy idea to the contrary that had grabbed him -- *without his consent* -- and urged him to give it all up.

Next, he chose to act as if God exists and as if Nature were full of select intentions. Finally, he chose to hold the thought that his soul is immortal, and he proceeded to make plans, including ethical choices, as if that were so.

For the next twelve months, he would build his life **"IN DOING AND SUFFERING AND CREATING"** -- with an eye toward determining whether his efforts would bear good fruit and dissuade him from suicide. Was it possible that acting as if freely chosen metaphysical[21] beliefs were true might have positive empirical consequences?

"My belief, to be sure can't be optimistic," he told his journal, "but I will posit life (the real, the good) in the self-governing resistance of the ego to the world." From now on, he and God, a force for good -- or whatever 'God' may be -- would 'do business' together and see what happens -- a kind of 'happy thoughts while contemplating suicide' approach.

He wrote: "*If this life be not a real fight, in which something is eternally gained for the universe by success, it is no better than a game of private theatricals from which one may withdraw at will. But it feels like real fight!*"

And fight he did! But when he used the word 'success' he didn't mean monetary success. Far from it. He frowned: "*The moral flabbiness born of the exclusive worship of the bitch-goddess success, with the squalid cash interpretation put on the word 'success' – is our national disease.*"

He went on to speculate that when his testing period was up, "*my callow skin being somewhat fledged, I may perhaps return to metaphysical study and skepticism without danger to my powers of action.*"

At the end of the year, he was neither depressed nor undecided. His life had more zing. He wanted to stay in the game. What's more, he believed that in the process of curing his own depression, he had given birth to a kind of 'radical empiricism.' He'd discovered that Pragmatism could, indeed, be expanded to include states of mind as well as factual experience.

He believed he had come up with a psychology that could help other *normal* people – typically troubled folks quite different from the psychotics, neurotics, and chemically-unbalanced people customarily treated by psychiatrists.

Through experimentation, James had discovered that his reasons for living were more intuitive and emotional than verbal and rational. From then on, he would strongly encourage the rest of us to answer life's difficulties "*by consents or non consents and not by words.*"

"*What wonder,*" he wrote, "*that these dumb responses should seem our deepest organs of communication with the nature of things! What wonder if the effort demanded by them be the measure of our worth as men! What wonder if the amount which we accord of it be the one strictly underived and original contribution which we make to the world!*"

As for the fruits of his chosen beliefs, he concluded that meaning and value came neither from God nor from Nature but from his existing and acting in a particular way, experimenting to see what worked for him in the interest of creation, not destruction.

Henceforth, he would hold that the meaning of ambiguous abstract ideas about God, freedom, immortality, and ethical values are determined, not by their factualness, but by the practical effect they have on a believer's life.

On the subject of God, his thoughts were mixed.

He liked the idea of an *intimate* deity: "*I myself believe that the evidence for God lies primarily in inner personal experience.*" Here, he seems to have been alluding to a possible portion of divinity in his psyche -- a sort of 'God spot,'[22] -- possibly related to a universal Spirit. He would argue further, after years of research into the religious experiences of others, that there is an innate *reflex action* in the human psyche urging us toward theistic conclusions.

Yet his skepticism as a scientist was always active.

Logic led him to a compelling, somewhat disconcerting[23], conclusion about a less comforting God. If there is a God, he suggested, this "*must be a God of universal laws exclusively, a God who does a wholesale, not a retail business. He cannot accommodate his processes to the convenience of individuals.*"

Ultimately, he would conclude, with Blaise Pascal[24] before him, that there are two opposing, but complementary kinds of 'truth' -- logical and emotional. Both needs *must be satisfied* , he said, if a person hopes to lead a balanced life. His own experience attested to that. Betting on the existence of a positive spiritual power had made a big difference in his attitude toward living.

His personal wager *meant* that he would

henceforth be able to dismiss certain kinds of fear and that ethical behavior mattered. He would clarify, however, that *"an act has no ethical quality whatever unless it be [freely] chosen out of several all equally possible."* In acting as if, he had won his bout with despair.

His anxiety disappeared the moment he made a decision to abandon his 'duty' to the practice of healing bodies and devote his life to the related study of rejuvenating spirits. He chose now to cultivate a gift far more suited to his temperament[25] -- teaching. He felt certain now that he could remain at Harvard and continue to grub among those metaphysical subtleties in which his soul took such delight, without danger to his 'powers of action.'

With teaching as his profession, he could not only earn enough money to comfortably maintain himself and any future family, but he could share ideas, travel, lecture, and, best of all, relate to peers who also loved to 'grub.'

The result: Satisfaction, if not downright joy.

A narrow and selfish decision? Not at all. James explained that in following our bliss we not only satisfy our own deepest creative needs, we also help to maximize the **"very largest total universe of good which we can see."**

But he was ever realistic. If he understood all too well that this world is a place of real gains and real losses, he also understood that there is a sense in which the earth, too, is striving to improve. That's because Nature produced *intelligence*,[26] and it's at least *possible* to use that intelligence in building a world nearer to our heart's desires.

Whatever James concluded, his father was relieved. Observing his son's recovery, he wrote: **"[William] saw that the mind does act irrespectively of material coercion, and could be dealt with therefore at first hand, and this was health to his bones ... He has been shaking off his respect for men of mere science as such, and is even more universal and impartial in his mental judgments than I have known him before."**

Apropos of this, James would speak of a 'mysterious tie' between thought and motor centers that comes into play and that, **"in a way which we cannot even guess at, the obedience of the bodily organs follows as a matter of course."** [27] Clearly, what healed him was a self-directed reintegration of powers in his psyche that had previously been in disarray.

His 'meaningful' ideas had helped him **"get into satisfactory relation with other parts of [his] experience."** Therefore, he came to regard the mind as a kind of antenna, an instrument for biological adaptation. By staying in the game, he believed, we not only learn to respect the processes of Nature, we gain self respect in what seems like a very heroic struggle to live creatively in a seemingly indifferent, occasionally downright hostile, world.

As for the inevitable *"sufferings and hardships"* he would write, *" [they] do not, as a rule, abate the love of life; they seem, on the contrary, usually to give it a keener zest ... Need and struggle are what excite and inspire us; our hour of triumph is what brings the void."*

And more: *"It is only by risking our persons from one hour to another that we live at all. And often enough our faith beforehand in an uncertified result is the only thing that makes the result come true."*

Now he was in full agreement with Renouvier, who had launched him on his quest in the first place. Renouvier taught that we must not allow our desires and emotions to run away with reason, but neither must we allow the intellect to suppress our emotional (including moral and religious) needs. To do the latter, as James discovered, could be suicidal.

"Believe that life is worth living," James concluded, *"and your belief will help create the fact. The 'scientific proof' that you are right may not be clear before the day of judgment ... but the faithful fighters of this hour ... may then turn to the faint-hearted, who ... decline to go on, with words like those with which Henry IV greeted the tardy Crillon after a great victory had been gained: 'Hang yourself, brave Crillon!*

We fought at Argos, and you were not there!'"

Four years after his breakdown, James was enthusiastically teaching Physiology, Psychology, and Philosophy at Harvard. In 1874, his classes were so successful that Psychology was taken from under the umbrella of Philosophy, where it had always been, and established as a separate discipline. To top it all, he established the first American psychology laboratory based on experimental method. Eventually, he became Harvard's most popular teacher and a world renowned lecturer.

He went on to assuage his insatiable metaphysical curiosity by studying religious experience through the ages. In the process, he interacted enthusiastically with all kinds of people willing to talk about their personal experiences and put it all together in a consummate book, *The Varieties of Religious Experience*. In it, he redefined religion as *"the feelings, acts, and experiences of individual men in their solitude"* and as *"a man's total reaction upon life."*

Most important, drawing from his own experience, he could say, with some authority, to a person contemplating suicide: *"Wait and see [your] part of the battle out ... the consent to live on ... is not the sophistical 'resignation' which devotees of cowering religions preach; it is not resignation in the sense of licking a despotic Deity's hand. It is, on the contrary, a resignation based on manliness and pride ... Are we not bound to take some suffering upon ourselves, to do some self-denying service with our lives, in return for all those lives upon which ours are built?"*

Besides, he could wink, you never know what the next postman might bring!

Yet there was an important caveat connected with all this subjectivity. James warned about *'a certain blindness'* in human beings, a blindness to the sometimes secret joys of others.

He illustrated what he meant in a talk to Cambridge teachers in 1892, after reading Robert Louis Stevenson's metaphorical essay called 'The Lantern Bearers.' In it, Stevenson told how he and his school mates would hide a shining bulls-eye lantern under their coats and dare to walk into the scary night. Only the boys themselves knew about the hidden lanterns on their belts, and they exulted in their secret. To ordinary onlookers, the boys were, as Stevenson put it, *'a mere pillar of darkness.'*

James went on to tell his audience that while *"our judgments concerning the worth of things, big or little, depend on the feelings the things arouse in us,"* we are all afflicted with a blindness regarding the feelings of creatures and people different from ourselves.

He explained, *We are practical beings, each of us with limited functions and duties to perform. Each is bound to feel intensely the importance of his own duties and the significance of the situations that call these forth. But this feeling is in each of us a vital secret, for sympathy with which we vainly look to others. The others are too much absorbed in their own vital secrets to take an interest in ours. Hence the stupidity and injustice of our opinions, so far as they deal with the significance of alien lives. Hence the falsity of our judgments, so far as they presume to decide in an absolute way on the value of other persons' conditions or ideals."*

He illustrated his point with quotations from the experiences of nature mystics like William Wordsworth, Richard Jefferies,[28] Walt Whitman, and Leo Tolstoy. Their souls, he said, had the capacity to feel *inner joy*. They were responsive to the 'secret life' of everyone and everything around. And *"life is always worth living,"* he went on, *"if one has such responsive sensibilities."*

Then he gave his fellow teachers a jolt: *"But we of the highly educated classes (so called) have most of us got far, far way from Nature. We are trained to seek the choice, the rare, the exquisite exclusively, and to overlook the common. We are stuffed with abstract conceptions, and glib with verbalities and* verbosities; and in the culture of these higher functions the peculiar sources of joy connected with our simpler functions often dry up, and we grow stone-blind and insensible to life's more elementary and general goods and joys."

Our human blind spot, he concluded, "is negative in one sense, but positive in another. It absolutely forbids us to be forward in pronouncing on the meaninglessness of forms of existence other than our own; and it commands us to tolerate, respect, and indulge those whom we see harmlessly interested and happy in their own ways, however unintelligible these may be to us.

"Hands off! Neither the whole of truth nor the whole of good is revealed to any single observer, although each observer gains a partial superiority of insight from the peculiar position in which he stands. Even prisons and sick-rooms have their special revelations. It is enough to ask of each of us that he should be faithful to his own opportunities and make the most of his own blessings, without presuming to regulate the rest of the vast field."

Equipped with such wisdom, James had risked marriage in 1878, seven years after choosing the path most suited to his temperament. It may just be that his commitment to matrimony stemmed from another attitude he considered most important.

This frame of mind involved "an element of active tension, of holding my own, as it were, and trusting outward things to perform their part so as to make it a full harmony, but without any guaranty that they will. Make it a guaranty – and the attitude immediately becomes to my consciousness stagnant and sting-less. With no guaranty, I feel ... a sort of deep enthusiastic bliss, of bitter willingness to do and to suffer anything."

Surely such a mind-set would be as important for persons contemplating marriage as James' previous outlook had been for persons contemplating suicide!

The following, from the author's Master's thesis, takes a critical look at existential aspects of the metaphysics of William James, based on the man's personal struggle for knowledge of God. James' pragmatic 'conclusion' is the result of what is arguably the most exhaustive exploration of the 'varieties of religious experience' reported in his book by that name. The author's own critique springs from her comparisons of the 'Existential knight of faith' with the 'Jamesian hero' who -- like James' (and the author's own) favorite writer, Robert Louis Stevenson -- is ever- willing to light his candle in a darkness wherein he is likely to stumble and fall but has the courage to continue …

'DOING' PHILOSOPHY:

CRITIQUING THE 'INSTINCTIVE RELIGION' OF WILLIAM JAMES

METAPHYSICS: THE GROUND OF POSSIBILITY
(WHAT MIGHT WE REASONABLY HOPE FOR?)

HAVING CONSIDERED what man *can*[29] do and what man *ought*[30] to do (with some emphasis on what, in fact, man *does* do), James turned to what man might reasonably *hope* for.

In view of the honest agnosticism or skepticism on which he and existentialists (and other empiricists) base their ethical philosophy, it remains to determine whether James had leanings toward theism or naturalism – whether he had more in common with religious or secular existentialists -- or whether he philosophized somewhere in between.

The term 'naturalism' is used here instead of 'materialism' because James himself stated that "the completion of present-day materialism" might better be called 'naturalism.'

Theists are defined, generally, as those who believe in a god or gods, and naturalists are defined as those who hold to the theory that the universe needs no supernatural explanation. They base hope on the belief that it is up to individuals to generate awareness and create values that will determine what will ultimately triumph in the world.

But to attempt to get at the heart of the philosophy of William James is like Plotinus' attempt to interpret Plato. Plotinus lamented, ***"The divine Plato … said many beautiful things – He makes us hope that he will have something clear to say on this matter. But unfortunately he does not everywhere say the same thing and so does not enable one easily to know his intent."***

James, too, said many beautiful things, but he was, like Plato, not always clear about his own particular views. It isn't easy to distill a 'doctrine' from random reading of James' more popular essays.

But to say that it is difficult to extract philosophical 'doctrine' from the writings of James and the existentialists -- because they are poets as well as technicians -- is not to say that it can't be done. There are common threads running through James' varied writings just as there are in those of existentialists. This, in spite of the fact that writers like James often gear their use of terms to their audiences, meaning one thing by a term in one lecture and something quite different by the same term in another.

For example, in one lecture, James denies acceptance of 'popular Christianity,' yet, four pages earlier, in the same lecture, he comments on 'us Christians,' seemingly lumping himself with the Christians of the 'popular' variety in the audience. In an entirely different essay, he speaks of the ***"hypocrisy, which church-Christianity brought in."***

As for God, James speaks of him as 'transmundane energies' in one essay, then, a little later, his 'God' goes from plural energies to possible selves. God, he says, might be 'a large and more godlike self' than our 'self,' or 'the universe might conceivably be a collection of such selves' of godlike variety – 'a sort of *polytheism*,' which 'has always been the real religion of common people.'

But in almost every one of his other essays, James speaks of God in the singular, like a good monotheist in a Christian society, perhaps, as he noted in one spot, because 'the word polytheism usually gives offence.'

James defines God in still another essay as the 'deepest power in the universe' and *"a mental personality ... to be regarded, like any other personality, as something lying outside of my own and other than me, and whose existence I simply come upon and find. A power not ourselves, then, which not only makes for righteousness, but means it, and which recognizes us."*

Elsewhere, he seems to identify with panpsychism, the theory that reality consists of minds or psychic entities. But, in an address before a group of ministers, he identifies with the theists, saying that theism *"always stands ready with the most practically rational solution it is possible to conceive."* Yet he turns around and calls the theistic God a 'sterile principle' in an essay on pragmatism.

Again, James classifies himself against the rationalists in favor of naturalism in one essay, but in another, he sides with the supernaturalists against the naturalists.

What did he really intend? Let's take a further look at the definition of theism. Webster defines it as 'belief in the existence of a god or gods,' specifically monotheism, which is 'belief in the existence of one God, transcending, yet immanent in, the universe.' The dictionary distinguishes theism (or monotheism) from pantheism and deism.

The Fuller-McMurrin volume, *A History of Modern Philosophy*, similarly defines theism as *"religious philosophy asserting existence of God as a living being. Usually identified with monotheism. Theism is opposed to pantheism, q.v., by holding that God is not identical with the world. Often used in opposition to deism, q.v., as indicating that God is at least partially immanent in the world rather than totally transcendent to it."*

If we apply the general definition (that theism is a belief in the existence of a god or gods), James was a theist. He wrote an entire book on man's religious experiences which, in James' words, *"has been regarded as making for the reality of God."*

Said James, *"I firmly disbelieve, myself, that our human experience is the highest form of experience extant in the universe ... we may well believe, on the proofs that religious experience affords, that higher powers exist and are at work to save the world on ideal lines similar to our own."*

But a perusal of his writings indicates that James' so-called theism, like that of some religious existentialists, was as unusual as his empiricism, as we shall show. In his unorthodox (anti-church, anti-establishment) treatment of God and man's relationship to deity, James had much in common with these existentialists.

His fundamental concept of a mystical 'reality' is, for example, similar to that of Karl Jaspers. After an exhaustive study of the religious experiences of others (and an experience of his own which he thought might have religious significance) James concluded, as an 'over-belief' (one that is held beyond empirical evidence), that *"the further limits of our being plunge ... into an altogether other dimension of existence from the sensible and merely 'understandable' world."*

This 'transcendence' aspect of man's being, reaching toward some 'mystical region' in Pure Experience, James thought, indicates that man belongs to this 'region' in a "more intimate sense than that in which we belong to the visible world."

Our 'ideal impulses,' he said, *seem to originate in this region "for we find them possessing us in a way for which we cannot articulately account."* And, he argued, *"We belong in the most intimate sense wherever our ideals belong."*

He further argued that this 'unseen region' is 'not merely idea' because it *"produces effects in this world."* Yet, it should be noted, it does not necessarily follow that the effects-producing 'idea' entails existence of a producer 'out there.'

His argument seems odd in view of the fact that James was not a Platonic idealist. One might say is that this is another pragmatic argument, based on possibility, without possibility of verification in this life. In a sense, all enacted 'ideas' produce effects, but the effects do not prove that the idea is more than a thought engendered from within, not participating in some region that has existence outside the mind.

Granted, however, that this so-called 'transcendent,' yearning aspect of man seems to 'produce effects' in him, and it could be argued that in this sense man has a real 'mystical, psychic energy world' inside him – a 'Holy Ghost' or deity, as it were. But the conclusion, on the basis of effects, that there is a mystical reality outside man remains questionable.

Indeed, James' over-belief seems to contradict his own 'reflex theory of the mind' in which he sees the mind as an essentially teleological mechanism functioning *"exclusively for the sake of ends that do not exist at all in the world of impressions we receive by way of our senses, but are set by our emotional and practical subjectivity altogether,"* man's volitional nature exerting *"constant pressure upon the other departments of the mind to induce them to function to theistic conclusions."*

His later study of the religious experiences of others seems to have conflicted with his psychological hypothesis or, at least, to have made him less definite about the lack of correspondence of the mind's 'reflex action' with a region 'out there.'

The study of such experiences led him to claim that for those who have communed with this so-called mystical region, *"work is actually done upon our finite personality"* in that *"we are turned into new men, and consequences in the way of conduct follow in the natural world upon our regenerative change."*

He concluded: *"But that which produces effects within another reality must be termed a reality itself, so I feel as if we had no philosophic excuse for calling the unseen or mystical world unreal."*

This is comparable with Karl Jaspers'[31] argument:

"It is wrong to play off against each other the question about man and the question about Deity. Although in the world only man is reality for us, that does not preclude that precisely the quest for man leads to Transcendence. That the Deity alone is truly reality does not preclude that this reality is accessible to us only in the world, as it were, as an image in the mirror of man, because something of the Deity must be in him for him to be able to respond to the Deity."

Jaspers claimed, as James did, that it is psychologically essential to man that he seek not only knowledge of himself but knowledge of Deity or Transcendence. Like James, Jaspers held that man is always *"related to something other than himself"* as, for example, being to the world, as consciousness intending objects, and as existence to Transcendence.

He strives, as Jaspers put it, *"for a certainty that he lacks, for the certainty that there is that which is eternal, that there is a Being through which alone he himself is."* If Deity appears only in ways man can grasp -- if man responds to Deity and if Deity produces effects – Deity must be real, for both James and Jaspers.

Jaspers agreed with James that philosophy can't establish a positive knowledge of Transcendence comparable with scientific knowledge, but it can demonstrate that consequences occur. Jaspers said philosophy can also clarify that Deity, or the Source, is possible, but it can't say what the Source is or what it speaks. Transcendence can't be grasped with any finality. With James, he held that *"philosophizing merely establishes the general right to trust in that which seems to speak to me as the light of Transcendence."*

But is there empirical evidence for holding to the notion of Transcendence as reality, or does one simply have the *right* to believe where one can't prove r disprove a statement about Deity if one needs Deity to make life worth living?

James thought there was ample evidence in religious experience through the ages. This conclusion, offered in The Varieties of Religious Experience, is convincing, particularly when coupled with W. T. Stace's exhaustive study, Mysticism and Philosophy. While James examined religious experience of all types, Stace examined mystical experiences (excluding sense images such as visions and voices). Both concluded that, regardless of the culture in which a person has his experience, such experience has a common core. James put it this way:

"This overcoming of all the usual barriers between the individual and the Absolute is the great mystic achievement. In mystic states we become one with the Absolute and we become aware of our oneness. This is the everlasting and triumphant mystical tradition hardly altered by differences of clime or creed. In Hinduism, in Neo-Platonism, in Sufism, in Christian mysticism, in Whitmanism, we find the same recurring note, so that there is about mystical utterances an eternal unanimity which ought to make the critic stop and think."

One critic, Professor C. D. Broad, who professed no religious belief and never had anything which could be called a religious or mystical experience, wrote in Religion, Philosophy, and

Psychical Research:

"*Finally I come to the argument for the existence of God which is based on the occurrences of specifically mystical and religious experiences. I am prepared to admit that such experiences occur among people of different races and social traditions … at all periods of history. I am prepared to admit that … there are probably certain characteristics which are common to them all … In view of this, I think it more likely than not that in religious and mystical experience men come into contact with some Reality or some aspect of Reality which they do not come into contact with in any other way. But I do not think there is any reason to suppose that this Reality … is personal.*'

It is questionable whether any philosopher worthy of the title can avoid admitting 'possibility, based on experience, which lends credibility.' But admission of a universal core in all mysticism (even in drug experiences such as LSD which have, for some, much in common with the mystical) does not refute those who assert that such experiences are illusory, regardless of their *value* for life.

However, the fundamental agreement of mystics does seem to indicate the existence of some universal element in the physical and/or mental (psycho-physical) makeup of human beings which leads to similar paradoxical (identity in difference) experiences. And when James speaks of the reflex action (some today call this a 'God spot') which craves deity or absolutes, and when existentialists speak of man's transcendence aspects or his longing for certainty, they seem to be referring to this seeming common element in man's nature.

Sigmund Freud, however, would interpret these 'transcendence' needs the 'longing for a father' – wish fulfillment -- or creation of a dreaded god whom man seeks to propitiate while trusting him for protection against consequences of human weakness. And yet, Freud was quick to admit that "*illusions need not necessarily be false – that is to say, unrealizable or in contradiction to reality.*"

He added, however, that it is "*an illusion to expect anything from intuition and introspection; they can give us nothing but particulars about our own mental life, which are hard to interpret.*" True. But when individual experiences studied at great length do come up with a common core, 'possibility' of some objective 'more' 'out there' must be allowed. And that is what James and the religiously-inclined thinkers among the existentialists argue for – possibility.

Martin Heidegger, in whose ontology[32] 'ontic'[33] existentialism seems to be rooted, attempted, too, to verify his metaphysics on the basis of subjective experience (i.e. 'dread,' uneasiness, fear of nothingness and the consequent grasping of being that may occur).

Heidegger's most influential teacher, Edmund Husserl, was, in turn, influenced by James. Herbert Spiegelberg, in an historical study, The *Phenomenological Movement*, comments: *The earliest evidence of Husserl's study of James can be found in an article of 1894 where, in his discussion of the contents of cognitive acts, he refers twice to James' chapter [in Principles of Psychology] on 'The Stream of Thought' and specifically to his doctrine of 'fringes.' In his later references to these early studies, Husserl seems to have spoken variously of his intention to review James' Principles … in order to study James more thoroughly … and even of having abandoned his plan of writing a psychology, 'feeling that James had what he wanted to say.'*"

Insofar as existential ontology has been influenced by the aspects of Husserl's phenomenology which emphasizes reliance on introspection and the data of immediate experience, largely through Heidegger and Sartre, and insofar as Husserl was influenced by encounter with James, it is not surprising that James and the existential ontologists have much in common. All hold to the method of examining the concrete subjective data of immediate experience. They recognize vagueness, confusion as factors in experience and consider reason man's apprehending power in the attempt to clarify.

For James, Heidegger and Jaspers, the ontological (pure experience for James – reality is life, as it is lived, experienced; 'being' for Heidegger; 'the encompassing' for Jaspers) provides the possibility of the ontic and is, therefore, primary to philosophy.

As Heidegger put it, being takes precedence over doing because every significant human action must take place within some context that is, some encompassing region of Being. The will-to-action, in other words, is determined by things as they are. But, as Heidegger held, the 'silent power of the possible' is always at work in man ensuring that the doors of the future are never completely closed.

Momentary or prolonged dread, some form of despair or sense of the meaninglessness of human activity, for all three thinkers, reveals 'nothing' and/or 'being.' Jaspers revealed kinship with these thinkers in asserting that it is when one dares to be *'shipwrecked,'* to be left standing *'unsatisfied as though one's hands and heart were left empty,'* yet *'by his own inner action'* is able to achieve a new relationship to himself and his world, that one experiences Being, *'an authentic feeling for the depths of reality.'*

Whether one sees in the encounter with one's own nothingness and consequent contingency on God via dread, as Soren Kierkegaard did, the possibility of the truth of Christianity (or Deity) beyond what Christendom (organized religion in general) has made of it, or whether one sees, as Frederick Nietzsche did, the greatest opportunity for man (he becomes a God himself) when faced with ultimate nothingness, there is, Jaspers said, common to both, "a will toward the substance of Being, toward the nobility and value of man." Or, as James put it, a calling forth of human dignity and courage -- the 'strenuous mood' of the authentic existential 'hero' as exemplified by Sisyphus.

When one sinks into the bottomless, Jaspers noted, he grasps hold of the Transcendent. Man is 'a mere perhaps' between something and nothing. Jaspers hopes man will grasp the Transcendent. It is of course possible that he might give up, commit suicide, go insane, or choose to live unauthentically. But there are no guarantees. Man lives dangerously. At this point, existential 'heroes' discover themselves (are saved by some power – their own or 'other') and are separated from the anti-heroes. The 'Overman' is separated from the 'herd.'

It is interesting, in connection with this, to note that Bertrand Russell held that **"the greatest men who have been philosophers have felt the need both of science and of mysticism."** And W. T. Stace also held that authentic mystical experience is not mere faith and emotion but *intellectual* union with some Reality – confidence in the ability of reason to grasp Being and receive power. Stace said, "It is possible that the superman of the future is to be the mystic man." This, because the direction of human evolution – if the races survive – may be toward **"the spread of mystical experience to most men and not merely its possession by a few rare individuals as now."**

Those who do experience what James and the existentialists have described as 'dread' seem to have much in common with what some mystics have called *'the dark night of the soul.'* And although many men are so busily engaged in projects that they neither reflect deeply on their lives nor experience despair (even when they do face uncertainty about meaning), those who do (and will to live authentically) experience feelings of rebirth, or what James called 'consequences.'

Many reflective, aware people, however, do experience, at some time, a sense of the 'absurdity' of life, without necessarily feeling anything akin to mysticism's 'dark night of the soul,' despair, or dread. They may stop, if only momentarily, to ask themselves, *"What am I doing? Why? What is the meaning of this routine I go through? What is the meaning of my life? Why go through all this if it ends in death? Am I just an ant in the heap? What difference does my life make?"*

They feel empty, uneasy, as if all the things they'd taken seriously don't really matter at all and don't have anything to do with their inner being. In dread (an uncanny feeling – a dread of one's own nothingness which may lead one to Being) one confronts this 'nothing' feeling. In sensing the absurdity of life – the paradox resulting from one's transcendent need for meaning that the world of facts cannot supply – or his seeming identity with a Transcendence from which he feels alienated – he comes to a crossroads where he either changes his life and lives with more care, responsibility, and awareness; goes on as before; or turns to some form of nihilism, escape from the reality of his predicament.

Some find comfort in being 'one' ('holding hands') and exhibiting empathy in view of their fate; others find comfort in looking at life as a testing ground; and some find comfort in the knowledge that nothing is certain but much is possible and that it is possible for man to live more creatively, in spite of suffering and death.

For better or worse, existentialists would have every man reflect (become aware of his predicament) when he comes to a crossroads and consciously decide between an authentic, personal, self-determining existence and an unauthentic, impersonal, other-oriented existence, leaning on dogma of others to obtain peace of mind and avoid the anxiety of responsibility.

They acknowledge, as James did, that the general mode of man's existence (in which he loses possession of himself) is unauthenticity. That is, he puts his freedom at the feet of the Establishment to have decisions made for him, in exchange for peace of mind; or he loses himself in work, drugs, alcohol,

162

sex, 'ivory towers.'

But there are those who, once aware, choose Being, the ground of their own existence. In so doing, they are able to muster courage to lead autonomous, responsible lives based on the 'nobility and value of man,' regardless of whether there is a God who cares. The authentic man is returned to (possess) himself. That is, he pays attention to what Socrates called the 'oracle' within' and D. H. Lawrence called 'the Holy Ghost within.'

Many existentialists write with an eye toward jolting the 'unawakened' (the unreflective) to reflection on what it means to be a man, to awaken them to the reality that man's transcendence (his insatiable appetite for the 'ideal'), whether ingrained self-deception or a response to some Reality 'out there,' is as much a part of his nature as facticity (existence as a physical object) and that his lack of recognition of subjective feelings (repression) in the interest of his objective, physical needs can result in a disoriented, split being who does not understand why he is anxious – what is missing, and that he may be searching for the inscrutable.

On completing his study, *Mysticism and Philosophy*, Stace observed: ***"We shall have to maintain that mystical consciousness is latent in all men but is in most men submerged below the surface of consciousness. Just as it throws up into the upper consciousness influences which appear in the form of ethical feelings, so must its influences appear there in the form of religious impulses."***

It is this sometimes latent 'mystical consciousness' (Transcendence, yearning, creative longing evoking a will-to-meaning) that existential ethicists, including James, would call forth in the service of man to stimulate him to set goals and act on them to fulfill his potential or, at least, approximate it. Why? Because if a man decides to affirm life and attempts to develop autonomy, making conscious choices in the light of reality, with willingness to accept vulnerability, it is possible that he may develop a maturity that will help him cope with himself and others in periods of anxiety.

It is possible that to the extent that people have deluded themselves into thinking that 'security' is to be had, they feel more stress. In stressing 'stress' as essential to life and development, existentialists hope to help men develop their psychological aspects along with their reason.

Both ethics and religion have stressed man's obligations to others but, with the exception of Aristotle's ethics, they have been naïve about man's obligation to himself. Psychologists tell us that tragic self-hatred can lead to hatred of others. And existentialists hold that most men have consistently lied to themselves about their own nature in order to conform to some image, usually idealized. They advocate an ethic of virtues (e.g. a combinations of altruism, power, empathy, responsibility, courage, and honesty) over a morality of rules. And they note, with James, that happiness is a by product of conscious growth and joyfully doing what one's nature intends.

But to return to the issue: Does Transcendence in man relate to some objective Reality or is it subjective self-deception? The question is moot. Nevertheless, it appears to be a psychological fact, one with which man must reckon if he is to be a 'whole man,' true to his nature.

Heidegger, too, for reasons akin to those of James and Jaspers, considered Transcendence a primitive fact in man just as solid bodies are facts, even though man's transcendence, however psychologically real it may be, may have no correspondence with any fact 'out there.' Transcendence may be a primitive psychological fact of consciousness derived from 'nothing' outside man, a self deception that appears to be essential to man's nature, a 'reflex action' of the 'teleological mechanism' of the mind, as James would put it.

Be that as it may, Heidegger believed that there is some enveloping presence in which both bodies and consciousness are present. For if a mental judgment is to match a physical fact, he argued, there must be a field in which both can meet, coincide. The field, he claimed, is Being itself – encompassing presence in which both subject and object meet – a field which is presupposed when the distinction is made between subject and object. The open field is neither physical object nor mental concept; it is openness of Being – the primordial sense of truth unhiddenness. And propositional truth, he said, is only possible through this unhiddenness of Being.

As for truth, he said, it is possible only through freedom – the freedom to let-be. This freedom is possibility in Being, the encompassing, itself, a kind of freedom which comes from relaxing the will rather than strenuously affirming it, something like James' experimental 'getting the feel of' a possibility (leaving oneself open to it), then acting and awaiting results to determine the wisdom involved.

But this relaxation of the will is on the ontological, not the ontic level. Though ontic existentialists speak of affirming the will – sustaining commitments and awaiting results to determine the wisdom of commitments – none of the ontologists, including James and Jaspers, would disagree that one ought to relax, as Heidegger said, and leave oneself open to Being – the Encompassing – to experience possibility. As Jaspers put it, *"Understanding the meaning of the Encompassing has the significance of creating a possibility."* He would preserve *"the open space of the Encompassing."* And it's doubtful whether creative men of science, the arts or religion would disagree with his saying, *"Do not lose yourself in what is merely known! Do not let yourself become separated from Transcendence!"*

Thinking beyond this Encompassing field, James proposed his own hypothesis that *"the conscious person is continuous with a wider self through which saving experiences come"* and that *"whatever it may be on its farther side, the 'more' with which in religious experience we feel ourselves connected is on its hither side the subconscious continuation of our conscious life,"* not unlike the latent /mystical consciousness' referred to by W. T. Stace.

James' use of the word 'self,' however, indicates that he held more to a personal Reality than did Jaspers or Heidegger, unless that 'self' is one's own latent 'possibility.' But his *eventual* conclusion about a personal deity is an *over-belief*, one imposed on what he called the nucleus of all religious experience which is 'an uneasiness' (i.e. there is something wrong with us as we naturally are) and its 'solution,' (i.e. we are saved from this wrongness by connection with a higher power). It's about the our bipolar struggle with a 'divided self.' He calls the 'higher part of the universe' God and proposes that this 'god' is a causal agent as well as a medium of communion. And he makes the charming suggestion: *We and God have business with each other; and in opening ourselves to his influence our deepest destiny is fulfilled."*

James sees this idea as an 'instinctive belief of mankind,' maintaining that 'God' is real because he produces 'real effects.' And yet, he seems to contradict what he has said elsewhere about there being no guarantee about the outcome of the world when he states, *"God's existence is the guarantee of an ideal order that shall be permanently preserved – where God is, tragedy is only provisional and partial, and shipwreck and dissolution are not the absolutely final things."*

This wishful thinking, combined with his study of religious experiences, leads him to say further: *"The whole drift of my education goes to persuade me that the world of our present consciousness is only one out of many worlds of consciousness that exist, and that those other worlds must contain experiences which have a meaning for our life also; and that although in the main their experiences and those of this world keep discrete, yet the two become continuous at certain points, and higher energies filter in ... Who knows whether the faithfulness of individuals here below to their own poor over-beliefs may not actually help God in turn to be more effectively faithful to his own greater tasks?"*

Who indeed! But James does admit that such notions are only 'poor over-beliefs.' He does not give the credence to them that he allows the experienced mystical consciousness, but his over-belief talk does very little to clarify the problem as to whether he was actually a theist, naturalist or whatever, beneath those 'poor over-beliefs.'

Both naturalists and theists might be willing to agree on a definition of deity as simply the 'higher part of the universe.' But in 'Reflex Action and Theism,' James notes that the word 'God' *"has come to mean many things in the history of human thought, from Venus and Jupiter to the 'Idea' which figures in the pages of Hegel."* He observed that *"even the laws of physical nature have, in these positivistic times, been held worthy of divine honor."*

And he admitted, in opposition to his own previous action (in *Varieties of Religious Experience*, he had stated: *"God is the natural appellation, for us Christians at least, for the supreme reality, so I will call the higher part of the universe by the name of God")* that *"we must mean something more definite than this"* – that we *"must not call any object of our loyalty a 'God' without more ado, simple because to awaken our loyalty happens to be one of God's functions."*

Apparently, then, in spite of all the foregoing, James has been leading up to something quite definite. Finally, in the postscript to Varieties, he admits that he couldn't *"accept either popular Christianity or scholastic theism."* He referred to God now as 'transmundane energies' which produce *"immediate effects within the natural world to which the rest of our experience belongs."* He was moot about the question of a personal god and personal immortality as understood by traditional Occidental theism. He further elaborated, after speaking of the traditional belief that any existing God must be 'one' and 'infinite':

"In the interest of intellectual clearness, I feel bound to say that religious experience, as we have studied it, cannot be cited as unequivocally supporting the infinitist belief. The only thing that it unequivocally testifies to is that we can experience union with something larger than ourselves and in that find our greatest peace."

So far, then, we only know that James held that man can experience union with transmundane energies which produce effects. As usual, his 'marketplace' works only serve to confuse the issue. Until one reads his major not-marketplace works, *Essays in Radical Empiricism* and *A Pluralistic Universe*, almost any theist could claim him as an ally in thought. There are, in his more popular works, only a few passages in which he hints at extreme unorthodoxy.

But in these books, he tightened up his thinking into a connected whole. In an initial lecture, 'The Types of Philosophic Thinking,' James distinguishes between two rival philosophies, materialism and spiritualism. He referred to materialism as *"defining the world so as to leave man's soul upon it as a sort of outside passenger or alien"* and spiritualism as insisting that *"the intimate and human must surround and underlie the brutal."*

Then he pointed to two distinct types of spiritualistic philosophy, monistic (the more intimate one) and dualistic (the less intimate). He explained the dualistic as the theism which reached its *'elaboration in the scholastic philosophy'* and the monistic as *'the pantheism spoken of sometimes simply as idealism, and sometimes as 'post-Kantian' or 'absolute' idealism."* Then he noted that the theistic concept pictures God and his creation *'as entities distinct from each other,'* leaving the human subject *'outside of the deepest reality in the universe.'*

In orthodox theology, he explained, God's action can affect us, but he can never be affected by us since he is from eternity complete and sufficient unto himself. In such theology, he observed, man's and God's relation is not a 'strictly social' one, although *"in common men's religion the relation is believed to be social, but that is only one of the many differences between religion and theology."*

In such theology, James said, God becomes our magistrate, not 'heart of our heart, and reason of our reason.' Truth is already instituted without man's help and the most man can do is acknowledge and adhere, though his doing so makes no difference to what is adhered to.

James held that *"this dualism and lack of intimacy has always operated as a drag and handicap on Christian thought."* And he noted that orthodox theology has constantly had to tone down *"the various forms of pantheistic heresy which the mystical experiences of religious persons, on the one hand, and the formal or aesthetic superiorities of monism to dualism, on the other, keep producing."*

He added that the *"vaster vistas which scientific evolutionism has opened, and the rising tide of social democratic ideals, have changed the type of our imagination, and the older monarchical theism is obsolete and obsolescent."*

He claimed, then, that the *"place of the divine in the world must be more organic and intimate."* And he sounds strangely like a prophet of the old 'God is dead' movement when he adds: *"An external creator and his institutions may still be verbally confessed at Church in formulas that linger by their mere inertia but the life is out of them, we avoid dwelling on them, the sincere heart of us is elsewhere."*

Because 'our contemporary mind' is grasping the possibility of a 'more intimate weltanschauung (world spirit),' he said, 'cynical materialism' and 'old-fashioned dualistic theism' would be left out of the discussion. He insisted that the only opinions 'quite worthy of arresting our attention' would fall under the 'pantheistic field of vision' which sees God as the *"indwelling divine rather than the external creator, and of human life as part and parcel of the deep reality."*

Here, at last, is a more definite, more articulate continuation of his kinship with Jaspers and Heidegger. And he had much in common with existential theologian Paul Tillich who also held that the God of traditional religion is 'dead,' that contemporary minds are searching for a more meaningful concept of God. Said Tillich, *"Only if the God of theism is transcended can the anxiety of doubt and meaninglessness be taken into the courage to be."*

Such a god, like the God of mysticism, transcends the theistic God who is a being. Paradoxes can only be resolved, say religious existentialists, in a God above the god of theism, 'a more intimate weltanschauung,' a God who has a more intimate relation with man, even though hidden.

Turning now to the 'pantheistic vision,' away

from traditional theism, James divided pantheism into two subspecies, the absolute (monistic) and radical empiricism (pluralistic). He explained that *"radical empiricism allows that the absolute sum total of things may never be actually experienced or realized in that shape at all, and that a disseminated, distributed, or incompletely unified appearance is the only form that reality may have achieved."*

Absolute pantheism, on the other hand conceives that "the divine exists authentically only when the world is experienced all at once in its absolute totality." In other words, he contrasted the 'all form' of pantheism with the 'each form,' and, for James, his over-belief was that 'God' is an Oversoul, greatest of the 'eaches.' His God has a history, suffers with men and understands their suffering, and we can *relate* to him.

It would seem obvious at this point that in spite of some previous public protestations in favor of being called a theist, James was no orthodox theist. He classified his own thinking as *pluralistic pantheism*, as opposed to absolute (monistic) pantheism, in another division process. Just where he ended up remains to be seen.

He dispenses with absolute pantheism this way: "*My conclusion, so far, then, is this, that although the hypothesis of the absolute, in yielding a certain kind of religious peace, performs a most important rationalizing function, it nevertheless, from the intellectual point of view, remains decidedly irrational. The ideally perfect whole is certainly that whole of which the parts are also perfect – if we can depend on logic for anything, we can depend on it for the definition. The absolute is defined as the ideally perfect whole, yet most of its parts, if not all, are admittedly imperfect.*"

A concept of this kind of Absolute, he pointed out, "*lacks internal consistency, and yields us a problem rather than a solution.*" It creates the philosophical problem of evil "*from which a pluralistic metaphysic is entirely free.*" The problem of evil bothered James because, he explained, when Absolutists say their '*belief affords them comfort,*' they mean '*that since in the Absolute, finite evil is 'overruled' already, we may therefore, whenever we wish, treat the temporal as if it were potentially the eternal, be sure that we can trust its outcome, and, without sin, dismiss our fear and drop the worry of our finite responsibility.*" Human responsibility concerned James as much as it concerned any existentialist.

But is it always true that a monistic system yields a 'problem of evil'? Is the ideally perfect whole one in which the parts are also perfect? Not if one subscribes to the Eastern 'Om' notion. That is, 'Om' – the whole as it is – is perfection, but not the perfection which insists that everything is 'good' in the human ethical sense. As Hermann Hesse explained in *Siddhartha:*

"In every truth the opposite is equally true ... The world is not imperfect or slowly evolving along a long path to perfection. No, it is perfect at every moment; every sin already carries grace within it, all small children are potential old men, all sucklings have death within them, all dying people – eternal life."

Perfection, for such a thinker, is positive *and* negative, yang *and* yin together, in complementary relationship, just as perfection, for James and the existentialists, involves the non-rational as well as the rational aspects of the being that is man. For Hesse, as for Heraclitus,[34] the river is the symbol of eternal change, like the sea of experience for James, the Encompassing for Jaspers. As Hesse put it, perfection includes "*all the voices, all the goals, all the yearnings, all the sorrows, all the pleasures, all the good and evil, all of them together was the world ... the steam of events, the music of life ... the whole, the unity ... Om – perfection.*" Only when 'Om' or an Absolute is personified and teleologically,[35] instead of cyclically, oriented does one have the 'problem of evil' to which James referred.

James' 'pluralistic pantheistic metaphysic,' however had points in common with the above. In this metaphysic, James said that "*the problems that evil presents are practical, not speculative.*" The problem becomes how men can lessen the amount of suffering and evil, not shy it exists. In this, again, he was not unlike Hesse and not unlike existentialists who speak not of ridding the world of evil (that is impossible in that 'evil' is relative to man) but of lessening the amount.

In his metaphysic, James' 'Absolute' is the wider cosmic whole including what is considered 'good' and what is considered 'evil' to man. And James' God, if he exists (*is but "the most ideal portion."*)

Any God, James argued, "*worthy of the name must be finite,*" working in an external environment, having limits and enemies, calling men "*to co-operate in his purposes, and who furthers ours if they are worthy.*"

Such a God may or may not exist, but James insisted that any Absolute which contains evil as well as good cannot e cons8idered a God or 'religious hypothesis'; it can only awaken 'cosmic emotion.'

And that is what the all-encompassing Being of the existentialists, like the 'Om' of Eastern philosophy and the sea of encompassing experience of James, seems to evoke.

Although James 'wider cosmic whole' has much in common with existential theories, his 'finite God' notion, or over-belief, has no parallel in existentialism. That is James' individual twist.

He attempted to clarify his views further in 'Conclusions' to his essays: *"The drift of all the evidence we have seems to me to sweep us very strongly towards the belief in some form of superhuman life with which we may, unknown to ourselves, be co-conscious. We may be in the universe as dogs and cats are in our libraries, seeing the books and hearing the conversations, but having no inkling of the meaning of it all."*

And he attempts to strengthen his argument by pointing to 'positive empirical evidence' – 'ordinary psychical research and religious experience.' Combine, he said, these establish a "formidable probability in favor of a general view of the world almost identical with Fechner's.[36]"

But he admitted the 'outlines of the superhuman consciousness thus made probable' are 'very vague' and problematic.'

James maintained, as an over-belief -- in the absence of possibility of verification in this life and because of psychological *'reflex action'* or need -- that in view of the modern temper of questioning of orthodox theism, the 'line of least resistance' in both theology and philosophy would be to accept a superhuman consciousness which is not all-embracing – a God that is finite, 'either in power or in knowledge, or in both at once."

And this, he said, has usually been the belief of common men in carrying on "their active commerce with God."

The 'monistic perfections,' he insisted, are the *"colder addition of remote professional minds operating in distans upon conceptual substitutes for him alone."*

With this, he clarifies what *he* means by 'theism' – meliorating (that is, taking the best of each in this case, with an eye toward lessening the problems involved in accepting one extreme or the other and synthesizing or bettering the situation), between empiricism and rationalism:

"May not the godlessness usually but needlessly associated with the philosophy of immediate experience give way to a theism now seen to follow directly from that experience more widely taken? And may not rationalism, satisfied with seeing her a priori proofs of God so effectively replaced by empirical evidence abate something of her absolutist claims? Let God but have the least infinitesimal other of any kind beside him and empiricism and rationalism might strike hands in a lasting treaty of peace."

But this is still not his final word. He speaks of **"the great empirical movement towards a pluralistic panpsychic view of the universe, into which our own generation has been drawn, [via the revolution in physics and vitalistic movement in biology] and which threatens to short circuit the methods of the churches and become their religious rival unless they are willing to make themselves its allies."**

Here James sounds like a prophet of things to come – of the religious existentialist's move to transcend organizations which are unwilling to change.

James said he felt that his radical empiricism is *"a more natural ally than dialectics ever were, or can be, of the religious life."* He stated:

"We are indeed internal parts of God [he seems to be referring here to 'God' as the absolute or cosmic whole] and not external creations, on any possible reading of the panpsychic system. Yet, because God is not the absolute, but is himself a part when the system is conceived pluralistically, his functions can be taken as not wholly dissimilar to those of the other smaller parts, -- as similar to our functions consequently."

His over-belief, then, as well as his panpsychic [theory that reality consists of psychic entities, not unlike the monads – souls or selves – conceived by Leibnitz[37]] ontology becomes more clear.

James' God has an environment, being in time, and works out a history like men, thus escaping the *"foreignness from all that is human, of the static timeless perfect Absolute"* that has been worshipped as God. He adds:

"No matter what the content of the universe may be, if you only allow that it is many everywhere and always, that nothing real escapes from having an environment; so far from defeating its rationality as the absolutists so unanimously pretend, you leave it in possession of the maximum amount of rationality practically attainable by our minds. Your relations with it, intellectual, emotional, and active, remain fluent and congruous with your own nature's chief

demands."

Here again, in his over-belief, James appeals to the *psychological* needs of man.

To repeat, he, like the existentialists, held that human beings have cravings on the level of mystical consciousness ('reflex action' of man's volitional nature – yearning for a god or absolute or unity) that cry for as much fulfillment as the physical and the intellectual and may or may not correspond to some psychic 'more' 'out there.' The question is open.

James, like most psychologists, held that all men may not be capable of existing without god substitutes, of resisting the reflex action, however ideal a goal this might be. Such people, he held, trying to decide whether he was a theist.

He was a theist on his own terms, by his own definition which did not turn out to be what is popularly known as theism at all. And he is a naturalist according to his own definition, although his definition of naturalism is somewhat closer to the conventional than is definition of theism is to the orthodox.

But the elusive James was 'ever not quite' a naturalist, just as he was 'ever not quite' a theist. Any attempt to fit him into an either-or category fails.

He was, like the existentialist who commits himself to living authentically, a 'whole man,' attempting to exist in the tension between polarities considered essential to his nature.

Meliorism, like his subjective ('giving human satisfaction' in this context) pragmatic method (which James explained, *'means the open air and possibilities of nature, as against dogma, artificiality, and the pretence of finality in truth"* in which science and metaphysics work together) is a major link in the thinking of James and that of existentialists of the secular persuasion.

It is a theory, opposed to both optimism and pessimism, that this world, being neither totally evil nor totally good from the human point of view, can be made better by human effort.

A meliorist holds that evil can be lessened but not totally eradicated – a non-utopian attitude shared by secular existentialists. James held, with them, that the fact of 'no' stands at the core of life and is not to be rationalized away.

Meliorism can also refer to a change of meaning for the better, as in James' use of his pragmatic method in arriving at a new idea that mediates between stock ideas and new experience

"and runs them into one another most felicitously and expediently,"

New 'truth' is a go-between, a smoother-over of transition, marrying old opinion to new fact *"so as ever to show a minimum of jolt, a maximum of continuity."*

Said James, **"We hold a theory true just in proportion to its success in solving this 'problem of maxima and minima.' But success in solving this problem is eminently a matter of approximation ... and individuals will emphasize their point of satisfaction differently."**

But, he added, *"the part played by the older truths ... is absolutely controlling."*

As for pragmatism, he admitted that his form and Schiller's[38] humanism have much in common.

But he and the existentialists' brand of pragmatic humanism is more 'caring,' more emotional in tone. That is, many existentialists are fallen or broken-hearted idealists (e.g. Nietzsche, Sartre, Heidegger, James) who, having once believed in an infinite God in an Ideal Realm, put their faith in question and 'cared' that the God of their childhood may be 'dead.'

These are in contrast to those humanists – the tough-minded – who appear to be happy and liberated by the so-called 'death of God' and optimistic about the future of man, putting their faith in man.

The existentialists and James, as meliorists, stand between this type of optimistic humanist and pessimists who feel that all is lost if God is dead and that life consequently, has no proximate or ultimate meaning.

If God is dead, secular existentialists do 'care.' They are not happy about it at all because they realize they must then bear 'awful responsibility' without a God-crutch, with no hope for an afterlife or for a God who will help set things straight.

They can't totally put their faith in man because they realize that he, like the universe revealed by the new physics, is subject to unpredictable behavior.

But they can accept the disjunctive-conjunctive (discord-harmony) aspects of the universe and of man as essential to the nature of things and commit themselves to live without illusions – to the growth and change that result from the disjunctive-conjunctive relationships – to lessening the amount of evil and suffering in the world while holding that it cannot be totally eradicated. Secular existentialists commit to ideals or goals as substitutes for faith in a God.

Religious existentialists, on the other hand seek a different concept of Deity more in tune with modern scientific temper or, like Kierkegaard, make a 'leap of faith' faith -- from an agnostic springboard -- in that which is 'absurd' (i.e. the traditional God of theism) but on a personal basis that transcends organized religion.

James and the existentialists claim to be closer to the 'truth' of humanity in being 'true' to the tough-minded factual as well as the tender-minded metaphysical aspects that characterize all men in greater or lesser degree.

But to rejoin the issue, if James was 'not quite' a naturalist, what was he? Is there one inclusive label that might cover the metaphysics of all three types?

There are at least two types of naturalism. In their book *Philosophy: An Introduction*, Randall and Buchler distinguished between contemporary 'materialistic' and 'critical' naturalism.'

According to them, the critical naturalist is the 'offspring of both materialism and its idealistic critics.' And what they come up with, utilizing the pragmatic method, is akin to James' notion of the 'supernaturalist' of the 'crasser' type with which he identified.

James was a down-to-earth supernaturalist and a transcending naturalist – a *'critical naturalist.'* Here is how Randall and Buchler speak of the latter:

"It [critical naturalism] *avoids above all the hypothesis of a supernature* [James' God, and his Cosmic Reality are not above nature but here with us] *but its conception of nature is far broader and far more comprehensive than that of materialism* [James spoke of the necessity of 'broadening and thickening up' the bases of discussion and his radical empiricism and panpsychism broaden the base]'.

"It finds a natural status for much of the subject-matter of idealistic philosophy [James allowed that the absolute might be the wider Cosmic Whole of which God is the ideal portion.] *It regards the concepts of mater and motion as grossly inadequate for a speculative philosophy* [James preferred panpsychic explanations.] *It agrees with idealism in point to mind as an important fact, but it defines mind in terms of nature, not nature in terms of mind.* [This would be one point on which James' panpsychism would be at odds with critical naturalism and one point on which

some existential ontology and Jamesian ontology might be disparate although Heidegger and Jaspers do not clarify their psycho-physical views to the extent that James does, and yet, both feel nature and mind are one.]

"Like materialism, it denies the existence of 'final causes' taken as one kind of efficient cause or force; yet it finds room for the notion of ends and teleology [for James, the universe is making itself valid, going somewhere with our help, not however a pre-determined 'somewhere,' with our help and God's], *which it interprets as one among other kinds of relation with the natural world."*

The authors point out that critical naturalism doesn't look at nature as something we can survey as a *'fixed, closed system of things, events, or laws … our knowledge is always partial and possesses vague boundaries.'*

For James, too, everything is 'ever not quite,' even 'truth' truth for man being, not fidelity to a fact or absolute standard – or coherence with a priori assumptions – but a *'class-name for all sorts of definite working values in experience.'*

Critical naturalism employs scientific method, rejecting the supernaturalistic hypothesis because it resorts to what is *'intrinsically incomprehensible and beyond possible experience.'*

But it *'accepts non-cognitive experience as well as cognitive – art and religion besides science – as contributing to a world perspective.'*

James, too, wanted to include all kinds of experience, as did Heidegger and Jaspers.

Like James and the existential ontologists, critical naturalism rejects 'appearance-reality' dualisms and monistic 'reductions.' Life, mind and values are phases of nature, neither more nor less natural than physical phases and there may be unlimited numbers of other phases potential in nature. Value is a result of experience, value being related to some given area of experience. No absolute formula suffices to explain all cases.

But although values are relative to specific situations, their reality is not thereby denied. A kind of 'property' belongs to a given situation, one property being no less 'real' than another. And critical naturalism arrives at conclusions, not by deducing them from a priori conceptions of what nature necessarily involves but by the attempt to form hypotheses on the basis of the results of science and the 'broadest implications of our total experience.'

There again, the 'broadest implications' make room for all modes of what Jaspers calls the Encompassing, Heidegger the Possible, James Pure Experience – the Given or Being itself – which provides the possibility for action of existing beings.

For James, Pure Experience, the instant field of the present, potentially or virtually either object or subject, is the primal 'stuff,' the *Cosmic Whole.*

Experience is separated by James into consciousness (name of a non-entity, a function in experience) and content (akin to Heidegger's notion that both bodies and consciousness are present in some enveloping presence.)

Ideally, the latter discover their possibilities and attempt to fulfill themselves, always open to possibility, change.

But particulars are not to be deduced from this Cosmic Reality or the Encompassing because, as Jaspers put it, the latter is in no form known in itself. *"The authentic idea of the Encompassing disappears with every attempt to establish, isolate, and absolutize it. An Encompassing which has become objective is no longer the true Encompassing."*

He added, *"If I were to soar beyond and conceive myself to be authentic Being itself, i.e. regard myself as transcendence over and above mere empirical existence, consciousness, or spirit, I should again lose myself in false self-divinization, and cease to be possible Existenz and its actualization ... I know this Other, just as with myself, only as it appears to me and not as it is in itself ... we must think about the Encompassing in order to make it really present."*

Heidegger similarly held that Being discloses itself to man only when man surrenders to the mystery of Being. He lets himself be claimed by Being which discloses itself in man's feeling, mood, in which he understands objects as part of a larger context. 'Dread' makes man aware of his own nothingness – leads man to understand Being.

As Jaspers held that the Encompassing is in no form known in itself, James held that there is no 'general stuff' of which experience at large is made, that there are as many stuffs as there are 'natures' in the things experienced, 'experience' being only a collective name for all sensible features, for 'possibility,' even relations being experiences to one another.

Like the existentialists, he held that the universe is originally ambiguous, that no one single type of connection runs through all experiences that comprise it, his radical empiricism, he thought, being fair to both the unity and the disconnection.

He held that ordinary empiricism tends to do away with the connections of things, insisting mostly on the disjunction, while rationalism is an attempt to correct incoherencies of such empiricism. He believed that his radical empiricism did 'full justice to conjunctive relations,' without treating them as true in some supernal way.

To continue, critical naturalists hold, with James and the existentialists, that 'experience articulates nature,' that experience is the nature of Reality. To wit:

"What the critical naturalist finds in nature he finds in that aspect of nature called man's experience ... Man's experience consists in his experiencing, and his experiencing consists in his doing, feeling, and participating. Experience is a process ... a dimension of nature, in which nature, so to speak, finds its expression ... for the critical naturalist the warp and woof is an indefinitely complex one. In experience he finds many experiences, to none of which he denies significance ... he acknowledges his wonder at the very fact of existence.

The latter statement is comparable with Heidegger's wondering *"Why is there any Being at all, why not far rather Nothing?"* which seems to acknowledge wonder at the very fact of existence.

James' contention is that one attains to the feeling of vital significance in an experience *"depending on the capacity of the soul to be grasped ... by what is given."*

Life, he said, is always worth living if one has such 'responsive sensibilities,' but too many of the highly educated have gone too far away from Nature to be grabbed. *"The remedy ..."* James said *"is to descend to a more profound and primitive level.'*

He expressed sorrow for the person who *"has never been touched by the spell of this mysterious sensorial life, with its irrationality."*

Like Heidegger (who saw man as *'a poet as well as a technician'*), James was concerned lest Nature might totally recede in human lives because, as Nature disappears, the sense of mystery disappears.

Both hoped than man would ever be open to the *'silent power of the Possible'* to produce a fundamental kind of thinking which complements – and offsets – technology in our lives.

Critical naturalism attempts, like the philosophy of existentialists, to rise above the old problem of freedom versus determinism. It mediates between the two in holding that freedom is a form of determination.

That is, the freedom of man consists not in his being undetermined but in his being determined by, as Randall and Bucher put it, *'forces and conditions arising from his own nature and within himself, as contrasted with his being determined by something that coerces him."*

Man, then, is self-determined, responsible for fulfilling his own potential, even though his determining factors are not only the state immediately preceding a choice, but bodily constitution, past development and present relation to his environment.

Man has intelligence and can modify his conduct to meet new situations; he can grow and change, profiting from experience. Freedom and responsibility involve determination by intelligence.

The authors conclude that critical naturalism is *"imaginative naturalism ... able to recognize not only the experience of the scientist but that of the mystic, if we use the latter to mean one who can experience what, though it be in the natural course of events, defies literal description and arouses some of man's deepest responses."*

Like existentialism, critical naturalism holds that man's transcendence -- his need to be free from mere physicality, to project and seek metaphysical meaning and purpose in life -- is as much a part of his nature, his essence, as his factual being which binds him.

As Heidegger put it, only when science itself *"proceeds from metaphysics can it conquer its essential task ever afresh, which consists not in the accumulation and classification of knowledge but in the perpetual discovery of the whole realm of truth."*

He added that it is *"completely out of our power to transport ourselves into metaphysics because in so far as we exist, we are already there."*

Yet the truth of metaphysics, he warned, *"is so unfathomable there is always the lurking danger of profoundest error."*

He explained that philosophy is the 'setting in motion of metaphysics,' in full knowledge, however, that man's truth is always (as James had said) approximate. The real of experience and possibility seems to be as given to change and spontaneity as to uniformity and intentionality.

James' ontology, like that of Jaspers and Heidegger, wouldn't allow him to look outside experience for transcendental metaphysical entities.

As we have seen, even relations are part of experience which flows, ebbs, sometimes erupts and disrupts. No personal God need be invoked except as an over-belief born of a human craving.

This craving, however, is not to be ignored, and James-the-psychologist said man has a 'right' to satisfy this need on the basis of the evidence of religious experience.

James-the-philosopher, on the other hand, could, presumably, live with the Cosmic Whole. There's little doubt that James-the-man longed for some contact with that mystical 'more' on the fringe of ordinary experience beyond his own inner experience.

James, then, and the existential ontologists are, fundamentally, critical naturalists. James was a theist only in the sense that he acknowledged a finite top god over lesser gods (men) as an over-belief.

In so doing, he meliorated between the religious and secular existentialists. He gave the religious existentialists their hidden God whom man can, on occasion, encounter in extraordinary personal religious experience. And he gave the secular existentialists their deification of man.

James' 'useful' God, however, unlike the Transcendence of religiously-inclined existentialists, was in danger of becoming the cultural appendage that existentialists decry.

When a God becomes 'useful' he is apt to be too closely associated with human culture and aspiration. He is in danger of becoming a power which allegedly comes alive in man when he 'thinks positively.' Such a deity is not transcendent enough to be an autonomous God who is not so involved in creation that he infringes on the freedom of others.

Although James spoke of his over-belief in a finite God as working side by side with men to make the world better – and was thus in danger of having his deity 'used' – he nevertheless held to a God who 'lived and let live,' a God who has deity enough, or is authentic enough, that he does not have to limit man's creativity.

But it seems that James' panpsychism actually left him closer to polytheism than to theism.

To answer the question posed at the beginning of this chapter, *"What might man hope for?"* according to James and the existentialists, it seems evident that if existentialists can be said to have 'hope,' it is the perennial hope of humanist prophets and philosophers that more, not all, men can live creatively and courageously, with or without a *caring* God.

Their hope is that more can become genuinely civilized as opposed to the sham civilized who admit they would murder, rape, and steal if there were no God or power to reward and punish.

They hope that more might walk, as W. T. Stace put it, *"straightly and … live honorably without the props and crutches of one or another of the childish dreams which have so far supported men."*

Such a life doesn't promise peace of mind or ecstatic happiness. But many have been able to live it through the ages, and it is possible that more individuals, awakened to conscious living and to the so-called 'human predicament' and its consequences, can live it in the future.

And if some Oversoul in the impersonal Cosmic Whole – some 'more' revealed in extraordinary experience to persons on a special 'psychic wave length' – is a reality, say the existentialists, with James, let him be the God of Ezekiel who bid man to stand on his own two feet, or the God who bids each man to first become an authentic human being, experiencing the honest, human doubt that can lead to Transcendence, before he can 'know' Him.

But whether men in general, the 'herd' or the 'masses' who live unauthentically (i.e. they are unthinkingly driven by values of others) can ever live without appeal to any props and crutches is doubtful.

James and the existentialists have no utopian hopes. They speak only to individuals.

But they do believe that suffering can be lessened, not eradicated. And some men can become better, though not perfect, unless, by perfection, one means *whole*. In these ways, they can be said to 'hope.'

But many of those who live authentically will probably say, as James did, at the end of their lives:

"There is no conclusion. What has concluded that we can conclude in regard to it? There are no fortunes to be told and there is no advice to be given. Farewell!"

Earth seen from space, the 'standpoint of Eternity'

ACKNOWLEDGEMENTS:

—•—

RESEARCH SOURCES

The author gratefully recognizes the following resources – persons and materials -- utilized not only in the lengthy process of writing this book but also in classroom dialogues with spirited students for more than thirty years:

D. H. LAWRENCE

Lawrence, D. H., *Phoenix, Posthumous Papers*, "Pan in America," "Taos," "New Mexico," "On Being Religious," (New York, Viking Press, 1936)

Lawrence, D. H., *Psychoanalysis and the Unconscious; Fantasia of the Unconscious* (New York, Viking Press, 1973)

Lawrence, Frieda, *Not I, But the Wind* (New York, Viking Press, 1934, reprinted by Scholarly Press, St. Clair Shores Michigan, 1972)

Luhan, Mabel Dodge, *Lorenzo in Taos*, (New York, Alfred A. Knopf, 1935)

RICHARD HENRY DANA, JR.

Dana, Richard Henry, Jr. *Two Years Before the Mast and Twenty Years After* (The Harvard Classics, New York, P. F. Collier and Son Corporation, 1937)

Jack London Estate, Glen Ellen, CA, and The Huntington Library, Pasadena, CA

GERTRUDE ATHERTON

Leider, Emily, 'A Tale of Two Gertrudes,' San Francisco Sunday Examiner & Chronicle, November 30, 1980

Atherton, Gertrude, *The Splendid Idle Forties: Stories of Old California*, dedicated to The Bohemian Club of San Francisco (New York, McMillan, 1902)

Atherton, Gertrude, *An Idyll of the Redwoods* [*Los Cerritos*], Heinemann, popular Shilling Edition (London, 1916)

ROBERT LOUIS STEVENSON

Barrie, J. M., *Peter Pan*, Puffin Books, Penguin books Ltd., (Harmondsworth, Middlesex, England, 1977)

Chesterton, G. K., *Robert Louis Stevenson*, Hodder and Stoughton Ltd., London.

Fitzpatrick, Elayne Wareing, *Robert Louis Stevenson's Ethics for Rascals*, Xlibris Corporation, Random House Ventures (Philadelphia, PA, 2000)

Lapierre, Alexandra, *A Romance of Destiny: Fanny Stevenson* (Carroll & Graf Publishers, Inc., New York, 1995)

Letters of J. M. Barrie, edited by Viola Meynell (Charles Scribner's Sons, New York, Copyright 1947 by Lady Cynthia Asquith).

Masson, Rosaline, *The Life of Robert Louis Stevenson* (Frederick A. Stokes Co., New York, 1923)

Stevenson, Robert Louis, *Across the Plains with other Memories and Essays* (Charles Scribner's Sons, New York, 1904)

Stevenson, Robert Louis, *Dr. Jekyll and Mr. Hyde* and *Weir of Hermiston* (Thomas Nelson and Sons Ltd., London, Edinburgh, Paris, Melbourne, Toronto, and New York,1956)

Stevenson, Robert Louis, *Virginibus Puerisque and Later Essays* (Heron Books, Geneva,

1969)

The Robert Louis Stevenson Companion, Edited by Jenni Calder (Paul Harris Publishing, Edinburgh, 1980)

JACK LONDON AND 'THE BUNCH'

Austin, Mary, *Isidro* (Boston, New York, Houghton, Mifflin & Co., 1905)

Genthe, Arnold, *As I Remember* (N. Y., Reynal & Hitchcock, 1936)

London, Charmian Kittredge, *Book of Jack London* (N. Y. Century Co., 1921)

London, Jack, *The Valley of the Moon* (N. Y., McMillan Co., 1913)

Sinclair, Andrew, *Jack: A Biography of Jack London* (New York, Washington Square Press, 1972)

Walker, Franklin, *Seacoast of Bohemia* (Santa Barbara and Salt Lake City, Peregrine Smith, Inc., 1973)

ROBINSON JEFFERS

Abbey, Edward, *Desert Solitaire* (New York, McGraw Hill, 1968)

Bennett, Melba Berry, *The Stone Mason Of Tor House* (Ward Ritchie Press, 1966)

Everson, William, 'Earth Poetry' (Special Edition for Jeffers Festival at Monterey Peninsula College July 30-31, 1971, designed and printed for *Oyez* by Graham Mackintosh, July 1971; photograph by Allen Say)

Karman, James, *Robinson Jeffers*, (San Francisco, Chronicle Books, 1987)

"The Californians: The Magazine of California History," Vol. 10, No. 2, Sebastopol, CA, 1992)

'The Carmelite,' Robinson Jeffers Supplement, Carmel, 1928

Beilke, Marlan. *Shining Clarity* (Amador City, CA, Quintessence Publications, 1977)

Jeffers, Lindsay and Jeffers Literary Properties, Carmel, CA

Jeffers, Robinson, *Themes in My Poems* (San Francisco, The Book Club of California, 1956; one of 350 copies printed, with woodcuts by Mallette Dean, Fairfax, CA. Copy courtesy of Greg Lehman, grandson of B. H. Lehman who wrote Preface)

Jeffers, Robinson, *Poems*, Introduction by B. H. Lehman (San Francisco, The Book Club of California, 1928; one of 310 copies signed by the author, courtesy of Greg Lehman)

Jeffers, Robinson. *Selected Poetry* (New York, Random House, 1959)

Jeffers, Robinson. *"Whom Should I Write For"* (Laguna, CA, Laguna Verde Press, 1979, printed on Albion hand press by Ward Ritchie for Tor House Foundation)

Jeffers, Robinson, *Not Man Apart* (San Francisco, CA, Sierra Club, 1965)

Vardamis, Alex, Tor House Foundation, Carmel, CA

JAIME DE ANGULO

A *Jaime De Angulo Reader*, edited by Bob Callahan (Berkeley, Turtle Island, 1970)

Abbey, Edward, *Desert Solitaire* (New York, McGraw Hill, 1968)

Bennett, Melba Berry, *The Stone Mason Of Tor House* (Ward Ritchie Press, 1966)

De Angulo, Gui, *Jaime In Taos* (San Francisco, City Lights Books, 1985)

De Angulo, Jaime, *Indians In Overalls* (San Francisco, City Lights Books, 1990)

De Angulo, Jaime, *Indian Tales* (New York, Hill and Wang, 1984)

Deloria, Vine, *God Is Red* (New York, Dell Publishing, 1973)

Hannah, Barbara, *Jung, His Life And Work* (New York, G. P. Putnam's Sons, 1976)

Highwater, Jamake, *The Primal Mind* (New York, New American Library, Meridian Books, 1981)

Jung, Carl, *Memories, Dreams, Reflections*, recorded and edited by Aniela Jaffe (New York, Vintage Books, 1965)

Karman, James, *Robinson Jeffers*, (San Francisco, Chronicle Books, 1987)

Lawrence, D. H., *Phoenix, Posthumous Papers*, "Pan in America," "Taos," "New

Mexico," "On Being Religious," (New York, Viking Press, 1936)

Lawrence, D. H., *Psychoanalysis And The Unconscious; Fantasia Of The Unconscious* (New York, Viking Press, 1973)

Lawrence, Frieda, *Not I, But The Wind* (New York, Viking Press,1934, reprinted by Scholarly Press, St. Clair Shores Michigan, 1972)

Luhan, Mabel Dodge, *Lorenzo In Taos*, (New York, Alfred A. Knopf, 1935)

Miller, Henry, *Big Sur And The Oranges Of Hieronymus Bosch*, (New York, New Directions, 1957)

'The Carmelite,' Robinson Jeffers Supplement (Carmel, 1928)

'The Californians: The Magazine of California History,' Vol. 10, No. 2 (Sebastopol, CA,1992)

JOHN STEINBECK

Steinbeck, John, *The Log From the Sea of Cortez* (New York, Viking Press, 1951)

Steinbeck, John, *The Short Novels of John Steinbeck* (New York, Viking Press, 1953)

Steinbeck, John, *The Acts of King Arthur and His Noble Knights* (New York, Ballantine Books, 1976)

Steinbeck, John, 'John Steinbeck's Plan for Cannery Row' Monterey Peninsula Herald Sunday magazine, May 13, 1972

Steinbeck, John, *To a God Unknown* (New York, Viking Press, 1933)

ERIC BARKER

Barker, Eric, *A Ring of Willows* (New York, New Directions, 1961)

Barker, Eric, *Looking For Water* (New York, October House, 1964)

Barker, Eric, *Under Orion* (Santa Cruz, Kayak Books, 1970)

HENRY MILLER

Burrow, Dr. Trigant, *The Social Basis Of Consciousness*, (London, Kegan Paul, Trench, Trubner & Co. Ltd., 1927)

Christon, Lawrence, "*An Interview With a Natural Resource*," (Los Angeles Times, Friday, September 9, 1977)

James, William, *The Varieties Of Religious Experience*, (New York, Collier Books, 1961)

Jung, C. G., *Modern Man In Search Of A Soul*, (New York, Harcourt Brace Jovanovich, 1933)

Lawrence, D. H., *The Works Of D. H. Lawrence*, (London, Longmeadow Press, 1985)

Lawrence, D.H., *Psychoanalysis And The Unconscious And Fantasia Of The Unconscious*, (New York, Viking Press, 1973)

Lawrence, D. H., *Phoenix, The Posthumous Papers Of D. H. Lawrence*, (New York, Viking Press, 1936)

Miller, Henry. *Big Sur and the Oranges of Hieronymus Bosch*. New York, New Directions, 1957.

Miller, Henry, *The World of Lawrence: A Passionate Appreciation*, Santa Barbara, CA, Capra Press, 1980

Miller, Henry, *First Impressions Of Greece*, (Santa Barbara, CA, Capra Press, 1973)

Miller, Henry, *The Colossus Of Maroussi*, (New York, New Directions, 1941)

Miller, Henry, *The Air-Conditioned Nightmare* (New York, New Directions, 1945)

Miller, Henry. *Reflections*. Santa Barbara, CA, Capra Press, 1981.

Miller, Henry. *Remember to Remember*. New York, New Directions, 1941.

Miller, Henry. *The Henry Miller Reader*. New York, New Directions, 1969.

Miller, Henry. *The World of Sex*. New York, Grove Press, Inc., 1965.

Miller, Henry, *Tropic Of Cancer*, (New York, Random House, Inc., First Modern Library Edition, 1983)

Miller, Henry, *To Paint Is To Love Again*, (Alhambra, CA, Cambria Books, specially bound edition, Copy No. 3, 'For Eve,' 1960

Miller, Henry, *The Smile At The Foot Of The Ladder*, (New York, New Directions, 1974)

Miller, Henry, *The Cosmological Eye*, (New York, New Directions Books, 1939)

Miller, Henry, *The Paintings Of Henry Miller: Paint As You Like And Die Happy*, (San Francisco, CA, Chronicle Books, 1980)

Miller, Henry, *On Turning Eighty*, (Santa Barbara, CA, Capra Chapbook, 1972)

Miller, Henry, *The Books In My Life*, (New York, New Directions Publishing Co., 1969)

Miller, Henry, Preface to *The Stranger*, "What's Doing," VOLUME III, NO. 2, (Monterey, CA, May, 1948)

Miller/Nin, A Literate Passion: Letters Of Anais Nin And Henry Miller, edited by Gunther Stuhlmann (New York, Harcourt, Brace, Jovanovich, 1987)

Nin, Anais, *D. H. Lawrence, An Unprofessional Study*, (Chicago, IL, Swallow Press, 1964)

Nin, Anais, *Henry And June*, (New York, Harcourt, Brace, Jovanovich, 1986)

Porter, Bern, Editor, *Henry Miller Miscellanea*, Copy No. 253, (San Mateo, CA, Greenwood Press, 1945)

'What's Doing' (Monterey Peninsula, preface to the French edition, 1949, of *The Stranger*, by Lillian Bos Ross, reprinted in the May, 1948 issue)

Wicks, George. "Henry Miller." *Writers at Work*, 'The Paris Review Interviews,' Second Series, edited by George Plimpton (New York, Penguin Books, 1977)

WILLIAM JAMES POSTSCRIPT

Anderson, Dr. Camilla M., *Beyond Freud* (New York, Harper & Brothers, 1957)

Barrett, William, *Irrational Man* (Garden City, N.Y., Doubleday & Co., 1962)

Barrett, William, *What is Existentialism?* (New York, Grove Press, Inc., 1965)

Camus, Albert, *The Myth of Sisyphus and Other Essays* (New York, Vintage books, 1955)

Davidson, Robert F., *The Search for Meaning in Life* (New York, Chicago, San Francisco; Holt, Rinehart and Winston, 1966)

De Beauvoir, Simone, *The Ethics of Ambiguity*, (New York, Citadel Press, 1964)

Frankl, Charles, *The Love of Anxiety and Other Essays* (New York, Dell Publishing Co., 1967)

Freud, Sigmund, *The Future of an Illusion* (Garden City, New York, Anchor Books, Doubleday & Co., 1964)

Fromm, Erich, Escape from Freedom (New York, Avon Books, The Hearst Corp., 1965)

Fuller, B. A. G. and McMurrin, Sterling M. A *History of Modern Philosophy* (New York, Henry Holt & Co., 1955)

Gittins, Alvin L., 'What is Aught But As 'Tis Valued?' (Bulletin of The University of Utah, Vol. 55, No. 18, Extension Division, University of Utah, 1964)

Grattan, Hartley, *The Three Jameses* (London, Longmans, Green & Co., 1932)

Herbert, Will, *Four Existentialist Theologians* (Garden City, New York, Doubleday & Co.,1958)

Hesse, Hermann, *Siddhartha* (Binghamton, New York; New Directions, Vail-Ballou Press, 1957)

James, William, *Essays on Faith and Morals* (Cleveland and New York, Meridian Books, World Publishing Co., 1962)

James, William, *Pragmatism* (Cleveland, Meridian Books, World Publishing Co., 1964)

James, William, *The Principles of Psychology*, Volumes I and II, Authorized Edition (New York, Dover Publications, Inc. 1950)

James, William, *Radical Empiricism and a Pluralistic Universe* (New York, London, Toronto; Longmans, Green & Co., 1943)

James, William, *The Varieties of Religious Experience* (New York; Collier Books, 1961)

James, William, *The Will to Believe and Other Essays* (London, New York, and Bombay; Longmans, Green & Co., 1899)

James, William, *Talks to Teachers* (New York, W. W. Norton & Co., 1958)

Jarrett, James, and McMurrin, Sterling M., *Contemporary Philosophy*, (New York; Holt, Rinehart & Winston, 1961)

Kallen, Horace M., *The Philosophy of William James* (New York, The Modern Library, 1953)

Kaufmann, Walter, *Existentialism from Dostoevsky to Sartre* (Cleveland and New York; World Publishing Co., 1963)

May, Rollo, *Psychology and the Human Dilemma* (Princeton, New Jersey; D. Van Nostrand Co., Inc., 1967)

Morgenbesser, Sidney, and Walsh, James, *Free Will* (Englewood Cliffs, New Jersey; Prentice-Hall, Inc., 1962

Perry, Ralph Barton, *The Thought and Character of William James* (New York and Evanston; Briefer Version, Harper Torchbooks, The Academy Library, Harper & Row, 1964)

Randall, John R., and Buchler, Justis, *Philosophy, An Introduction* (New York; Barnes & Noble, Inc., 1963)

Russell, Bertrand, *Mysticism and Logic and Other Essays* (London; Longmans, Green & Co, Inc., 1921)

Sartre, Jean Paul, *A Collection of Critical Essays*, edited by Edith Kern (Englewood Cliffs, New Jersey; Prentice-Hall, Inc., 1962)

Schrader, George Alfred, Jr., *Existential Philosophers: Kierkegaard to Merleau-Ponty* (New York; MacMillan Co., 1967)

Spanos, William V., *A Casebook on Existentialism* (New York; Thomas Y. Crowell Co., 1966)

Spiegelberg, H., *The Phenomenological Movement* (The Hague: Martinus Nijhoff, 1965)

Stace, W. T., *Mysticism and Philosophy* (Philadelphia and New York; J. B. Lippincott Co., 1960)

White, Morton, *The Age of Analysis: Twentieth Century Philosophers* (New York; New American Library, 1961)

ENDNOTES:

INTRODUCTION:

[1]George Santayana (1863-1952), Spanish-U.S. philosopher, poet, and humanist who taught with William James at Harvard University.

JEFFERS:

[2]Dr. Rex L. Campbell, manager of KUED, Utah's public television station and University of Utah Philosophy professor, sent the *Not Man Apart* book to me while I was on leave from the University to teach summer philosophy classes at Monterey Peninsula College. After experiencing that book, with its magnificent photographs and equally magnificent lines from Jeffers – I sought guidance from Jeffers scholar Dr. Robert Brophy, a Jesuit who admitted that Jeffers kept him 'honest.' Together we spearheaded four summer Jeffers Festivals that not only 'resurrected' Jeffers in his own territory, but led to formation of Tor House Foundation.

[3]Oswald Spengler (1880-1936), German historian and philosopher who held an organic cyclical theory of the rise and decline of civilizations.

MILLER:

[4]D. H. Lawrence died in 1930.

[5] James Joyce (1882-1941), Irish author of the popular and controversial *Ulysses*

[6] Marcel Proust (1877-1922), French author of *Remembrance of Things Past;* typically, in the case of both Joyce and Proust (as with Lawrence), Miller had much in common with the very writers he was protesting at the time.

[7] Miller considered *vitality*, not consistency or smoothness, a mark of great writing

[8] While Miller was living in Big Sur, he used a quote attributed to St. Francis on the back flap of his envelopes. It read, *"Don't try to change the world, change worlds!"*

[9] St. Francis was a Thirteenth Century Italian mystic who once led a carefree, worldly life as son of a wealthy merchant but discarded his rich garments for a rustic cloak to live close to nature and preach sermons, some say, to the birds.

[10] It's interesting that he chose the name 'Auguste.' St. Augustine, a licentious 'sinner' like Miller, spent years shopping around for a religion, praying *"Oh Lord, make me chaste, but not yet!"* Augustine felt he was eventually 'chosen,' undeservedly like St. Paul, to become a Christian. After his transformation, he proclaimed, like Miller in Big Sur, "O, my tardy joy!"

JAMES:

[11] The thesis committee was chaired by Peter C. Appleby, Head, Department of Philosophy; supervised and read by Sterling M. McMurrin, Dean of the Graduate School and former U. S. Commissioner of Education under John F. Kennedy; and Kenneth E. Eble, Head, Department of English.

[12] These seminal thinkers had moved beyond the Calvinistic Puritanism that came over on the Mayflower

toward forms of nature mysticism not unlike that of the American Indian and the 'divine Logos' of ancient Greek Stoicism. Instead of a harsh God commanding unconditional obedience from genetically sinful, predestined men, they believed in a God of integrative love that encouraged self-reliance and 'allowed' men the freedom to think for themselves with the possibility of bringing about a better world through ethical value choices. Religion, for them, was the *adoration of goodness*.

[13] Consequently, James became the American forerunner of Existentialism, a movement in philosophy which athered force in the 1950s drawing attention to the perennial shadow that surrounds all human enlightenment. This, in an era of unbridled post-war optimism about the possibilities of creating a better world through science, technology, and the Pollyanna-ish spread of unrestrained capitalism.

[14] His father was a Swedenborgian theologian who enjoyed the friendship of Ralph Waldo Emerson and other New England Transcendentalists. One of his brothers was novelist Henry James, a close friend of Fanny and Robert Louis Stevenson.

[15] His 'philosophic pessimism' is comparable to 'dread' or existential *angst*, resulting from recognition of the pit of insecurity beneath the surface of life.

[16] Charles Bernard Renouvier (1815-1903), French philosopher, who disliked the 'Unknowable' in all its forms and believed in reliance on personal *experience*. He held that liberty is man's fundamental characteristic and that belief is determined by an act of will affirming what we hold to be morally good. He also held that we are rationally justified in affirming human immortality and the existence of a *finite* God who is not a despot but a constitutional ruler over the souls of men. He regarded atheism as preferable to a belief in an infinite Deity due to the problem of infinite regress. James wrote: *"But for the decisive impression made on me in the 1870s by [Renouvier's] masterly advocacy of pluralism, I might never have got free from the monistic superstition under which I had grown up."*

[17] He later maintained that *"no man is educated who has never dallied with the thought of suicide."*

[18] In his *Principles of Psychology*, James would advise, apropos of this matter: *"Keep the faculty of effort alive in you by a little gratuitous exercise every day. That is, be systematically ascetic or heroic in little unnecessary points, do every day or two something for no other reason than that you would rather not do it, so that when the hour of dire need draws night, it may find you not unnerved and untrained to stand the test."*

[19] He eventually concluded, that *"the philosophy which is so important in each of us is not a technical matter; it is our more or less dumb sense of what life honestly and deeply means. It is only partly got from books; it is our individual way of just seeing and feeling the total push and pressure of the cosmos."*

[20] From this came James' term 'stream of consciousness,' the concept that thoughts or ideas are shifting and fluid, rather than fixed. The term is a description of mental life at the borderline of conscious thought.

[21] James defined 'metaphysics' as *"the discussion of various obscure, abstract, and universal questions which the sciences and life in general suggest but do not solve; questions left over, as it were, questions, all of them very broad and deep, and relating to the whole of things, or to the ultimate elements thereof."*

[22] This can be compared with Socrates 'unknown god' -- an inner voice -- that warned (as James' 'revelatory' dark night of the soul seemed to do) when he was about to take a wrong turn. It can also be compared with D. H. Lawrence's 'Holy Ghost within' that led him in the quest for his own Morning Star.

[23] Disconcerting in that many prefer to believe their God is an all-powerful, omniscient, caring, and just *being* who has a *personal* interest in everyone and everything that happens.

[24] Pascal was a Seventeenth Century mathematician and philosopher who observed that the 'heart' has its reasons which reason does not know. He is famous for his 'reasonable' wager in favor of religious belief: If God doesn't exist, the agnostic loses little by believing and gains little by not believing. If God does exist, the agnostic gains eternal life by believing and loses an infinite good.

[25] James came to believe that temperaments and their cravings determine men in their philosophies.

[26] Others, of course, would argue that it is the other way around: Intelligence produced nature.

[27] One can't resist observing here that, Biblically speaking, James had unintentionally sided with St. James -- who taught that faith without works (acts) is dead -- against St. Paul, apostle of predestination, who taught that man is justified by faith alone, not works, *"lest any man should boast."*

[28] He especially liked these words of Jefferies written while he was on a hill-top: *"I was utterly alone with the sun and the earth. Lying down on the grass, I spoke in my soul to the earth, the sun, the air, and the distant sea, far beyond sight … With all the intensity of feeling which exalted me, all the intense communion I held with the earth, the sun and sky, the stars hidden by the light, with the ocean, -- in no manner can the thrilling depth of these feelings be written, -- with these I prayed as if they were the keys of an instrument … I was rapt and carried away … Had any shepherd accidentally seen me lying on the turf, he would only have thought I was resting a few minutes. I made no outward show. Who could have imagined the whirlwind of passion that was going on in me as I reclined there!"*

[29]For James, the future is open, and trials of human decision can make a difference in history. Yet – after all intelligence can do has been done, there still remains a shadow surrounding human enlightenment. The excesses that constitute 'evil' – in ourselves and in Nature -- are never wholly banished. Like Nature, we attempt to create in the eternal tension between polar opposites – if, that is, we decide to opt for Life.

[30] James held to an ethic of self-commitment and autonomous action. Once a caring person is fully conscious of – and possibly humbled by -- his ambiguous position in the world, he becomes responsible for *giving* meaning to his own existence – and developing his best talents -- instead of looking for meaning 'out there.' And although he has the right to make a leap of faith (from an honest agnostic springboard), for which he is also responsible, he needn't do that in order to undertake his ethical work. For James, *Ethical* decisions (unlike *rules* handed down from 'on high' by an absolute authority) are made by reasoning about consequences to oneself and others for which the individual is fully responsible.

[31] Karl Jaspers (1883-1969) was a German-Swiss philosopher and psychiatrist who believed, with James, that the aim of philosophy is practical. He held that philosophical illumination is most often achieved through experience of extreme situations that define the human condition – conflict, suffering, guilt, and death. In confronting these extremes, a person achieves authentic existential humanity.

[32] Theory of Being as such, the nature of Reality

[33] Concern with the factual, existing *being* who dies, not with the ontological or nature of Reality

[34] Heraclitus (540-480 B.C.), Greek philosopher who held to the persistence of unity despite eternal change. This is illustrated by his analogy of life to a river.

[35] Idea that a full explanation of anything must consider its final cause – the *purpose* for which a thing exists or was produced. Science today tends to appeal only to efficient causes in which an effect is dependent on prior events, not ends or purposes.

[36] Gustav Fechner (1801-1887), German physicist and philosopher who founded the science of psychophysics that was useful in James' experimental Psychology.

[37] Gottfried Wilhelm Leibniz (1646-1716), German philosopher and mathematician who invented the differential and integral calculus and, like James, espoused a pluralistic metaphysic.

[38] Friedrich Von Schiller (1759-1805), German dramatist, poet, literary theorist, and friend of Goethe. Schiller examined the inward freedom of the soul that enables the individual to rise above physical frailties and the pressures of material conditions.

[35] Idea that a full explanation of anything must consider its final cause – the purpose for which a thing exists or was produced. Science today tends to appeal only to efficient causes in which an effect is dependent on prior events, not ends or purposes.

[36] Gustav Fechner (1801-1887), German physicist and philosopher who founded the science of psychophysics that was useful in James' experimental Psychology.

[37] Gottfried Wilhelm Leibniz (1646-1716), German philosopher and mathematician who invented the differential and integral calculus and, like James, espoused a pluralistic metaphysic.

[38] Friedrich Von Schiller (1759-1805), German dramatist, poet, literary theorist, and friend of Goethe. Schiller examined the inward freedom of the soul that enables the individual to rise above physical frailties and the pressures of material conditions.

Cosmos and the dance of ecstasy: By dancing, by spinning around his own axis, in figures of eight or around a sun, man incorporates the movements of the universe, of planets and atoms, of galaxies and electrons. As he winds, he creates the still point in is heart and turns the universe into being; as he unwinds, he turns his spirit back to his divine source. (Dore Hoyer, drawing by Johannes Richter, 1968)